Political Loyalty
and Public Service
in West Germany

Political Loyalty and Public Service in West Germany

The 1972 Decree against Radicals and Its Consequences

GERARD BRAUNTHAL

The University of Massachusetts Press

AMHERST

Copyright © 1990 by
The University of Massachusetts Press
All rights reserved
LC 89–28435
ISBN 0–87023–707–1
Set in Primer 54 at Keystone Typesetting, Inc.
Printed and bound by Thomson-Shore
Library of Congress Cataloging-in-Publication Data

Braunthal, Gerard, 1923–
Political loyalty and public service in West Germany : the 1972
decree against radicals and its consequences / Gerard Braunthal.
p. cm.
Includes bibliographical references.
ISBN 0–87023–707–1.
1. Germany (West)—Officials and employees—Selection and appointment.
2. Germany (West)—Officials and employees—Political activity.
3. Allegiance—Germany (West) 4. Civil rights—Germany (West)
I. Title.
JN3971.A69A613   1990
354.43001′3242—dc20   89–28435
CIP

British Library Cataloguing in Publication data are available.

Contents

List of Tables

Preface

In the history of the Federal Republic of Germany, few government actions have produced controversy as emotional, polemical, and long lasting as the Ministerial Decree of 1972 concerning left and right radicals in the public service. The decree was intended primarily to prevent communists, but also fascists, from entering national, state, and local civil service posts and to dismiss those already in public employment. Entitled "Basic Principles on the Question of Anticonstitutional Personnel in the Public Service," it is known more simply as the Decree against Radicals (*Radikalenerlass*) or, by its opponents, the Ban on Careers (*Berufsverbot*).[1] The decree spawned a massive loyalty check of about 3.5 million persons, including most applicants for public employment and numerous civil servants. Since the decree went into effect, intelligence agencies submitted the names of 35,000 suspect applicants to the hiring authorities, who barred approximately 2,250 applicants for political reasons. In addition, 2,000 to 2,100 public servants were subject to disciplinary proceedings, and 256 were dismissed.[2] The decree led to a controversial and supportive Constitutional Court decision in 1975, to federal guidelines in 1976 and 1979 limiting its scope, to increasingly acrimonious inter- and intraparty debates on its merits and the excesses committed in its execution, to divergent interpretations and administration by the Länder (states), and to international protests and legal actions that have continued into the 1980s. It created a climate of intimidation, snooping, and fear, affecting particularly youth.

In retrospect, one writer noted that many students and intellectuals attacked the decree as a pernicious attempt to stifle dissent and block social change. Some politicians and editorial writers responded by questioning the loyalty of the critics, seeming to confirm the latter's charge that fear and distrust were sweeping the land. Other commentators saw the whole enterprise as a cycle of overreaction: the government overreacting to the security threat in the first place, the critics responding with gross exaggerations of the decree's impact, and the critics of the critics retaliating in language far more robust than enlightening.[3]

As part of this study, the charges, countercharges, and the degree of overreaction must be assessed. Defenders and opponents of the decree in the Federal Republic have written many partisan books, pamphlets, articles, flyers, and legal briefs in German, but none has done a comprehensive survey. Scholars in other countries have not studied the decree in detail either, except for writing a few articles. I seek to present a full overall assessment, including the views of both sides; however, I cannot remain detached in the controversy that touches on the fundamentals of human rights. I am one of the critics. My reasons for taking this position will become evident in the course of the narrative and especially in the concluding chapter.

The chief thesis of this volume is that a democratic government, while protecting its internal security and upholding the rule of law, must provide maximum freedom to political dissenters not sharing the prevalent norms and values. Legal restrictions should be confined to actions against those few found guilty of sabotage, conspiracy, or espionage, according to due process. If repression is extended to dissenters who seek to create peacefully another political, economic, and social order, civil liberties will be inexorably limited.

In this case study of West Germany's practices in examining the loyalty of its potential civil servants and those already in service, I will seek answers to a number of questions grounded in democratic theory: In a liberal democratic polity, where should the line be drawn between the security of the state and individual rights? Should there be limits to the right to dissent, the right to advocate a different system? Should the government deny jobs to civil service applicants if they are, as labeled by public officials, "political extremists"? Does the government, the largest employer, have the right to withhold employment from any person and thereby bar him or her from a chosen profession? Should the government have the right to fire civil servants who are political dissidents?

Conversely, should the government allow into the ranks of the public service members of leftist or rightist parties or organizations who, once gaining control over it, might eliminate the freedom of others? Should there not be tough loyalty tests to prevent them from entering the service? Would it suffice for the government to bar political extremists from holding positions in sensitive posts such as police, intelligence, and defense?

In short, as one American journalist put it, "How democratic can a democracy be if it wants to remain democratic?"[4] Henry Steele Commager once raised the same issue: "To draw the line between the exercise of freedom and the limitations on freedom is one of the most delicate tasks of statesmanship and philosophy."[5] Isaac Balbus, in a study of the American legal order and the black ghetto revolts of the 1960s, notes the difference in views between liberals, who contend that civil liberties mitigate the severity and arbitrariness of legal repression by a benign state, and radicals, who see such repression as the "fascist core" of a liberal state.[6] The controversy over the Ministerial Decree of 1972 represented similar clashing views between conservatives and radicals (with liberals in between) on where to draw the line on the spectrum ranging from repression to freedom. Neither critics nor defenders of the 1972 decree denied the right of the state to protect itself from individuals committed to attack it through terrorism and other illegal acts, but the issue becomes more complex when individuals in peacetime advocate a fundamental change of political or economic system without presenting a "clear and present danger" to the constitutional order.[7]

Defenders of the decree attacked the critics' argument that the government should assume the loyalty of its citizens unless it has compelling evidence to the contrary and that the excesses committed during the loyalty investigations and the resultant political repression weaken rather than strengthen the democratic system. They also disagreed with the argument that individual rights were being dismantled or that the issue was linked to maintaining the capitalist economic and social system, which was facing increasing crises.

The whirlwind of arguments raised in the wake of the decree must be seen within the context of a political culture that evolved under the imprint of a strong bureaucratic state and was marked through much of German history by protracted periods of government authoritarianism, intolerance toward and repression of dissenters, uniformism, law and order, and restrictions on human rights. From 1918 to the present, it also featured strong ideological and political anticommunism. Klaus von Beyme, characterizing some of these traits as stereotypes, nevertheless contends that "there is no other West European democracy as highly suspect throughout the world so far as the extent of its tolerance towards deviant marginal groups is concerned."[8]

If, as most observers argue, the present political system is democratic, stable, and pluralistic, can it weather crises that might shake its firm value orientation and its institutions? Rainer Lepsius notes, "The structure and performance of political institutions exercise an influence upon the political culture, just as political culture influences the character and functioning of institutions."[9] This interdependence means that value orientations do not develop in empty space, nor can institutions develop without legitimizing commitments.

The difficulty with this interpretation is that not all West Germans hold the same values regarding tolerance toward dissenters, partly because many insist that given the country's history of extremism and intolerance and its vulnerability to the Soviet Union, it is prudent to curtail the freedoms of some individuals in order to maintain the democratic political system. On the other hand, Ramsey Clark (not referring to the West German case specifically) argues: "It is the idea of the enemy, the bad man, the sinister force that we use to deny freedom. Until we overcome our need for enemies, we will fear freedom, and through fear, deny it."[10]

To examine the thesis advanced—the necessity of maximizing, within certain limits, the freedom of political dissenters—the introductory chapter surveys the loyalty of civil servants to the state during the Empire, Weimar, and Nazi eras and up to 1960 of the Federal Republic. The following chapters discuss the antecedents and setting of the 1972 decree, domestic reactions to the decree from 1972 to 1976, foreign reactions, and the role played by supranational organizations. The last chapters consider domestic developments between 1976 and 1980, the decree's decline in salience since 1980, comparative practices in selected West European countries and the United States, broader aspects of the status of civil liberties in the Federal Republic, and conclusions to be drawn from the effects of the decree.

This case study focuses on the extent of civil liberties for one segment of the West German population. Whether another democratic state under similar circumstances would similarly limit entrance into the civil service or oust some of its political extremists can only remain a matter of speculation, although, as will be shown, some parallels exist. The study emphasizes civil liberties, but the controversy surrounding the subject also illuminates the interplay among a number of institutions and political actors in the national and Länder executive, legislative, and judicial branches as well as between interest groups and the government. Thus it also adds to the information about the political process and power relations in the

Federal Republic during a period when orthodox political values were challenged by a new generation of critical youth.

I obtained data for the study from the Bundestag library and archive and from archives of parties in Bonn, of the *Spiegel* in Hamburg, and of the *Sozialistisches Büro* in Offenbach. I also interviewed fifty-four individuals who had direct knowledge of the decree or had been affected by it. Among them were officials of the Ministry of Interior in Bonn and Munich, the Ministry of Finance in Munich, and the State Chancellery in Stuttgart, as well as a Constitutional Court judge in Karlsruhe; Christian Democratic Union/Christian Social Union (CDU/CSU) and Social Democratic party (SPD) officials and staff members; journalists in Bonn and Frankfurt; academicians in Berlin, Cologne, Bonn, Frankfurt, and Freiburg; officials and staff members of the German Trade Union Federation (DGB) in Düsseldorf; the teachers' union in Frankfurt, Berlin, Hamburg, and Bonn; the railroad workers' union in Frankfurt and the public service union in Stuttgart; staff of the German Federation of Civil Servants (DBB); and lawyers and those denied entry into or dismissed from the civil service, including teachers and a postal employee. I am very thankful for the generous cooperation of the respondents—many of whom were either strong proponents or critics of the decree—and the library and archive staffs.

I also gratefully acknowledge a grant in 1979–80 from the American Philosophical Society and in 1987 from the German Academic Exchange Service (DAAD) to pursue field research in the Federal Republic. I thank the staff of Inter Nationes, the Deutsche Forschungsgemeinschaft in Bonn, the German Information Center in New York, and the University of Massachusetts library for their invaluable help.

I am indebted to Klaus Dammann, Gregg Kvistad, and Wolf-Dieter Narr for their careful reading of the entire manuscript and constructive comments, and to John Brigham, Arthur Gunlicks, Klaus Peter, and Jeremiah Riemer for their comments on parts of the manuscript. Many thanks to Terri Gozeski and Vera Smith for their able secretarial work in various stages of the draft. The editors of the University of Massachusetts Press also deserve praise for their unflagging support and assistance in the preparation of the manuscript for publication. The final acknowledgment goes to my wife, Sabina, for her constant aid and encouragement to see the study to completion.

Abbreviations

APO	Ausserparlamentarische Opposition (Extra-Parliamentary Opposition)
BMI	Bundesministerium des Innern (Federal Ministry of Interior)
CDU/CSU	Christlich-Demokratische Union/Christlich Soziale Union (Christian Democratic Union/Christian Social Union)
CGT	Confédération Générale du Travail (General Confederation of Labor)
DAG	Deutsche Angestellten-Gewerkschaft (German Salaried Employees Union)
DBB	Deutscher Beamtenbund (German Federation of Civil Servants)
DFG	Deutsche Friedensgesellschaft (German Peace Society)
DFU	Deutsche Friedens-Union (German Peace Union)
DGB	Deutscher Gewerkschaftsbund (German Trade Union Federation)
DKP	Deutsche Kommunistische Partei (German Communist Party)
DM	Deutsche Mark
DPG	Deutsche Postgewerkschaft (German Postal Workers Union)
EC	European Community
ECJ	European Court of Justice
FDGO	freie und demokratische Grundordnung (free and democratic basic order)
FDP	Freie Demokratische Partei (Free Democratic Party)
FRG	Federal Republic of Germany
GdED	Gewerkschaft der Eisenbahner Deutschlands (German Railroad Workers Union)
GDR	German Democratic Republic
GEW	Gewerkschaft Erziehung und Wissenschaft (Union of Teachers and Scientists)
ICJ	International Court of Justice

ILO	International Labor Organization
IMSF	Institut für Marxistische Studien und Forschungen (Institute for Marxist Studies and Research)
Jusos	Jungsozialisten in der SPD (Young Socialists in the SPD)
KGD	Komitee für Grundrechte und Demokratie (Committee for Basic Rights and Democracy)
KPD	Kommunistische Partei Deutschlands (Communist Party of Germany)
MSB-Spartakus	Marxistischer Studentenbund-Spartakus (Marxist Student League-Spartakus)
NPD	Nationaldemokratische Partei Deutschlands (German National Democratic Party)
NSDAP	Nationalsozialistische Deutsche Arbeiterpartei (German National Socialist Workers Party)
ÖTV	Gewerkschaft Öffentliche Dienste, Transport und Verkehr (Public Service and Transport Workers Union)
RAF	Rote Armee Fraktion (Red Army Faction)
RCDS	Ring Christlich-Demokratischer Studenten (Circle of Christian Democratic Students)
SA	Sturmabteilung (Storm Detachment, Storm Troopers)
SDS	Sozialistische Deutsche Studentenbund (German Socialist Student Federation)
SEW	Sozialistische Einheitspartei Westberlins (Socialist Unity Party of West Berlin)
SHB	Sozialistische Hochschulbund (Socialist University League)
SPD	Sozialdemokratische Partei Deutschlands (Social Democratic Party of Germany)
SS	Schutzstaffel (Defense Echelon, Blackshirts)
UNESCO	United Nations Educational, Scientific and Cultural Organization
VDJ	Vereinigung Demokratischer Juristen (Association of Democratic Lawyers)
VDS	Verband Deutscher Studentenschaften (Association of German Student Governing Boards)
VVN	Vereinigung der Verfolgten des Naziregimes (League of Victims of the Nazi Regime)
WFTU	World Federation of Trade Unions

Political Loyalty and Public Service in West Germany

1

Prelude to 1972

The controversy that raged around the 1972 Decree against Radicals can be understood only within a historical context. A survey of the groups and individuals that gained entry into the public service shows that discriminatory hiring practices did not begin in the 1970s but had antecedents in previous German regimes. Then and now, the power wielders codified their own norms and values. Those who dissented from this political culture and advocated radical transformation of the existing order had to battle entrenched interests intent on maintaining it. Often the dissenters were barred or discharged from the civil service, whose members were expected to be loyal to the regime.

In this chapter, we first survey the nature of the state in which the civil service operated in the Prussian, Empire, Weimar, Third Reich, and postwar West German eras. Then articles in the Basic Law (constitution) of the Federal Republic are discussed, as well as provisions in the civil service laws that deal with the loyalty of the public servants in terms of the legal norms established for them. Finally, a government loyalty decree of 1950—a harbinger of the 1972 Decree against Radicals—is examined.

The Prussian State

From the eighteenth century on, German rulers defined the nature of the state and laid down the perimeters of liberties that different groups in society, ranging from the landed aristocracy to the peasants, were to possess. These "state-societies," as Kenneth Dyson characterized them, did not evolve from the people but rather from the absolutist rulers who set the standards of society and whose efficient bureaucrats, recruited primarily from the nobility but containing some upwardly mobile commoners, had a special relationship of loyalty to the ruler.[1]

During Frederick the Great's reign (1740–86), the absolute but enlightened ruler viewed himself as "the first servant of the state." He kept close control over the administration of every department, while at the same time appointing capable and conscientious men to the expanding bureaucracy. In 1770, a Prussian civil service commission proposed rather courageously that civil servants should be independent of the arbitrary authority of the kings. Only in 1794, when absolutism was weakening, did King Frederick William II sign the Prussian Code of General State Law (*Allgemeines Landrecht*), establishing a nominally independent civil service. Its members were no longer royal servants but "servants of the state." Nevertheless, they still had to maintain a special loyalty and obedience to the ruler and were expected to remain monarchists.[2]

The Prussian reforms of 1807–11, set in motion by the 1794 law, Napoleon's defeat of the Prussian armies in 1806, and the stirrings of liberalism among the bourgeoisie, created the modern professional service that has endured to the present. Enjoying a special caste position in society, the career civil servants, then imbued with both aristocratic and bureaucratic values, were entitled to life tenure, incremental pay, automatic promotions, a generous pension, and dismissal only through judicial disciplinary proceedings. The governing authorities established four classes of civil servants—higher, executive, clerical, and basic—with different educational requirements. Thus, the study of law, normally taught by conservative professors, was a prerequisite for appointment to the elite higher service. Because of their special status, the civil servants had an excellent reputation for individual incorruptibility.

This bureaucratic elite functioned as an authoritarian center of power while it simultaneously aided in the modernization of Prussian politics and society, including the push for a constitutional state to limit the ruler's absolute power as a means of protecting its own rights.[3] It claimed to operate within the mantle of the *Rechtsstaat* (literally "rule of law state") based on the 1794 code and on Roman law, which was predicated on the idea that all governmental organs are governed by principles of justice and on the grant of private, civil, and political rights to individuals if these rights do not contravene state power. But rule of law in practice was not yet characteristic of the Prussian state, although its Chamber of Deputies contested executive absolutism until 1866. In addition, Baden, the Rhineland, and East Prussia adopted some liberal policies after 1815.

An emphasis on state rights in the *Rechtsstaat* doctrine, enunciated by a number of writers (e.g., Robert von Mohl) in the first half of the nineteenth century, signified that the monarchical governing elite, including the powerful bureaucracy, could resist the claims of the liberal bourgeoisie demanding more individual liberties. One writer aptly noted, "Society can find the personal freedom, the moral and spiritual development of the individual, only in permanent subordination to a constant higher power."[4]

When pressure increased, the rulers gradually allowed more liberties, but only those that did not undermine their own independent authority. Unlike other Western states, where individual rights were won at the expense of state power, in Germany they were linked to the state. In nineteenth-century Germany the strong state was thus the giver and protector of liberty, albeit limited, rather than a threat to it.[5]

The linkage of state and liberty stunted the development of a democratic society and a strong civil libertarian tradition. Under the rule of law, citizens were considered "free" only when they obeyed the government's rules and regulations. Although detailed legal codes and laws defined individual rights and duties and limited state power, and although administrative and other courts were expected to enforce equal justice under law, their narrow interpretations constricted rather than enlarged individual freedoms.

As a consequence, tolerance of political views hostile to the established order was low, and political repression was high.[6] The Carlsbad Decrees of 1819 restricted freedom of the press and established controls over universities to ferret out "subversive" elements. In 1837, the king of Hanover dismissed seven progressive professors at the University of Göttingen who had protested the abrogation of the state constitution. On other occasions, politically unreliable civil servants were dismissed. In the wake of the failed revolution of 1848–49, in which the Frankfurt Parliament promulgated a catalog of basic rights, disciplinary measures, including dismissals, were taken against civil servants who espoused the revolutionary cause.

The Second Reich

The founding of the German Reich in 1871 did not lead to any appreciable liberalization or democratization because the constitution, lacking a bill of rights, granted executive power to a powerful emperor and chancellor at the expense of a weak Reichstag and because a governing coalition of Junkers, army officers, industrialists, and bureaucrats stymied most reform efforts. In this conservative elite coalition, the civil servants were pledged to protect the antidemocratic constitution and to take an oath of loyalty to the reigning monarch, representing the state.

Typical of the restrictions on personal freedoms was Chancellor Bismarck's campaign against the Catholic church and Center party from 1870 to 1887 and his ban from 1878 to 1890 of the SPD, which was becoming increasingly popular among voters. The SPD could not continue as an organization, hold assemblies, print its newspapers, or distribute its literature. The ban led to a wave of arrests and to dismissals of social democratic teachers and other civil servants. Even after 1890, known social democrats had no opportunity to enter the civil service, despite a steady growth in voter support for the party, because they were considered enemies of the Reich.

The antisocialist policy in the civil service was buttressed by the Prussian Superior Administrative Court, which ruled in 1894 that it was an infraction for civil servants to favor social democratic movements. Six years later, the Prussian State Ministry dismissed a University of Berlin faculty member because of his SPD membership. In Bavaria, no social democrat could hold any town office.[7]

Not surprisingly, the national and state civil servants, most of them holding university and law school decrees, were sympathetic to a conservative policy designed to root out the social democratic and other political opposition and to maintain the status quo. The personnel consisted mainly of young men whose fathers came from the ranks of the elite—the aristocracy, the upper bourgeoisie, the landowners, the army, the upper civil service, and academia.[8] Politically conservative, they were loyal executors of the antidemocratic and antiliberal policies of Bismarck and successor governments to the bitter end, even though in theory they were supposed to be nonpartisan.

Although during the Empire era individual rights were still severely curtailed, a gradual liberalization process took place in local administration, including instances in which civil servants decided for an individual and against the state. In addition, the government adopted national penal and civil codes, established administrative courts, and created a social welfare network that provided for some equity and justice to the population.

The Weimar Republic

World War I led to the downfall of the Second Reich and the birth of the Weimar Republic. During the period of upheaval, 1918–19, fully 90 percent of civil servants remained in their posts and provided expertise, continuity, and stability to the new democratic government. Because soon thereafter political leaders wanted to limit the privileged position of civil servants, many sons of aristocratic families no longer automatically chose the service as a career. Thus in later years the proportion of civil servants from the lower strata of artisans and working-class families increased appreciably, to 44 percent, clustered primarily in the lower civil service grades.[9]

Few of these new civil servants had entered universities and studied law, a prerequisite for a career in the upper service. As a consequence, most senior civil servants remained conservative, were hostile to or passive vis-à-vis the Republic (for which they felt no personal loyalty), and considered the constitution too democratic and political parties too divisive and antithetical to the state's interests. In the Prussian Ministry of the Interior, for instance, Minister Carl Severing estimated that there were only thirteen reliable republicans among the sixty-five higher public servants.[10]

Conservative senior civil servants had opportunities in their advisory and administrative roles to limit political, economic, and social reform proposals promulgated by the governing coalition parties in the national and state cabinets and parliaments. Yet, because from 1919 to 1933 the civil servants had less significant powers in the governments and because the political parties were catapulted into a major policy-making position (except for the last years of emergency rule), scholars have categorized Weimar Germany as a "party state" (*Parteienstaat*) in which politics was democratized. As part of this process, the governing parties developed a modest influence over the public service and set unofficial quotas for top posts.

The constitution, then one of the most democratic in the world, granted citizens an impressive number of basic rights. Two provisions dealt with civil servants: Article 128 allowed any qualified citizen to enter the public service, and Article 130 guaranteed civil servants the freedom to express any political views and to participate in public assemblies. Subsequently a court ruled that civil servants could be members of any political party. Adherents of leftist and rightist parties gained entry into the public service, even though in later years some, as noted below, were ousted. In addition to these expanded freedoms, civil servants no longer had to pledge loyalty to an individual (the monarch, during the Empire period) but did so to the state and the constitution.[11]

Although these changes were important at a symbolic level, the Weimar governments were too fragile to permit civil servants full political freedoms. Following right-wing assassinations of Finance Minister Matthias Erzberger in August 1921 and Foreign Minister Walter Rathenau in June

1922, the government issued a law in July 1922 obliging civil servants to uphold the republican state order and not to support monarchical restoration or antirepublican movements. Yet, conservative judges, disregarding this law, meted out only light sentences against right-wingers responsible for continuing acts of terror but heavy sentences against communists found guilty of similar or less serious acts.[12]

The Weimar governments did not take action against these antirepublican judges or against civil servants who were members of the Communist or Nazi parties. In the key state of Prussia, two court cases guided its government: the Superior Administrative Court's decision of November 10, 1921, that public servants would be guilty of a service misdemeanor only if they intended to promote through positive acts the goals of a party seeking the overthrow of the state order, and its June 18, 1923, decision that membership in the Communist Party of Germany (KPD), whose goal was such an overthrow, was not compatible with holding a civil service post. It did not cite the Nazi Party (NSDAP). On the other hand, in June 1930, the Prussian Ministry of State decreed that public servants could not support either the KPD or the NSDAP or participate in their activities, because such actions would violate their obligation of loyalty to the state. Even though in theory the decision did not differentiate between the two parties, in practice communists (the few that even held jobs) but hardly any Nazis were ousted.

Only one state, Baden, took the same position as Prussia, while others, such as Bavaria, warned civil servants about NSDAP membership but decided on possible dismissal only on an individual basis. These Länder often found it difficult to prosecute Nazi members, because Hitler did not publicly advocate the elimination of the Republic through illegal means. As a result, NSDAP members were sometimes merely suspended temporarily from the service. Throughout the Reich, the Nazi members in the civil service constituted only a minority. Many of those who had joined were motivated by the Great Depression and cuts in civil service salaries or because they held that party strife had damaged Germany.

The majority of civil servants were not members of the NSDAP or the KPD. Some feared the rise of the NSDAP but kept silent, while most, facing a choice between a takeover by the Left or Right, preferred the latter.[13] Few protested when the conservative Chancellor von Papen overthrew the Prussian government in July 1932 and when many civil servants belonging to the SPD lost their jobs. One month later, the new Prussian government lifted the June 1930 civil service decree aimed at the extremist parties, ostensibly on the ground that the NSDAP was trying to change the system legally, and replaced the ousted SPD members with Nazis.

Whether the Weimar federal and state governments were too lax in their treatment of the NSDAP remains a matter for historical debate. Since 1949 conservative politicians and scholars in the Federal Republic have insisted that the Weimar Republic failed because its governments decided too late and without enough conviction to take action against parties hostile to the constitution and against NSDAP or KPD members who had entered the public service and violated civil service regulations. They have contended that by being too democratic, the Weimar governments dug their own graves. They have cited these arguments repeatedly as a warning that the Bonn Republic must keep political extremists out of the public service to prevent a repetition of Weimar.

On the other hand, liberal politicians and scholars have argued that the Weimar Republic fell, not because Hitler and his followers had undermined the state and its civil service, but for a host of more important reasons. Among them were the Great Depression, the inability of democratic leaders to transform the system into a real democracy, and, toward the end, the defamation of the Republic by President von Hindenburg, Chancellor von Papen, and Nationalist party leader Alfred Hugenberg and their invitation to Hitler to take power. Alfred Grosser, a German émigré and French scholar, has argued that to blame the civil service, containing few Nazis at the time, for the Weimar defeat is highly exaggerated. It is actually low on the scale of causes of the downfall. He also has assailed conservatives in the Federal Republic who use the Weimar defeat as an excuse for a new form of "inquisition" against left radicals.[14]

The Nazi Era

When Hitler became chancellor in January 1933, the civil servants saw the handwriting on the wall. According to one estimate, 80 percent of them joined the party before May 1 to beat the deadline set by its leaders.[15] On April 7, the new government issued a decree announcing that non-Aryan civil servants were to be pensioned unless they had been in the civil service before August 1914 or had been veterans of World War I, and that civil servants whose political activities showed that they did not at all times support without qualification the national state might be dismissed. On July 20, the government, in a supplementary law to the Professional Civil Service Law, announced that "civil servants who were members of the

Communist party or of communist organizations were to be dismissed unless they proved to have been outstanding supporters of the 'national movement.'" In addition, civil servants were to be dismissed "who in the future will be active in the Marxist (communist or social democratic) sense."[16] The reference to Marxists was a pretext to remove any civil servant whom the Nazis did not like, although in practice many were disciplined, pensioned, or transferred instead. These government announcements engendered a climate of fear and uncertainty among most civil servants, who were not able to influence public policies significantly. Hitler, demanding total obedience, was able to use to his advantage their traditional ethos of loyalty to the state they were sworn to uphold. On January 26, 1937, the Nazi government issued a law amending earlier ones. Only those who guaranteed that they unreservedly and at all times supported the national socialist state (the previous formulation had read "national state") could be civil servants. Those who no longer could provide this guarantee were to be pensioned or dismissed.

Nazi leaders, intent on erasing the image of a politically neutral civil service, expected positive support and inner conviction from public servants, who had to take a personal oath to the new state and the Führer. They also expected public servants to join the party or its organizations as proof of loyalty and used the party to check on the members' commitment prior to any personnel action. Their efforts were successful; nearly all civil servants continued to support the regime until its collapse at the end of World War II. One writer commented aptly, "It is probably no exaggeration to say that the German civil service has never before been so much instrumentalized or played so subservient a role."[17]

Allied Occupation, 1945–1949

Attempts by the Western Allies (United States, Britain, and France) to prevent a resurgence of fascism in Germany meant that, among other policies, the German bureaucracy should become more democratic. This policy met with only moderate long-range success against the entrenched interests and traditions of the held-over senior civil servants. During the initial occupation period, the Western Allies had to deal with the staffing of agencies. They lifted the Nazi regulations against non-Nazis' becoming civil servants and simultaneously weeded out from the public service the most active NSDAP members who had been jailed as war criminals. But to provide administrative expertise and continuity they retained up to an estimated 90 percent of former civil servants in certain categories. Most teachers, judges, lawyers, police and security officers, and other civil servants remained at their posts after a token de-Nazification process.[18]

By 1950, throughout the Federal Republic, in a continuing restoration process, former membership in the NSDAP, SA, or SS no longer was an important criterion for being kept out of the civil service. According to one account, applicants were questioned about their Nazi organizational memberships, but their statements were not checked either locally or at the American Documents Center in West Berlin, where such files on the Nazi period were kept. To be hired, former Nazis only had to produce a police certificate of good conduct.[19]

In May 1951, the Bonn CDU/CSU-led government promulgated a law, based on Article 131 of the Basic Law (to be discussed below), which allowed reinstatement of civil servants who had been dismissed or suspended after 1945 for Nazi connections or activities. This provision applied to any individual, regardless of earlier position, except for former Gestapo officials. Not surprisingly, a latent conflict developed between these civil servants and the smaller group of democratic and anti-Nazi civil servants appointed to many top posts by the Allies after 1945.[20] At first, the veteran civil servants, whose social background hardly differed from that of their predecessors in earlier regimes, remained apolitical. But in later years one may assume—on the basis of polls showing an increasing commitment to the multiparty system on the part of respondents of all occupations—that most became convinced democrats. Once again, the bulk of civil servants in the higher ranks came from the upper and lower middle class, with no significant representation from the lower class.[21]

While U.S. and British officials, and eventually West German policymakers, had to deal with public-service personnel questions, the Allies also tried to impose reforms on the service. In February 1949, they issued Military Government Law No. 15, which proved most unpopular among civil servants who had held their posts in former regimes. The law eliminated the distinction among civil servants, salaried employees, and manual workers; created a personnel office that would function independently of individual department heads; and prohibited civil servants from running for parliamentary seats.[22]

The Basic Law's drafters, representing all political parties, rejected these reforms as they set out to write a temporary constitution. They were under strong pressure from civil service organizations not to agree to Allied reforms, although trade unions favored democratization of the service. Thereupon the Allies reluctantly accepted the provisions of both the Basic Law of 1949 and a later transition bill drafted by the new West German government, which envisaged no fundamental changes in the character of the public service.

The Basic Law

The constitution contained a number of articles that touched directly or indirectly on the public service. Much of the legal controversy that developed after the signing of the Decree against Radicals in 1972 revolved around the question of priority of constitutional articles when they seemed to contradict one another.

In the Weimar constitution, basic rights and freedoms were placed at the end of the document and often were disregarded in practice. In 1949, the drafters of the Basic Law symbolically put twenty of them at the beginning: the familiar freedoms against the state found in Western liberal democracies—freedom of speech, press, religious belief, association, and movement—and other provisions dealing with equality before the law, freedom of expression and information, privacy of mail, the right to petition, and the right "to resist any person or persons seeking to abolish the constitutional order, should no other remedy be possible" (Article 20). These guaranteed and inalienable rights are binding on the three branches of government and cannot be amended.[23]

The opponents of the Decree against Radicals repeatedly cited several other articles to support their contention that it violated the spirit and letter of the Basic Law. They mentioned Article 3: "No one may be prejudiced or favored because of his sex, parentage, race, language, homeland and origin, faith, religious or political opinions." Article 12 guarantees all Germans "the right freely to choose their trade, occupation, or profession, their place of work and their place of training." Article 21 provides for the free formation of political parties, but with limitations (to be discussed below). Article 33, paragraph 2, states, "Every German shall be equally eligible for any public office according to his aptitude, qualifications, and professional achievements." In brief, the decree's opponents maintained that a person should be able to enter the public service freely, regardless of political views or party affiliation.

For the decree's supporters, other articles had priority. They cited Article 33, paragraph 5, "The law of the public service shall be regulated with due regard to the traditional principles of the professional civil service." They interpreted this article to mean that public servants, appointed for life, are expected to serve and be loyal to the state and the constitution and to remain politically neutral and impartial in their official duties. Article 33, paragraph 4, deals with loyalty, "The exercise of state authority as a permanent function shall as a rule be entrusted to members of the public service whose status, service and loyalty are governed by public law." These constitutional provisions have been construed to mean that the civil servants owe a greater degree of loyalty to the state than does the ordinary citizen. By perpetuating this historical difference, contested by many delegates to the Parliamentary Council, the architects of the Basic Law in effect created one set of civil liberties for civil servants and another set for the rest of the population. In anchoring the behavior and beliefs of civil servants in the constitution, as the Prussian state had done in the early nineteenth century, the founders hewed to a statist political ideological and legal tradition, one that is hardly evident in other contemporary Western democracies.

To prevent a repetition of the situation when extremist groups undermined the Weimar Republic, the drafters of the Basic Law included three articles that are the basis for the concept of "militant democracy" (*streitbare Demokratie*). Articles 9, 18, and 21 grant the government the right to deprive political parties, associations, and individuals of their freedoms and rights if they abuse these rights in order to destroy the free and democratic basic order (*freie und demokratische Grundordnung*, FDGO). Article 21, for instance, stipulates that parties judged by their "aims or the behavior of their adherents to impair or abolish the FDGO or to endanger the existence of the Federal Republic of Germany (FRG) shall be unconstitutional," and that the Federal Constitutional Court shall decide on the question of unconstitutionality upon petition of the Parliament or government. Supporters of the decree cited the 1952 and 1956 decisions of the Constitutional Court outlawing extremist parties as setting the legal foundation for the FDGO. They also cited a 1970 decision that interprets articles 9, 18, and 21 to mean that citizens must defend the basic order and not misuse basic rights to abolish the order.[24]

Militant democracy became a battle cry of the CDU/CSU, the senior governing party from 1949 to 1969 and since 1982. Its leaders coined such slogans as "no freedom for the enemies of freedom," "tolerance except vis-à-vis intolerance," and "renunciation of terror, but not of self-defense against terror." The first two slogans applied to political extremists applying for civil service positions.

Some critics of the Decree against Radicals, on the other hand, contended that the constitutional articles on which the concept of militant democracy was based were included in the Basic Law in order to wage a campaign not against the Left but against the Right, which had been responsible for undermining the Weimar Republic and for producing the excesses of capitalism, which in turn had contributed to the rise of fascism. They warned that legitimate criticism of the existing system would be curbed for partisan advantages, ostensibly to safeguard freedom and democracy. Then militancy would become intolerance.[25]

These sharply clashing views of the meaning of some constitutional articles manifested a deep ideological gulf separating radicals and conservatives that could not easily be bridged. When the government began its loyalty programs, the gulf widened.[26]

The Public Service

Once the federal government was formed in 1949, it issued new laws and regulations dealing with the public service that signified primarily cosmetic rather than systemic changes to those promulgated under earlier German regimes. On May 17, 1950, a federal civil service law was signed; it hardly differed from its predecessor of 1937 except for the removal of all references to the Nazi regime. One clause stipulated that civil servants through their "entire behavior" must acknowledge the democratic (rather than national socialist) state concept. After years of discussion, the 1950 law was supplanted by the federal civil service law of July 14, 1953.

Under this law, an applicant must "be able to guarantee that he will defend at any time the FDGO in the spirit of the Basic Law." Once appointed, the new civil servant must swear an oath to support the Basic Law and all laws applying to the Federal Republic and must "through his entire behavior acknowledge the FDGO and be ready to maintain it."[27] The law also provided for rules of procedure and the uniform application of principles, guaranteed due process, and allowed applicants to verify in the courts whether proper grounds were used to deny them appointment.

In subsequent years, further revisions in civil service laws were made, including laws of 1957, 1961, 1965, and 1971, which set guidelines for Länder legislation. The Länder in turn passed similar laws for their personnel. These laws contain the FDGO clause but also stipulate that a civil servant is beholden to all people rather than one party, fulfills all tasks in a nonpartisan manner, and considers the general welfare. The civil servant is permitted to be active politically during off-duty hours but must show moderation and reserve.[28]

Thus the civil service laws passed since 1950 have maintained the traditions of the professional service built up over the centuries. Predemocratic structures of the Prussian civil service have hardly been altered, although the loyalty (*Treuepflicht*) of a public servant must now center on a democratic order. As noted, Western Allied and union attempts to achieve a fundamental change during the reconstruction of the civil service between 1945 and 1949 failed because most civil servants were retained from the Nazi era and were not interested in a reorganization that would have limited their status and power. The FDGO clause did not constitute a barrier to former Nazis remaining or being reinstated in the service. Most had been "small fry" who had joined the party under pressure or for opportunistic reasons. After the war they became apolitical and conducted themselves correctly. They had no difficulty switching allegiance to a new political system and thus were kept on, as they could be expected to defend the FDGO. On the other hand, as we shall see, many members of the revived Communist Party of Germany (KPD) who entered the public service after 1945 were weeded out a few years later because their views were held to be incompatible with the FDGO clause.

The reconstructed public service after 1945 is made up mainly of those working for the federal, Länder, or local governments (see table 1). In 1972, when the Decree against Radicals was issued, the total number of personnel was about 3.7 million. In 1976 it had risen to 3.9 million, and by 1984 to over 4.5 million. This sizable number, many of whom were subjects of loyalty investigations, is about 17 percent of the total economically active population.[29]

To achieve some coordination in this mammoth bureaucracy, the federal government has the right to issue framework legislation for the Länder that deals with appointments, training, conditions of service, and legal responsibilities. As stated earlier, the public service at all levels retains its traditional division into three groups: the civil servants (Beamten), normally comprising about 42 percent of the total personnel; salaried employees (*Angestellten*), 34 percent; and manual workers (*Arbeiter*), 24 percent. At the federal level, the percentage of employees and workers is higher than in the Länder because of the great number of personnel working for the federal railways and postal service. On the other hand, the Länder and local governments have a high percentage of civil servants because that status covers not only administrative staff in ministries, departments, or agencies but also police agents, teachers, health and social workers, television and radio station staffs, trash collectors, municipal swimming instructors, and a host of other categories. Thus, in Lower Saxony, for instance, 69 percent of personnel in 1974 were civil servants; 26 percent, salaried employees; and 5 percent, manual workers.[30] Because the Decree against Radicals applied especially to civil servants—although it also covered salaried employees and manual workers in the public service—the number of loyalty investiga-

Table 1
Personnel in Public Services,
June 30, 1972
(in thousands)

Federation	
Federal Ministries	314
Railways	423
Post	430
	1,167
Länder	
Central Administration	91
Finance	107
Police	156
Administration of Justice	110
School Teachers	388
University Staff	172
Medical Personnel	63
Others	172
	1,259
Local Authorities	741
Social Insurance Funds	177
State-owned Enterprises	365
	1,283
Total	3,709

Source: Figures supplied by Statistisches Bundesamt, Wiesbaden, letter to author, Nov. 16, 1987. See also Statistisches Bundesamt, Finanzen und Steuern, Fachserie 14, Reihe 6, *Personal des öffentlichen Dienstes, 1985* (Stuttgart: Kohlhammer, n.d.), pp. 148–59.

Note: Figures exclude armed forces.

tions was far greater than would occur in other Western countries, where the number of public servants is restricted to fewer categories of personnel.

The three-tier public service in West Germany perpetuates a division among personnel that favors the civil servants with high status in society and numerous privileges—early permanent status, high salaries and pensions—not enjoyed by the salaried employees and manual workers. The civil servants, aware of the state authority vested in them, are expected, however, to have a special loyalty to the state, as well as, according to one observer, "integrity, a strong sense of duty, and a narrow but vigorous professionalism."[31] Applicants for the administrative higher civil service must pass a rigorous state examination in law and the social sciences, followed by a minimum of two years of practical training and a second state examination. They receive permanent status after a maximum of six years in probationary status and when they are at least twenty-seven years old. Lacking a central civil service commission, each ministry or agency at the three levels of government selects its own personnel. Although the system is fragmented, public service law and regulations provide some uniformity, enabling personnel to transfer, for instance, from one Land to another. Civil servants are protected against arbitrary decisions of public authorities and are entitled to make use of administrative courts in grievance cases.[32] Only a disciplinary court can remove a civil servant from office if a serious breach of duty, such as lack of loyalty to the FDGO, can be proved.

Salaried employees and workers have a lower status and fewer privileges and rights than those accorded civil servants. For instance, employees receive permanent status only after fifteen years of service and their fortieth birthday. They cannot advance to the top nonpolitical posts in the ministries. As will be noted below, a number of personnel involved in loyalty screenings moved laterally from civil servant to employee classification or, when applying for a government position, chose the latter because, according to collective bargaining accords, the loyalty criterion was less rigorous than for civil servants.

Although the traditional public service structure was maintained, attitudinal changes have been visible among many civil servants in recent decades. As political parties assumed a greater policy-making role at the expense of the civil servants and as West Germans became more involved in political affairs and more interested in noneconomic, "postmaterialist" issues (such as participatory democracy in all organizations), civil servants became increasingly "advocates of the public" rather than "servants of the state." The "classical bureaucrats" (as Robert Putnam calls them), who still identify with the traditional values of the civil service state, are losing ground to the "political bureaucrats," who have become more responsive to the demands of individuals, interest groups, and parties. The political bureaucrats are usually younger, although Putnam has concluded on the basis of a transnational study that "top level civil servants in Germany in 1970 displayed great sensitivity to and support for the imperatives of politics in a democracy. By all the measures now available, they are hardly less egalitarian, hardly less liberal, hardly less politically responsive or programmatic in their outlook than their British or Swedish counterparts."[33]

Public Service Unions

The attitudinal schism among public servants that became more pronounced in the 1960s was present to a lesser degree in their views toward becoming members of associations or unions formed to protect their interests. The "classical" civil servants usually join the unaffiliated German Federation of Civil Servants (*Deutscher Beamtenbund,* DBB), with a membership in 1972 of about 713,000. The DBB is a powerful organization, which normally succeeds in its lobbying efforts to protect the gains made for its politically conservative members, most in the upper ranks of the service.

The "classical" employees and some civil servants (mostly former salaried employees) join the German Salaried Employees Union (*Deutsche Angestellten-Gewerkschaft,* DAG), which in 1972 had nearly 470,000 members, of whom 106,000 were salaried employees in the public service and 65,000 were technical employees and civil servants.

The more liberal pro-union public service personnel join the national unions affiliated with the largest peak organization, the German Trade Union Federation (DGB), with a total membership in 1972 of nearly 7 million and close ties to the SPD. Four of the then sixteen national unions organized mostly public servants (see table 2). (The fifth, the Police Union, joined the DGB in 1978, increasing the number of affiliated unions to seventeen.) These public service unions on occasion coordinate their lobbying and programmatic activities; their power in the DGB is significant because they constitute about 30 percent of total membership.

In 1972, the four public service unions were the Public Service and Transport Workers Union (*Gewerkschaft Öffentliche Dienste, Transport und Verkehr,* ÖTV), most of whose members are salaried employees and workers; the German Postal Workers Union (*Deutsche Postgewerkschaft,* DPG), mostly civil servants and some manual workers; the German Railroad Workers Union (*Gewerkschaft der Eisenbahner Deutschlands,* GdED), with a rather even division between civil servants and manual workers; and the Union of Teachers and Scientists (*Gewerkschaft Erziehung und Wissenschaft,* GEW), mostly civil servants and a sizable segment of employees. Most of these unions were strongly involved in the controversy surrounding the 1972 decree, partly because they had to deal with communist members in their own ranks.

The Adenauer-Heinemann Decree, 1950

Not only the unions but the government became concerned about communists in their midst during the emerging Cold War between the West and the East. Chancellor Konrad Adenauer (CDU) pursued a staunch anticommunist policy at home and abroad while putting the Federal Republic

Table 2

Membership of DGB Public Service Unions, 1972

Union	Total	Civil Servants	Salaried Employees	Manual Workers
Public Service and Transport	997,771	110,314	350,813	536,644
Postal Workers	390,788	247,218	33,404	110,166
Railroad Workers	434,889	188,513	10,463	235,913
Education and Science	125,745	106,563	19,182	0

Source: Statistisches Bundesamt, *Statistisches Jahrbuch für die Bundesrepublik Deutschland, 1973* (Stuttgart: W. Kohlhammer), p. 153.

Note: In 1978, the Police Union (GdP) had 152,486 members, of whom 133,474 were civil servants, 11,818 salaried employees, and 7,194 manual workers (*Statistisches Jahrbuch, 1979*, p. 549).

squarely into the Western Alliance system. A substantial majority of the populace favored this policy because of the historic anti-Soviet propaganda in Germany during the Weimar and Nazi periods, the association of communism with national socialism as twin totalitarian menaces, the millions of refugees who had fled from the Eastern territories at the end of the war, the behavior of the Soviet army during the war, and the record of the Soviets in their occupation zone (East Germany; after 1949, the German Democratic Republic, GDR).

Adenauer's policy meshed with that of the United States in its anti-Soviet policy. It also meshed with the vigorous U.S. postwar efforts to promote capitalism in Western Europe. One component of Adenauer's policy was to free the public service of political "extremists," a harbinger of the 1972 decree. On September 19, 1950, the cabinet issued a "decision (*Beschluss*) on political activity by members of the public service directed against the democratic basic order." The decision stated that the country's enemies were redoubling their efforts to undermine this order and that any involvement—such as participation, membership, or activity—in such endeavors was incompatible with the duties performed by public servants. It listed thirteen organizations, such as the Communist party (KPD), the League of Victims of the Nazi Regime (VVN), and other left groups, as well as three fascist groups, and called on the heads of the public service "to take appropriate action against civil servants, employees, and manual workers who breach their obligation of loyalty to the Federal Republic by involvement in such organizations or activities."[34] (Ironically, the KPD had participated in the drafting of the Basic Law, which created the democratic order.)

The cabinet decision stipulated that those found guilty "must be removed immediately from government service," although acknowledging that civil servants with permanent status could only be suspended without pay while formal administrative proceedings were instituted against them. Civil servants with probationary status (nonestablished appointments) would have their appointments cancelled, while personnel in clerical grades and manual workers would be dismissed without notice. The cabinet decision covered only those already in public service; it did not extend to applicants, because cabinet members assumed that the hiring authorities would not fill positions with political "extremists." When such persons did apply, they were normally told that because of a shortage of positions, they could not be hired. They began to get suspicious when a teacher shortage developed and less-qualified applicants received the positions.

To put the cabinet decision into effect for federal personnel, Minister of the Interior Gustav Heinemann (then CDU; later SPD and federal president, 1969–74) issued the so-called Adenauer-Heinemann decree (*Erlass*). The cabinet recommended to the Länder governments that they take corresponding action immediately, which all but one (Württemberg-Hohenzollern) did in the course of time.

There are no statistical data on the number of public servants who were dismissed, but the information is that there were few—most of them communists. Unlike the 1972 decree, the 1950 decree raised little discussion in public because political extremism was not yet a salient issue and a consensual atmosphere then prevailed between the major parties on the question of civil servants' loyalty to the state. Indeed, seven months earlier, on February 15, 1950, the SPD had already introduced in Parliament a bill labeled "Against the enemies of democracy," which mandated jail sentences for public servants found guilty of violating the Basic Law. (The bill was not passed.)

Left or right "extremists" who faced dismissal publicly objected to the 1950 decree; in addition, well-publicized criticisms in legal circles came from many judges and law professors, including conservative ones, who had doubts about some of the decree's provisions, such as making loyalty to the state more important than the civil servants' right to belong to a radical party that had not been outlawed. But their objections did not stop the government from drafting a federal civil servants law in November 1951 and a law on the political loyalty of public servants in April 1952. The latter did not receive the assent of the Bundestag (lower house of Parliament) because of constitutional objections. Hence the federal civil servants law was revised, with bipartisan support, to include a clause that only persons who pledged to support the FDGO could enter the service.[35]

In the early 1950s, the labor courts in numerous decisions did not initially support the Adenauer-Heinemann decree. But soon the tide turned. For instance, on December 11, 1951, the Rhineland-Palatinate Labor Court decided that the KPD membership of a public employee was a breach of his obligation to the service; to cancel his appointment was neither unconstitutional nor an error of judgment. On December 20, 1955, the Bavarian Supreme Administrative Court ruled that a civil servant who was a KPD town councillor could not be in government employment. On March 10, 1960, the Federal Administrative Court rendered the same decision as the Labor Court in a case concerning a postal civil servant.[36] But despite these court judgments, the Adenauer-Heinemann decree to test the civil servants' loyalty was not taken too seriously in the 1960s, once a period of liberalization set in.

Conclusion

This overview of civil servants' loyalty to the state in German history to the 1950s indicates that a remarkable continuity has existed in their loyal support of every regime, whether totalitarian, authoritarian, or democratic. Normally, civil servants are to be nonpartisan and serve any administration that comes into power in a democratic state. They are expected to execute the policies initiated by the political decision makers and not sabotage policies they personally disagree with. In Germany, however, their failure during the Empire and Nazi periods to be openly critical of policies that violated human rights, their willingness to serve under such administrations, and their failure to support fully the Weimar governments reveal their political conservatism, their authoritarian bureaucratic tradition, their high social status, and their insensitivity toward upholding basic democratic principles. Consequently, they had no qualms about accepting policies designed to keep dissenters out of the civil service or to oust those who were in it already. An exception was the Weimar era, when many of them tolerated Nazi colleagues in their midst who had violated civil service regulations. In the Federal Republic era, the Adenauer-Heinemann decree reflected a continuing concern with political left extremists in the public service, which, unlike the Weimar era, was soon populated primarily by personnel becoming more dedicated to the principles of democracy.

2

The 1972 Decree against Radicals

The Adenauer-Heinemann Decree of 1950 set the tone for the Decree against Radicals of 1972. The earlier decree showed that policymakers were convinced their system was potentially threatened by dangerous political foes within the public service. Then after a period of political quiescence, the turbulent late 1960s convinced them even more of the rising danger of the Left's gaining more influence and eventually taking over the institutions of the state. Whether their fear was legitimate or merely another stage in the repression of dissent will be examined.

The late 1960s witnessed, in many parts of the world, the rise of a student generation dissatisfied with aspects of the technological age, the horrors of the Vietnam War, the increasing poverty of the Third World, and the "faceless" bureaucracy. In West Germany, this antiestablishment group, known as the Extra-Parliamentary Opposition (APO), consisted primarily of a sizable number of university students, most of whom were members of an array of pacifist-neutralist, radical democratic, Marxist socialist, and New Left groups. The APO opposed national rearmament, the emergency legislation, capitalism and monopolies, government backing of U.S. intervention in Vietnam, the conservative media, and tradition-bound universities. One of its leaders, Rudi Dutschke, called on its adherents to "march through the institutions" of the state in order to produce at the minimum their democratization and at the maximum their radical transformation.

This call for youth to enter the teaching, social service, health, and other public service professions in order to change and improve society was not viewed with equanimity by conservatives (including right-wing social democrats) in the government, academia, and the media, who feared that the democratic state and the social market economy were threatened. Some of them were less worried about right radical groups, which seemed of no immediate threat to the state.[1]

Neo-Nazism

West Germany has seen the rise and decline of several minor neo-Nazi parties. In 1949, the German Reich party and the Socialist Reich party surfaced, but in 1952 the Constitutional Court declared the latter unconstitutional. In 1964, the German National Democratic party (NPD) was founded and five years later claimed twenty-eight thousand members. From 1966 to 1969, it received more than 5 percent of votes in seven Länder elections and therefore seats in their parliaments. But it never obtained that percentage in any Bundestag election (the highest total was 4.3 percent, based on nearly 1.5 million votes in 1969). By 1976 the faction-ridden party, a shadow of its former self with less than ten thousand members, mustered a mere 0.3 percent of the total vote.

In its programmatic declarations, the NPD claimed to support the FDGO, yet it glorified the rebirth of Germany through the formation of a "national democracy" and a "real Volk community of national solidarity." It emphasized the need for individuals to subordinate their interests to a collective weal. These ideas approximated closely those of the NSDAP, which the party did not criticize. Thus, its failure to support the individuals' inalienable rights in a democratic system ran counter to a cornerstone of the Basic Law. In addition, it denounced democratic institutions and "the oligarchy of party bosses," while espousing law and order, and jobs only for Germans and not foreigners.

Although the NPD's program had limited electoral appeal, the party never called for the overthrow of the Bonn government or advocated the commission of unlawful acts. Thus by skirting on the edge of legality, the Constitutional Court might have had difficulty outlawing it as an unconstitutional party. Whether NPD members supporting the party's program should be allowed into or remain in the civil service became an issue dividing the established parties, as will be noted below.

In 1977, the right-wing movement, with a total membership of about 17,000, included the weakened NDP, eighty-three small groups of the Old Right (the great majority of which had fewer than 100 members each), and a cluster of young, provocative activist groups of the New Right.[2] Despite the concern of many government officials, in the 1960s a number of rightists, of whom a majority were NPD members, had entered the ranks of the

Bundeswehr (army), had become teachers or judges in the administrative court system, or held other posts. By 1972, there were 1,487 in the public service, but of these the membership of 662 in rightist organizations was in doubt. (By 1978, the number of rightists had declined to 427, and by 1984, to 256, apparently because most had dropped their party membership, become politically inactive, or retired.) In 1972, of the 1,487 in the public service, 829 worked for the federal government, 387 for the Länder, 109 for local governments, and 162 for semiautonomous institutions. Close to half of NPD members in the federal service were in the permanent professional cadres of, or worked as civilian employees for, the Bundeswehr. In the Länder, one in four rightists was a teacher, while the rest were in justice, finance, police, and other branches. At all levels there were only 120 rightist civil servants and professional soldiers (8 percent) in the higher civil service and 294 (20 percent) in the executive class, but 756 (51 percent) in the clerical class and 317 (21 percent) in the basic class.[3]

Although the number of rightists in the public service seems to have declined swiftly after 1972, perhaps because that year's figures were inflated as a result of wrong data, the government made few attempts to remove those remaining, insisting at times that there was insufficient evidence against them. When efforts were made, as will be seen, the NPD members often won their appeals in courts or in disciplinary proceedings. In some instances they contended that they were not yet NPD members when they entered the public service in the 1960s but only joined thereafter and then remained nominal members.

Critics asked why the government did not take any measures to bar known NPD members who applied in the 1960s but became concerned only when left-radical applicants applied for positions in the late 1960s and early 1970s. By then few NPD members applied, because they were older and were working already, many times in occupations outside the civil service. New Left members, on the other hand, were younger and were more interested in starting their careers, often in such civil service fields as teaching and social work. Despite disclaimers by government hiring agencies that they were waging a one-sided campaign against leftists, in some CDU/CSU-governed Länder a double standard seemed to prevail; in a number of cases, leftists had more difficulty getting a position than rightists.[4]

Left Radicalism

The rise of left radicalism in the late 1960s eclipsed that of right radicalism, especially in the universities. A plethora of left groups mushroomed on fertile campus soil as a result of the already-cited dissatisfaction with a range of local, national, and international developments. In September 1968, the German Communist Party (*Deutsche Kommunistische Partei,* DKP) was founded as a successor organization to the KPD, which had been outlawed by the Constitutional Court in 1956. Given the more liberal international atmosphere, including a West German rapprochement with the East (Ostpolitik), which might have been endangered if the pro-Moscow DKP had been banned, the party hoped that it would not suffer the same fate as its predecessor. (The Grand Coalition government [CDU/CSU–SPD], in office from 1966 to 1969, had initiated the Ostpolitik under the aegis of Foreign Minister Willy Brandt [SPD].)

The DKP tailored its program to conform to the democratic principles of the Basic Law in order not to be banned as an unconstitutional party. In its basic program published in 1969 and at its convention in 1971, it contended that the democratic and social bases of the Basic Law could be realized only if socialism, standing for the principles of Marxism-Leninism and the governance of the working class, was achieved.

The Ministry of the Interior maintained that the DKP, a tool of the USSR and the GDR, camouflaged its program to prevent a ban; that it was in fact a disciplined cadre party, which received financial support from the GDR. Its aim was to overthrow the basic order through class struggle and to set up a communist dictatorship. It had no interest in a basic free, democratic order that, according to the ministry, stood for respect for human rights, popular sovereignty, separation of powers, government responsibility to Parliament, the independence of the judiciary, a multiparty system, and maintenance of a parliamentary opposition.[5]

Just as for the NPD, the DKP's alleged loyalty to the FDGO was to become a controversial issue that sparked a discussion on the members' right to enter or stay in the public service. As a result of the decree, the DKP received a good deal of publicity, but much of it was negative. The party never obtained more than token electoral support (0.6 percent of the total vote in the 1969 election) and had only a modest membership of about thirty-six thousand in 1972. Nevertheless, the Ministry of the Interior was concerned about the party and the 364 other radical left groups, whose membership, including the DKP, totaled about seventy-eight thousand.[6] Among them were the Maoist KPD, the Socialist Unity Party of West Berlin (SEW), the Marxist Student League-Spartakus (MSB-Spartakus), the Socialist University League (*Sozialistische Hochschulbund,* SHB), small ultraleft communist K-groups (*K-Gruppen*), and Trotskyite and "dogmatic New Left" factions.

The less organized and less dogmatic New Left groups (formerly German Socialist Student Federation [SDS], among others) and the youth organizations of the SPD (Young Socialists or Jusos) and FDP (Young Democrats), which also advocated radical anticapitalist system changes in the Federal Republic, were excluded from the ministry listing. When all the left groups began to organize students on campuses and to form coalitions, CDU/CSU students were outnumbered. In 1971, for instance, the left groups captured nearly 58 percent of the seats in forty-five university student parliaments—although three years later their strength had dwindled to less than 35 percent.[7]

Many left-radical university graduates and other left radicals sought public service positions in the late 1960s. According to the Ministry of the Interior, by the end of 1972 there were 1,307 left radicals in the public service, of whom 235 worked for the federal government, 695 for the Länder, 236 for municipalities, and 141 for semiautonomous institutions. About eighty percent were DKP and SEW members or members of DKP- and SEW-allied and influenced organizations, and the rest were New Left members. How these individuals managed to enter or stay in the public service despite the Adenauer-Heinemann and the Radical decrees must be examined later.

Of those in federal employment, nearly 50 percent worked for the post office, 40 percent for the federal railways, and others for the Bundeswehr. Of those in Länder employment, 44 percent were teachers; 21 percent, professors and nonacademic professionals at universities; 12 percent, other personnel in schools and universities; 6 percent, in justice; and 17 percent, in other administrative branches. There were no known leftists in the Federal Border Guard (*Grenzschutz*) or in the police forces, which in West Germany are under Länder jurisdiction.

In 1978, of all left radicals, 50 percent were civil servants; 42 percent, employees; and 8 percent, workers. The distribution of the civil servants into the four classes shows a significant difference from that of the NPD civil servants. There were 619 (54 percent) left radicals in the higher civil service (the right—NPD—had only 8 percent in 1972), 426 (37 percent) in the executive class (the right, 20 percent), 86 (7 percent) in the clerical class (the right, 51 percent), and 28 (2 percent) in the basic class (the right, 21 percent).[8] The marked difference between the distribution of left radicals and right radicals in the four classes was the result of different educational achievements—most left radicals had a university degree and thus could compete for the top class, while most right radicals, lacking such a degree, were restricted to the lower classes. Many left radicals attempted to become teachers, but right radicals were more interested in the Bundeswehr and police.

The rise of left radicalism in the Federal Republic was paralleled in 1968 by the rise of left terrorism. Andreas Baader and Ulrike Meinhof led one group, which in 1971 became known as the Red Army Faction. This group, rivaled by other small groups, launched a mini–guerrilla war against the Establishment. In April 1968, in its first terrorist action, the Baader-Meinhof group set fires in two Frankfurt department stores. There followed a series of bank holdups as well as kidnappings and murders of government officials and businessmen. The actions were designed to shatter the people's support for the capitalist government and to put fear in those governing the nation, but the terrorists were unable to achieve their goals. Instead they strengthened rather than weakened the anticommunist cause. They inspired government overreaction, civil liberties restrictions, and fear among the populace (see chapter 8). They contributed to nonterrorist radicals' being labeled "enemies of the state," despite the radical left's denunciation of terrorism.

The Conservative Challenge

The terrorists were seen as a serious threat by conservatives in the major parties, who used the activities of terrorists as a pretext for action against the radical left, viewed as equally or more threatening to the body politic in the long run. Once again, these conservatives held the communists—and Nazis—responsible for the end of the Weimar period. To prevent the Federal Republic from suffering a similar fate, they contended, actions against extremists seeking entry into the public service must be taken. The neo-Nazi NPD had already peaked in the early 1960s; hence the radical left represented the real danger.[9] Implicit was the fear of young, nonconformist intellectuals challenging the prevailing political culture, the neocapitalist economic system with its worldwide investments, the military establishment with its alliance to the Western bloc, and the political nonsocialist Establishment.

Helmut Schelsky, a sociology professor, supplied the academic arguments for the establishment parties' campaign against the radical Left: In its march through the institutions, the Left's strategy is to capture first the key nongovernmental positions in universities and teachers' colleges, then in other educational sectors, churches, and information and entertainment sectors. Such strategy must be stymied at all costs.[10]

In concurrence, one writer noted that neo-Marxists had infiltrated especially the political science and sociology departments of universities. They had radicalized a significant portion of students, who were ready to resist the constitutional order, as witnessed in the demonstrations against the Shah of Iran. The writer concluded, "Our state cannot afford to have teachers, who are effective as multipliers, opposed to the constitution."[11]

These views were shared by most SPD and Free Democratic party (FDP) as well as all CDU/CSU leaders. Following the 1969 election, the latter had to give up governing the nation after two decades in power. In political opposition to the social-liberal coalition of SPD and FDP, which had embarked on a major domestic reform policy, the CDU/CSU leaders needed an issue that would have popular backing and that might embarrass the governing coalition. In October 1971, CDU leader Rainer Barzel, at the party convention, accused left radical teachers of spending more time denouncing the military junta in Greece and American intervention in Vietnam than the "totalitarian communist system of the German Democratic Republic." He spoke of a consensus among 90 percent of West Germany's citizens to sustain democracy and fight radicalism.[12]

At the same time, in a major Bundestag debate, Barzel warned the country about the radical left's intention to undermine and sap the societal order. He called on all democratic parties to wage a common struggle against it. In reply, Chancellor Brandt (in office from 1969 to 1974) contended that social democrats do not need a reminder to take issue with communists or that a hunt against the latter was necessary.[13] He rejected Barzel's implication that the SPD was soft on communism and provided an opening to the communists at home.

When CDU/CSU leaders spoke of an opening, they were referring to the radicals' entrance into the civil service, especially into schools, where pupils were said to be exposed to communist propaganda. The CDU/CSU leaders, in discussing ways of keeping the radicals out, thought first of a judicial route. They considered requesting the federal government or Parliament to initiate proceedings against the DKP, to which many civil service applicants belonged, before the Federal Constitutional Court. The leaders hoped that if the court declared the radical party unconstitutional, its adherents could be barred legally from the public service.

As noted, Brandt, intent on maintaining a détente policy with communist states, did not want to alienate the Soviets by making DKP members outlaws in the Federal Republic. Unwilling to take any step against the DKP, he stated publicly that he did not want to interfere in the free competition of political parties or to overuse the sword of prohibition against an extremist party.[14]

But Brandt faced another problem within the SPD, which the CDU/CSU exploited to the full. The neo-Marxist Jusos were challenging the SPD's domestic policies, viewed as being too moderate and too system conforming. To gain a greater foothold in the policy-making organs of the party and the government, Juso members became the activists in the party, ran for public offices, and sought positions in the civil service. But as a minority in the party, the Jusos had to contend with powerful center and right wings, which had their own ideological differences. According to one newspaper account, Brandt, a leader of the center wing, feared that the Jusos would stream into the civil service and entrench themselves in local, state, and national administrations as a prelude to challenging the more orthodox SPD policies. To prevent such a challenge, he concurred with the proposal set forth primarily by CDU/CSU leaders to bar radicals from entering the public service.[15] Although some SPD officials had strong misgivings about the need for such a step and its consequences, they wanted to defuse CDU/CSU charges that the SPD was not tough enough on communism and left radicalism, the latter espoused by the Jusos.

SPD leaders who were critical of a possible ban supported the statement made by Günter Nollau, former president of the Federal Office for the Protection of the Constitution (*Bundesamt für Verfassungsschutz*—the domestic intelligence service), that no basis existed for the fear that enemies of the constitution would invade the public service and systematically undermine the Federal Republic.[16] A few SPD and FDP officials, in the left or center wings of their parties, were of the opinion that the country would not change much if the radicals, who had little political support, were allowed into the public service, because a healthy democracy could profit from their critiques and because they often tempered their critical views in their later professional life. Political scientist Kurt Sontheimer, who is personally critical of the radicals, reinforced such a position: "There can in any case not be any talk of a real threat to German democracy by radical parties in the manner of the Weimar Republic."[17]

The Hamburg Decree

The more conservative SPD officials disagreed with the view that left radicals were not a threat. They took the initiative against left radicals, including sizable communist groups, in the SPD stronghold of Hamburg, one of many cities where parents feared that their children would be exposed to "Red propaganda" in schools by the 1968 generation of young progressive teachers who had been appointed on probation. The right-wing

SPD mayor Peter Schulz and his associates in the city-state administration were wary both of Juso accusations that they were not responsive to the demands of youth and of CDU accusations that they were blind to leftist machinations. They were also cognizant of the publicity generated by the *Verfassungsschutz* concerning the many left radicals who were in the public service throughout the Federal Republic. They did not want to act as the Trojan horse responsible for the Left's capturing schools and eventually the city administration.

Left critics viewed the threat as exaggerated. They said that leftist teachers were primarily interested in introducing antiauthoritarian and democratic reforms, humanism, and an understanding of the Nazi past into a traditional curricular system that had withstood similar Western Allied attempts at reform more than two decades earlier. They wanted more workers' children to have an opportunity to enter *Gymnasien* (academic high schools) and universities. From 1970 on, the teachers' union (GEW) authorized a warning strike should no reforms be undertaken, and it organized meetings and demonstrations.

The Hamburg Senate, making only minor concessions, considered the teachers' demands a threat to cultural values and the stream of left radicals into the public service a threat to state security. Because the threats were national rather than local, it tried to gain support for joint action from other Länder (see below).[18] In the meantime, it decided to act on its own. On November 23, 1971, the senate (the city's executive body) issued a decree that became the model for the Decree against Radicals of 1972.[19] The decree prohibited entry into the civil service, especially the educational sector, of candidates who had been politically active in an extreme leftist or rightist group. It sparked protests: the Hamburg University Senate sharply criticized the decree's limits on academic freedom; left-wing SPD leaders assailed its antileft bias and its unfairness toward applicants. Without warning, applicants were informed that their party membership (usually DKP) would be held against them and that they would be prohibited from entering the profession for which they had been trained.

Before the city-state decree was issued, the Hamburg and North Rhine-Westphalia SPD government chiefs urged the Standing Conference of Länder Minister-Presidents to consider national action. Supported by Federal minister of the interior Hans-Dieter Genscher (FDP), the minister-presidents, convening on October 14, requested the Standing Conference of Ministers of the Interior to prepare a report on political loyalty of public servants for the December 3 meeting. The ministers of the interior set up a working group that drafted a lengthy experts' report, which became the basis for the 1972 decree.[20] Federal minister of justice Gerhard Jahn (SPD) and SPD deputy chairman Herbert Wehner warned about possible unconstitutional aspects but reluctantly accepted the draft decree once the SPD executive committee gave its approval.[21]

The 1972 Decree

On January 27, 1972, Genscher and the Länder ministers of the interior met to discuss at length, and to make compromises on, the draft of the decree. On the following day, the eleven minister-presidents (six SPD, four CDU, one CSU), convening as the Standing Conference of Länder Minister-Presidents, concurred on the text, published first as a declaration (*Erklärung*), "Basic Principles on the Question of Anticonstitutional Personnel in the Public Service." Then they met with Chancellor Brandt, who later claimed to have played a passive role in the talks. To justify his position, he insisted that ministers of the interior merely sought an understanding to concur on uniform procedures, which would also circumvent any possible ban on the DKP.[22]

Brandt put his signature on another joint declaration issued the same day, which was nearly identical to the first one but extended coverage to employees and workers in the public service. The declaration, which dealt with applicants to the public service as well as personnel already in it, stated: "Only persons who can guarantee that they are prepared at all times to uphold the FDGO as laid down in the Basic Law, may be appointed to the public service. Civil servants, whether on or off duty, are required to take an active part in maintaining this constitutional system."[23]

The declaration also stipulated that each case must be examined and settled on its own merits and that a candidate "pursuing anticonstitutional (*verfassungsfeindlich*) activities" shall not be appointed. If a candidate belongs to an organization pursuing "anticonstitutional aims," doubt is cast on "the candidate's readiness at all times to uphold the FDGO. In most cases such doubts would justify rejecting the candidate's application." In the section on personnel already in government employment, the declaration reiterated the civil servants' obligation in their "total behavior" to support and maintain the FDGO. If in their actions or in their membership in an organization with anticonstitutional aims they are not fulfilling the Civil Service Act provision concerning support of the FDGO, then the employing authority will review their case to see whether their dismissal from the public service should be initiated. For manual workers and salaried employees in the public sector, nearly similar principles applied.

Both declarations, soon called decisions (*Beschlüsse*), were said to be restatements of existing civil service statutes rather than new policies or legal documents. According to official justification, they were issued only to set up uniform procedures throughout the Federal Republic, but, as will be noted, they did make some policy changes.

On February 18, the minister-presidents and Land ministers promulgated a joint decree (*Gemeinsamen Runderlass*) that formalized their earlier declaration. On April 28, the ministers of the interior met to approve guidelines for the Länder, which between 1972 and 1973 issued their own decrees based on the January 28 declarations. These implementing decrees differed slightly from Land to Land.[24]

Unlike the Adenauer-Heinemann decree of 1950, the 1972 decrees did not list any prohibited organizations or parties. This omission gave the authorities greater flexibility to set their own standards but also produced more uncertainty among applicants. When Genscher sent to Land officials and the courts a report about the anticonstitutional goals of the DKP and the duties expected of its members, all knew that the party would be on the "hit list." This had not been the case in October 1967, when the Länder ministers of the interior, basing their views on Constitutional Court decisions affirming that a minority had a right to existence and a chance at equality, had no objections to the reconstitution of a German communist party as a quid pro quo for the new détente policy with the East. In the years thereafter no civil servant was dismissed for such membership.[25] But in 1972 the political realities had changed.

Extremism and Radicalism

One indicator of the changing times was the deep ideological schism in the body politic among conservative, liberal, social democratic, and radical forces. The schism was reflected in the dispute that arose over the terminology of the decree, with some asserting that it was not a decree but merely a declaration of policy. A more correct statement is that it started as a declaration and a decision and was soon codified into a decree (or series of Länder decrees). Given the lengthy title of the decree, a shorthand term was necessary. CDU/CSU officials began to call it a decision against extremists (*Extremistenbeschluss*). Noncommunist left radicals objected because the term implied that the decree was going to be restricted to "extremists" (DKP or NPD members) who favored the revolutionary, forceful overthrow of the existing system and the creation of a dictatorship of the Left or Right.[26] The left radicals, made up of the Jusos (SPD), Young

Democrats (FDP), and other "radical democrats," contended that the decree was directed against them too, even though they favored a peaceful change of the order. The conservatives retorted that most of the left radicals were DKP extremists whose avowed goal was to abolish the old order. The decree was aimed against such extremists rather than against noncommunist left radicals.[27]

Thus conservatives not only used the terms "extremists" and "radicals" interchangeably but put the moderate leftists in the same left radical pot as the DKP and at times named them all as potential helpers of terrorists. Government officials shared in the obfuscation. They labeled extremists and radicals "enemies" of the constitution who lacked "loyalty." The DKP, with its own vocabulary, seldom used the term "communist"; instead it opted for "engaged" or "critical democrats," "democratic forces," and "active unionists." Opponents of the decree called it *Berufsverbot* (ban on careers), because applicants certified to become teachers, mail carriers, or locomotive engineers had little or no opportunity to work in the private sector. The government in turn objected strenuously to the term "Berufsverbot," finding it loaded and exaggerated and labeling those who used it as suspected radicals. In some other West European countries it found its way into the local languages, making it almost as well known as *Blitzkrieg, Panzer, Kindergarten,* and *kaputt.*[28]

Critiques of the Decree

Once the decree was issued, the Left criticized its substance. The DKP maintained that it discriminated against the party and its members. Given the party's support of the Basic Law, the threats against its members were undemocratic, politically untenable, and unconstitutional. According to the DKP, the real purpose of the decree, behind which stood reactionary capitalist forces, was to limit the democratic rights of the working class and to prevent open discussion, a basic democratic principle. If communism were equated with Nazism, public opinion would tolerate the decree more willingly. The DKP called on the SPD not to make joint cause with the CDU/CSU, which was responsible for mobilizing reactionary forces.[29]

A number of left-radical university professors, critical of the decree, argued that progressive students could not champion socialism without the ruling elite calling them enemies of the state and making the "fight against radicals" the government's most important task. Such a fight was timed to coincide with a difficult economic and social situation in order to distract the population with a nonexistent problem. In no other European state was the term "radical" used in such a derogatory manner. If in these other states government officials wanted to dismiss communists from teaching positions, the officials would be regarded as foes of democracy. The decree will lead to discrimination against radicals and might be a stepping stone to a police state, such as seen then in Spain, Portugal, Greece, and Turkey. To prevent the establishment of a police state, a broad solidarity of those affected and potential victims, such as unionists, was necessary.

The League of Democratic Academics (*Bund demokratischer Wissenschaftler*), a DKP-dominated organization of left-radical university professors and professional staff, maintained that the decree furthered ideological repression, narrowed the pluralism of views, and impoverished serious controversial discussions at universities.[30] The Association of German Student Governing Boards (*Verband Deutscher Studentenschaften*, VDS), the confederation of university student bodies, sharply attacked the decree, seeing in it a "signal for an official chase after democrats and socialists." It urged support for petitions circulating on campuses and for protest demonstrations in university towns, in which thousands of students were expected to participate.[31]

The association of graduate student assistants contended that the decree would keep progressives out of the civil service and accelerate conformity with government policies among dissenting groups. None should be deemed enemies of the constitution as long as the Constitutional Court had not rendered a decision.

In the year following the decree's publication, other groups joined part of the academic community in the protests. In an open letter to the Bundestag presidium, fourteen prominent writers questioned the decree's constitutionality; it did not precisely define radicalism and did not discriminate against right radicals as much as left radicals. In a resolution, the PEN-Center of the Federal Republic (the association of writers) stated that the decree would make the work of academics, writers, and journalists in the media more difficult.[32]

The Jusos and Young Democrats strongly criticized the decree at their national conferences. The Jusos, in a resolution of February 27, 1972, accused their parent organization of coresponsibility in initiating the decree. They feared that the decree would intimidate people working for anticapitalist societal changes. The decree's equation of constitutional loyalty with support of the laissez-faire economy represented the triumph of reaction. The SPD ministers, putting themselves in the service of anticommunist forces, should have heeded Wehner's warning in early January

1972 that if one starts the process of labeling certain groups as anticonstitutional, there is no end in sight. The Jusos called on the decree's opponents to put political pressure on the government decision makers through demonstrations, flyers, signature campaigns, informational meetings, and contacts with deputies.[33]

The Young Democrats (FDP), in a resolution of June 24–25, 1972, echoed the Juso arguments. They charged that the decree endangered the citizens' basic rights in order to prevent progressive changes and intimidated the younger generation from engaging in political activities. Its demand for constitutional loyalty discriminated against socialists and communists in the civil service and demanded conformity to the political and economic status quo.[34]

Defense of the Decree

The decree had its defenders among all establishment parties, although it soon became a weapon that the CDU/CSU used against the governing SPD and FDP. A CDU official, Rainer Barzel, used the Juso critique as ammunition against the SPD. He called upon SPD leaders to put an end to the Juso campaign; if they failed to take action, suspicion would arise that they were not energetically behind the decree.[35] Hans Filbinger, right-wing CDU chairman of Baden-Württemberg, stated that whenever the SPD had governed the nation or certain Länder, communists had infiltrated the judiciary, the police, and the army. According to Friedrich Vogel, the legal expert of the CDU/CSU Bundestag *Fraktion* (group), the decree's promulgation was a victory for his party; if it was executed vigorously, communists would no longer march through the institutions.[36]

On March 13, 1972, CDU chiefs, in a strategy meeting on the decree, called on all democrats to maintain solidarity against the radicals, who were intent on subverting the Federal Republic by establishing a totalitarian system. The CDU chiefs welcomed the assurance by DGB labor leaders that radical unionists would not be supported for elections to shop councils.[37] One week after the CDU meeting, the SPD chiefs met to reaffirm their support of the decree. They insisted that it did not signify a departure from previous regulations concerning civil servants or the beginning of a new witch-hunt but rather that it was designed only to provide uniformity in execution.

On June 7, a Bundestag debate indicated the absence of substantial interparty schisms, despite open dissent by the Jusos and Young Democrats. Minister of the Interior Genscher, reflecting this parliamentary consensus, stated that a democratic state can fulfill its function to promote freedom only when it is free of the enemies of freedom. He called on all Länder to issue the implementing regulations as soon as possible. CDU/CSU deputies pointed to the lack of unity within the SPD, which SPD deputies glossed over, especially because of the growing opposition to the decree among some SPD Land executive committees and subdistrict conferences.[38]

The conservative German Teachers Association (*Deutscher Lehrerverband*), composed primarily of *Gymnasien* teachers, announced as soon as the decree was published that it would not tolerate DKP and NPD members in its ranks. Its affiliated branches were requested to enforce this ruling.[39] In the universities, the League for the Freedom of Science and Research (*Bund Freiheit der Wissenschaft*), the conservative professorial counterpart to the League of Democratic Academics, and the Circle of Christian Democratic Students (RCDS), associated with the CDU, responded to the criticisms of the decree's opponents with arguments mirroring those of the CDU/CSU.

The major independent labor federations, DBB and DAG, supported the decree, but the public service unions in the DGB had increasing doubts. The DGB unions, well aware of the problem of communists in the public service, had to resolve a similar problem within their own ranks. In October 1973, as a result of DKP and other left radicals becoming active in the unions, the DGB passed a resolution declaring membership in a DGB-affiliated union to be incompatible with support of left-extremist parties, associations, or groups. DGB leaders feared that if DKP and other left-radical members captured union leadership posts, the public image of the unions would be damaged and nonleftist members would leave. But this incompatibility clause was applied laxly against rank-and-file DKP members unless they became politically active in the unions. On the other hand, members of more extremist Maoist K-groups were often ousted, and some of them subsequently lost their jobs if their names were published in union newspapers.

In the teachers' union (GEW), on the political left within the DGB, the total membership included about 5 percent communists, but the GEW leaders did not see that number as a threat to their own incumbency.[40] They knew, however, that they had to take a position on the Decree against Radicals. As a result of the discussion preceding the Hamburg decree of November 1971, the GEW executive committee (*Hauptvorstand*) announced the union's continued support of the FDGO. The enemies of the constitution had no place in either the union or the public service. But membership alone in an extremist party could not be a factor for excluding an applicant to the service; concrete evidence of views hostile to the constitution must be shown to refuse anyone entry. The union would provide legal assistance to all its members who were denied entry or who might be ousted, even though it did not identify itself with the political views of those affected.[41]

The DGB at numerous congresses since the 1950s had passed resolutions upholding the principle of civil servants' loyalty to the state and to the FDGO. At the ninth congress, held in Berlin in June 1972, the DGB reaffirmed this principle but pledged legal support to members in its constituent unions who were adversely affected by the decree. It insisted on an individual review of each case and the maintenance of due process.[42]

The unions' qualified initial support of the decree in 1972 must be understood in the broader context of their determination to be in the forefront of the defenders of the FDGO. As in the case of the SPD, the DGB unions did not want to be accused by their opponents, including the conservative media, of being soft on communism. Yet, as will be noted below, in the succeeding years their consensual position began to weaken.

Execution of the Decree

Government decision makers were heartened by initial widespread support for the decree and minimal, if vocal, opposition from left-radical groups; they did not know that in its implementation there would be mounting administrative and political problems. The chief one was the continuing lack of uniformity among the Länder, compounded by the failure of a number of Länder to issue implementing guidelines within one year of the decree's promulgation.

SPD-governed Länder, in general, applied the decree less strictly than did CDU/CSU-governed Länder, although there were variations among them too. In the left-wing SPD stronghold of Hesse, the government, during the initial two years, interpreted the decree loosely. It promised not to deny positions automatically to radical applicants but to examine each application carefully. Minister-President Albert Osswald (SPD) said that applicants would not be required to sign loyalty oaths, partly because "subversive opponents of the constitution" would not hesitate to sign them.[43] The SPD-led governments in Berlin, Lower Saxony, Hamburg, Bremen, and North Rhine-Westphalia announced that mere membership in an extremist organization would not necessarily be reason for disbarment but that applicants who held posts in one would be barred from employment.[44]

In the CDU/CSU-governed Länder, nominal membership in an extremist organization was normally ground for disbarment; in Rhineland-Palatinate the government allowed exceptions dependent on the nature of each case. To provide a minimum of uniformity among all Länder in the Federal Republic, the ministers of the interior issued a supplementary decree on April 28, 1972, requiring the hiring authorities in each Land to check with their *Verfassungsschutz* whether it had a file on an applicant containing any entries for the previous five years that would justify refusing an appointment. If the *Verfassungsschutz* could not provide any negative facts, the applicant had to sign a loyalty oath to the FDGO as a condition for employment. Should the applicant refuse to sign, doubts about his or her loyalty would lead to a ban on employment. Should the applicant once hired violate a signed oath, such an individual would be subject to dismissal.[45]

The supplementary decree was not always obeyed. In the SPD-governed city of Munich, for instance, the hiring authorities, objecting to the Bavarian practice of automatically barring members of extremist organizations, refused to ask the CSU-controlled Bavarian Ministry of the Interior and its *Verfassungsschutz* whether any negative entries were in its files.

In the initial year of the decree, the federal government and the Länder usually refrained from taking any action against members of extremist organizations already in the public service as long as they did not engage in antidemocratic actions, such as infraction of the duty to be loyal.

Conclusion

The birth of the 1972 decree must be viewed in a historical and political-cultural context, especially in terms of the strength of dissident movements challenging the prevailing norms. While neo-Nazism has had its ups and downs in the history of the Federal Republic, the Bonn and many Länder governments were less concerned about its renewed growth in the 1960s than about the mushrooming of the radical left, especially at universities. Driven by fear of subversion from the GDR and imbued with a virulent anticommunism, the SPD, FDP, and CDU/CSU leaders were afraid, or professed to be afraid, of the Left's infiltrating the public institutions and capturing them. When the CDU/CSU leaders, who were genuinely concerned about the preservation of the political democratic and neocapitalist system, were in the parliamentary opposition after 1969, they put pressure on SPD and FDP policymakers in the government, first, to request a ruling from the Constitutional Court to ban the most visible symbol of the radical Left, the DKP, and, second, to issue a decree to prevent radicals from entering the public service.

The policymakers yielded to the second demand, although most of them did not expect the Left to be successful in an institutional takeover. Rather, they feared a voter backlash against their parties at the next election for being weak on communism, as the CDU/CSU repeatedly charged. The charge was false; SPD and FDP chiefs were as anticommunist as their conservative counterparts. Despite shades of differences between the two party blocs on anticommunist tactics, they concurred on the need to keep radicals, especially leftists, out of the public service. Symbolically, right-wing SPD chiefs in Hamburg issued a decree against radicals only months before Chancellor Brandt and the minister-presidents, in a multipartisan move, announced their accord on the declaration—followed soon by a joint decree. Predictably, sharp reaction came from left political forces, but not from NPD leaders, who even paid lip service to it, perhaps hoping that their party members would not be adversely affected.

In their crusade against left radicals, the policymakers maintained a policy of repression and social control against dissenters. They did not make a sharp distinction between Leninist-imbued elitist and authoritarian radicals, who were committed to seeing a state socialist system replace the capitalist system, and New Left radicals, who demanded that political, economic, and social institutions become more participatory and conform with democratic, progressive clauses in the Basic Law.[46] By not differentiating between these two major strands of left radicalism, the policymakers created a multitude of problems in the wake of the Decree against Radicals.

The decree symbolized the government's giving priority to safeguarding the state by requiring loyalty of its civil servants over constitutional protection of individual rights. The decree also demonstrated the importance of the state's political culture, its anticommunism in this instance, which had a direct bearing on the degree of government repression of political dissidents. Although observers might assume that the more conservative the government in a democratic system, the greater the restrictions on civil liberties, in this case, the social-liberal SPD-FDP government was coresponsible for the formulation and initiation of the decree. Several factors— the politically exposed state since the end of the war, the perceived German vulnerability on issues related to political democracy, the anticommunist ideology, the maintenance of the neocapitalist system, and the fear of subversion from the GDR that might lead to the undermining of the Federal Republic—permeated all establishment parties, regardless of their differences on other issues. These were the compelling reasons for the genesis of the decree.

3

The Aftermath,
1973–1976

The controversy surrounding the 1972 decree intensified in the following years, and it became one of the most hotly contested domestic issues in the postwar period. Proponents and opponents waged bitter campaigns that left scars not easily healed by the passage of time. This chapter first concentrates on some of the reasons why the opponents attempted to gain support for a repeal of the decree—the activities of the *Verfassungsschutz*, the scope of the hearings, the nature of the court decisions, the number of individuals affected by the decree, and its effect on some of them. Then the focus turns on the public's reaction to the decree and the constellation of those opposing it (citizens initiative groups and segments of the unions, the SPD and the FDP) and those supporting it (the CDU/CSU and conservative groups and scholars, and the SPD and FDP establishments). Finally, the Constitutional Court decision of 1975 bearing on the decree and legislative and executive attempts to amend it are examined.

Verfassungsschutz

In 1950, at a time when spies from East Germany posed a problem to the nation's security, the Federal and Länder Offices for the Protection of the Constitution (*Verfassungsschutz*) were established. Charged with keeping subversive activities in the Federal Republic under observation, they were especially interested in the activities of leftist groups. According to statute, they are responsible for compiling and assessing intelligence information, reports, and other material on attempts to undermine the constitutional system. (The Criminal Investigation Bureau or police handle investigations, arrests, and prosecutions of individuals charged with violation of laws.)

When applicants for the public service seek positions, they apply directly to the government agency for which they want to work. As part of a security investigation, the agency asks the *Verfassungsschutz* to check its central computer data bank in Cologne to see if the applicant's name appears in it. If the answer, available in a few seconds, is negative, as is usually the case, security clearance is normally granted. If a file exists (*Erkenntnisfall*), the information is forwarded to the agency, which then evaluates the information and possibly holds an informal hearing (see below). The *Verfassungsschutz* is forbidden at that stage to obtain more data on the applicant.

Controversy has arisen about the methods used by the *Verfassungsschutz* to collect materials for its political data files, which numbered more than 2 million in 1975 and reportedly more since then. Critics insist that the agency has exceeded its legal restrictions. In addition to gaining information from open sources—public speeches, pamphlets, doctoral theses, lists of candidates for public offices, and information in the press—it has engaged in covert surveillance, concealed photography, mail opening, and telephone tapping and has used agents provocateurs and informers.[1]

It receives much information from twenty to thirty thousand contact persons and informers active in political groups, as well as from police, state registrar's offices, universities, and other administrative bodies. Some of this information is based on hearsay evidence, malice, or mistaken identities. According to a former Constitutional Court judge, "Often the files of the intelligence service are not worth the paper on which they are written."[2]

The *Verfassungsschutz* has been especially interested in the political views of university students. According to some critics, it hired a number of students to spy on fellow students and professors. These informers are said to collect flyers and pamphlets, report on public lectures, and take notes on student reports and discussions in political science and sociology seminars.[3] The well-known use of informants in universities eventually had a dampening effect on academic freedom and led to students' being afraid to voice dissenting views openly. The students knew that their names would then be stored in an intelligence file, diminishing their chances of obtaining a position in public service.

To obtain the mass of data, the federal *Verfassungsschutz* in the 1970s and 1980s requested and received more budgetary and personnel support. In 1969, its budget was nearly 30 million Deutsch Mark, and it had over 1,000 personnel. By 1978, its budget exceeded 100 million DM, and it had more than 2,100 personnel.[4] In the 1980s, it has continued to receive substantial support. The Länder *Verfassungsschutz* agencies expanded correspondingly.

The question whether this expansion of the *Verfassungsschutz* was necessary to keep up with its surveillance activities became the source of much debate. Government supporters insisted that there was no danger of the growth of an authoritarian state crushing freedoms with a powerful secret police. They avowed that the *Verfassungsschutz* generally has not exceeded its powers and that the ministries of the interior keep tabs on it. But critics contended that the growth of the intelligence service did not correspond to any greater danger to the Federal Republic. The service had developed a dynamic of its own, which meant that parliamentary controls became less effective. The critics also noted the antileft bias of the *Verfassungsschutz*, whose president in 1971 was Hubert Schrübbers (CDU). Under the Nazis he had been a prosecuting attorney who demanded that judges jail antifascists for several years for minor offenses. The critics' complaints of the expansion of the intelligence service, improvements in its technical knowhow, and conservative political bias must be examined further in the context of restrictions on civil liberties (see chapter 8).

Irrespective of the criticisms, the *Verfassungsschutz* played a key role in the administration of the 1972 decree because of its extensive files, its data bank, and its yearbooks, which listed the activities of left- and rightextremist groups. Government agencies hiring applicants for public service used these lists as guidelines in the screening process.[5]

Hearings

The top bureaucrats in the agencies, rather than the politicians, made the key decisions on how the 1972 decree would be applied to security screenings, including an average of six hundred informal or formal hearings per year from 1972 to 1976.[6] When an applicant's name appeared in the *Verfassungsschutz* computer, the agency that had received the application reviewed the *Verfassungsschutz* file and decided whether there would be a hearing on the basis of any incriminating evidence. If there was sufficient evidence, normally true in only a minority of cases, then one or more closed hearings, each lasting from a brief time to three hours, were held.

At a typical hearing, or "conversation" (as it was called at times), high civil servants, usually politically conservative, made up the examining commission. (On occasion, only one civil servant examined the applicant.) The applicant was expected to answer all queries and to defuse accusations made by unknown sources; failure to reply was viewed as an admission of guilt. The examiners asked a series of questions concerning the applicant's former and present political views and assumed guilt unless the applicant could prove otherwise. If a respondent tried to give lengthy explanations, the examiners demanded short yes-or-no answers. Typical questions concerned the applicant's views on Marx, Engels, and Lenin; on the Warsaw Pact armies marching into Czechoslovakia; on the GDR serving as a model for a new society; and on party affiliation. If the applicant was a DKP member, questions were asked about the party's statute, program, and goals and how these related to the FDGO. Invariably, the applicant had to deal with questions about the dictatorship of the proletariat or democratic centralism and whether he or she concurred with the party's tactics and goals. Examiners also might ask a hypothetical question such as, "In your view, can a civil servant belong to the DKP or the KPD pursuing anticonstitutional goals, even if such parties are not outlawed?" rather than the more direct question of the applicant's party affiliation. Or they might ask the applicant, "When did you last sign a petition?" as a way of elucidating information not available to the commission.

The examiners, in these inquisitorial and intimidating sessions, often pried into the private lives of applicants to gain more political insights. Not atypical were questions about the applicant's attitude toward sexual permissiveness outside of marriage, or the following questions asked of a potential teacher in Berlin:

"Are you a member of a household commune?"
    "No, I am a roomer."
"Do you have contacts with other roomers?"
    "I know the other roomers."
"Do you know whether the persons living in your apartment are working in a political group?"
    "No, I do not know that."
"Do you engage in political conversation with them?"
    "No, I am seldom home; I have little contact with the other roomers."
"Thus, you do not know anything about their political motivations?"
    "No. I do not understand what your questions have to do with your doubts about my legal rights to enter the civil service."
"You do not need to understand this. Why do you live together with people about whom you know nothing?"[7]

This is but a small sample of the questions, which encouraged evasive answers and led to increasing criticism of the decree's administration.

To maximize chances of receiving an appointment in the public service, applicants were primed by their lawyers, often union appointed. They were told to provide minimum information; otherwise, it might be used against them. They were reminded that the examiners determined their guilt or innocence. Should they convincingly repent of their past political mistakes, if they were so inclined, the examiners might look upon their case more favorably. But often, not knowing the evidence against them until the time of the hearing made an adequate preparation exceedingly difficult and increased their anxiety. Ironically—although it happened seldom—trained and camouflaged communists who wanted to infiltrate into the public service avoided joining any radical group and slipped through the net by swearing allegiance to the FDGO.[8]

Whether or not an applicant received a security clearance and was hired after a hearing depended on what weight the examiners attached to "political sins" (e.g., signing radical manifestos) committed during student years, to party activities, and to possible future disloyalty—a vague and subjective concept that could be applied arbitrarily and indiscriminately. Normally, the hearing commission recommendation would be accepted by the hiring agency but could be countermanded by top officials in a ministry, the chancellery, or the cabinet.

The Courts

If the decision was negative, the applicant had the right to file suit in a district administrative court, which has jurisdiction over civil servants, or a district labor court, which deals with salaried employees and workers. If the court upheld the negative decision of the agency, the applicant could appeal the verdict to a Land court and then to the Federal Administrative Court or Federal Labor Court. Conversely, if the applicant's appeal was upheld, the government agency could appeal the verdict to a higher court. The likelihood that applicants could win a case in the courts averaged 35 percent, but at least they had a chance to have their cases reviewed by an independent branch of government.[9] This right of citizens to secure a review was limited, however, by numerous instances of state governments, especially Bavaria and North-Rhine Westphalia, repeatedly appealing court decisions requiring applicants to be hired, even when the governments' loss of cases was predictable. Government officials hoped that the years of appeals would force the applicants to seek employment elsewhere. In the meantime, agencies might fill vacancies, if not abolish them entirely.

Critics of the 1972 decree also were outraged that some judges who had served the Nazis in various capacities were holding office, pledging to support the FDGO, and sentencing dissidents once again. Among the judges sitting on the Federal Administrative Court was Edmund de Chapeaurouge, who had incarcerated hundreds of Jews under the Nazi Nuremberg laws, and Rudolf Weber-Lortsch, who had joined the NSDAP and the SA (paramilitary organ) in 1933. During the war, Weber-Lortsch had become a high SS-führer in the police service of the Reich commissioner's office for the Ukraine and had held a leading post in the Reich commissioner's office for the occupied Norwegian territories. Helmut Fuchs, a judge of the administrative court in Karlsruhe, who during the Hitler era had been a volunteer member of the Waffen SS, after 1972 permitted a NPD schoolteacher to retain his post but decided on the ouster of a teacher who had been a member of a communist party.[10] Defenders of the decree contended that a judge's Nazi past should have no bearing on his record as a committed democrat in the Federal Republic era.

Although most older judges in the Federal Republic could not match the former devotion to the Nazi cause of these judges, their verdicts in cases dealing with the 1972 decree often showed political conservatism.[11] They were influenced by legal commentaries written by conservative scholars and created case precedents that became the base for the legitimation of the decree, even though it was not supposed to have created a new law. With exceptions, the judges were tougher on leftists than on rightists, regardless of whether these were applicants for public service positions or were already in the service. When hearing examiners concluded that an applicant was a potential enemy of the constitution, chances that an older judge in a higher court would reverse the decision were slim. (In the 1980s, as a result of the influx of new, young judges, the administrative courts became somewhat more liberal, especially toward radicals protesting nuclear power production.)[12]

Applicants seeking entry into the public service as salaried employees or workers had to file appeals in the labor courts if administrators had denied them entry. The judges, who are appointed by the ministers of labor in each Land, were often sympathetic to the applicants and overruled the negative decisions of the hiring authorities. The judges put more weight than colleagues in the administrative courts on the applicants' "total personality" profiles, their minimal activity in political groups or parties, and their exemplary behavior in the preparatory service. Unlike some administrative court judges, labor court judges would not normally conclude that if plaintiffs distanced themselves from a radical party, they were feigning a change in political attitudes.

Although the district and Länder labor courts often rendered verdicts favorable to plaintiffs, the Federal Labor Court verdicts were less predictable. In November 1979, judges from the top labor and administrative courts reportedly held talks to see if the divergent decisions in the lowest and appeals courts could be bridged, but they could not agree.[13] Despite the lack of agreement and the many administrative court verdicts upholding the hiring authorities' decisions, the courts in a number of instances over-turned the negative decisions of the administrative agencies and put them on notice to follow guidelines set by the ministers of the interior.

Number of Screenings

The decree became the fulcrum of controversy partly because of the sheer number of automatic screenings. According to the Federal Ministry of the Interior, in the period from January 1, 1973, to June 30, 1975, federal, state, and local agencies screened 454,000 persons. (Other estimates run higher.) Of these, the *Verfassungsschutz* had negative findings on 5,678. After reviewing their files, the agencies rejected 328 (see table 3). Many of those rejected thereupon appealed the decision to the courts.

Most striking is the high number of applicants in West Berlin and Hesse for whom the *Verfassungsschutz* had a negative file. Both Länder had become centers of dissent among a sizable group of university students who upon graduation wanted to enter the teaching or other civil service profes-sions. In West Berlin, the government, controlled by the conservative wing of the SPD, barred about 5 percent of those applicants tainted by a negative

Table 3
Screenings of Applicants to Public Service, 1973–1975

	Screenings[a]	Negative Files	Rejections
Federal Government	32,000	445	8
Baden-Württemberg	70,000	487	50
Bavaria	55,000	342	23
Bremen	20,000	421	15
Hamburg	40,000	103	29
Hesse	50,000	970	26
Lower Saxony	28,000	249	16
North Rhine-Westphalia	84,000	523	30
Rhineland-Palatinate	25,000	131	22
Saar	6,000	34	0
Schleswig-Holstein	20,000	173	16
Berlin	24,000	1,800	93
Total	454,000	5,678	328

Source: Adapted from BMI, *Innere Sicherheit,* no. 33 (Apr. 13, 1976): 5.

Note: Figures for 1972 are not available.

[a]Figures rounded off to nearest thousand.

file. On the other hand, the Hesse government, controlled by the left wing of the SPD, rejected only about 2.7 percent. In other Länder, conservative SPD and CDU/CSU governments both rejected a relatively high number of applicants with negative files.

At least 92 percent of the applicants barred were leftists. More than one-third tried to obtain positions as teachers, about 20 percent as university lecturers, and the remainder as social workers, lawyers, and other professionals.[14] Thus most applicants applied for posts under Länder rather than federal jurisdiction. In addition to screening applicants to the public service, government agencies also screened personnel already in the service who were being considered for permanent status, promotion, or transfer to another agency. From 1973 to 1975, the agencies initiated 129 disciplinary proceedings against nonpermanent public servants who were suspected of not upholding the FDGO. In only a few of these cases did the government have enough evidence for dismissal after a lengthy legal procedure, although a number of individuals were denied promotion. The screenings, disciplinary proceedings, and court trials of applicants to the public service and of career servants were costly; they added more than $4 million yearly to government budgetary outlays.[15]

Individual Cases

To mobilize mass support against the decree, the critics publicized its adverse effects on individuals caught in the screening process. Among the first affected were left-leaning university professors whom the CDU/CSU accused of infecting students with Marxist concepts. The *Verfassungsschutz* had been busy collecting materials against them.

One well-publicized case against a university professor occurred even before the passage of the 1972 decree. Horst Holzer, sociologist at Munich University and a DKP member, had received an offer in April 1971 to teach at the newly founded Bremen University. Two months later the SPD-led government of Bremen, afraid that the opposition would capitalize on its hiring a communist, rescinded the offer, despite the backing he had received from the minister of education of Bavaria, Hans Maier, a CSU member who had lauded his academic qualifications and his support of the FDGO. An administrative court in Bremen sustained the government decision. In 1973, the Hesse Ministry of Education also rejected his candidature for a post at Marburg University. One year later, Maier, in a reversal, ousted him from the Munich position, accusing him of Marxist-Leninist indoctrination and linkage of scientific work to DKP goals.[16]

Another case that attracted attention in academia was that of Prof. Wolf-Dieter Narr, who had been teaching political science at the Free University in Berlin since 1971. A left-wing member of the SPD, he headed a list of candidates considered in 1975 for appointment to a teaching post at the new law institute of the Technical University in Hanover. The minister of the interior, Rötger Gross (FDP), a member of the SPD-FDP government of Lower Saxony, received Narr's personnel file from the Berlin senator of the interior (SPD). The file contained copies of political petitions that Narr had signed on Vietnam, on the government's ban against a communist university group, and on the incarceration of political prisoners in isolation cells. The file also contained incriminating material indicating doubts about his constitutional loyalty, on the basis of insinuations by conservative colleagues and denunciations by the League for the Freedom of Science and Research.

Lower Saxony's minister of education, Joist Grolle (SPD), favorably inclined to Narr's appointment, requested him to appear before ministry officials in Hanover. In February 1975, in a three-hour hearing, or "inquisition," as Narr put it, the officials questioned him about his political beliefs but apparently concluded that Narr's loyalty to the FDGO was beyond reproach. Yet, when Grolle presented the case to Minister-President Alfred Kubel (SPD) and his cabinet, all members but Grolle voted against Narr's appointment. They feared that the CDU would win the Landtag election if he were appointed. In Grolle's letter of rejection to Narr, the minister assured him that the cabinet members had no doubt about his qualifications but stated that they had been interested in a "balanced" composition of the law faculty.

The university rector, most law school professors, several Landtag deputies, and other politicians and professors protested the cabinet's decision, but in vain. Narr requested the Berlin senator of the interior to expunge several statements in his file. When the request was denied, he appealed the decision in the courts. He lost the first round, won on appeal in the second round, and lost in the Federal Administrative Court. He weighed taking his case to the Constitutional Court but refrained when told his chance of winning approached zero. Narr also appealed the decision of Lower Saxony authorities not to hire him for political reasons and the cabinet's arbitrary decision. In 1976, an administrative court in Hanover sustained the decision, but twelve years later the Land Administrative Court found for the plaintiff.[17] By then Narr had no intention of applying for any future vacancy and remained at the Free University in Berlin.

Left-wing lawyers who sought judgeships attracted as much attention as did professors denied appointment at universities. In July 1973, Volker Götz, a twenty-eight-year-old lawyer, applied for a judgeship in Düsseldorf. Initially, the SPD-FDP cabinet of North-Rhine Westphalia, headed by Minister-President Heinz Kühn (SPD), upon the favorable recommendation of Minister of Justice Diether Posser (SPD), considered Götz to be highly qualified for the post, especially when he affirmed his loyalty to the Basic Law and asserted that his political views would not influence his decisions. Posser contended that Götz's DKP membership was not sufficient cause for barring him from the post. But the cabinet action was rejected by the president of the Land supreme court, who refused to give Götz the nomination papers and was criticized by the league of judges, the chamber of lawyers, the CDU Fraktion in the Landtag, and the press.

In August, Kühn changed his mind when faced with this massive opposition and, in a reversal of position, a threat by Minister of Interior Willy Weyer and other FDP ministers to leave the cabinet if Götz was appointed. Kühn convinced the SPD cabinet members to set aside the appointment. Protesting the cabinet's action, the Jusos contended that the FDP was calling the tune. Chancellor Brandt, who feared the Götz controversy could lead to a breakup of the SPD-FDP government in Bonn, supported the decision of Kühn, one of the vice chairmen of the party, and warned the Jusos not to attack the Land decision. Brandt feared an increase of Juso influence in the Land SPD, which could lead to a loss of SPD power in North-Rhine Westphalia, the most populous Land in the Federal Republic. The SPD could then face negative electoral consequences in other Land elections scheduled the following year.

In the meantime, the SPD executive of North-Rhine Westphalia, after listening to forty members making statements at a six-hour meeting, reaffirmed the cabinet decision. Minister of Justice Posser, in an attempt to shore up the controversial cabinet decision, announced the receipt of additional information on Götz that cast doubt on the applicant's intention to support the Basic Law in all instances. Götz appealed the decision to the courts.

In March 1980, the Superior Administrative Court in Münster ruled against Götz. It said that no functionary in the DKP, whose goals are anticonstitutional, can become a judge. Götz's activities in the party meant he closely identified with its goals, regardless of his declaration of loyalty to the FDGO. After the court verdict, Götz remained a lawyer; under federal law, the lawyers' examining committee has the power to disqualify applicants to the bar only if they fight the FDGO in a culpable manner.[18]

The Götz case demonstrated the ease with which the administration of the 1972 decree could precipitate a political crisis among coalition partners, in this instance an SPD minister of justice pitted against an FDP minister of the interior. The case also showed how the SPD leaders in Düsseldorf, in order to preserve their political power, had to set aside their moral opposition to what they privately called "snooping" investigations conducted by the FDP minister of the interior.

National SPD chiefs began to have more doubts about the decree when an SPD member was caught in its net in CSU-governed Bavaria. In September 1975, Charlotte Niess, an assistant to a judge in Munich, was denied a judgeship by the CSU minister of justice. At issue was not her membership in the SPD but her seat on the executive committee of the Association of Democratic Lawyers (*Vereinigung Demokratischer Juristen,* VDJ). The VDJ was founded primarily to protect individuals opposed to conservative laws reinforcing the status quo, such as the nation's emergency legislation, but the *Verfassungsschutz* labeled the VDJ as a DKP-front organization. Federal minister of the interior Werner Maihofer (FDP)—more liberal than his colleague Weyer in North-Rhine Westphalia—declared in Parliament that even though communists belonged to the VDJ, there was no reason to doubt the organization's loyalty. He viewed the Niess case as "an alarm signal warning that in the defense of our legal state we are near to trespassing on the limits of this legal state."[19]

Niess took her case to the courts. In 1976, the Munich Administrative Court instructed the Bavarian government to employ her as a judge on probation. The government appealed the ruling; in December 1977, the Bavarian Administrative Court sustained the original government decision not to hire her. In 1978, Niess appealed the ruling to the Federal Administrative Court, but two years later dropped the appeal after having moved to the then more hospitable North-Rhine Westphalia, where she received a civil service post in the Department of Agriculture.[20]

Public Reaction

Media coverage of individuals negatively affected by the decree, as well as the controversy surrounding the *Verfassungsschutz,* the hearings, court verdicts, and the scope of loyalty screenings, left an imprint on the public. Opinion polls indicated that the decree's supporters, whose views were shaped by the anticommunist political culture, outnumbered its opponents, who held strong libertarian views. In one poll taken in October 1973 by the conservative Allensbach Institute, 52 percent of the respondents were in accord with the statement that one could not expect a member of an extremist party to support the FDGO, 27 percent disagreed, and 21 percent had no opinion. To the question of whether a DKP member should be named judge, 58 percent answered in the negative and 18 percent in the affirmative. Young persons (sixteen to twenty-nine years old) and SPD voters opposed the decree in greater numbers than did CDU/CSU voters; FDP voters were in the middle.[21]

Polls taken by a liberal institute, Infratest, indicated swings in public opinion. Forty-two percent of respondents in May 1972 opposed the decree, contending that political views should not be a bar to hiring. By October 1973, when arguments of the decree's supporters had become more convincing, only 28 percent opposed it. By October 1976, however, the ranks of opponents had increased to 45 percent, perhaps because by then the governing parties had become more critical. Respondents between eighteen and twenty-one years old were the most critical—72 percent in 1972, 50 percent in 1975, and 66 percent in 1976.[22]

Later polls revealed one cause for the opposition: many of those interviewed considered members of radical groups to have a high degree of social responsibility and to support basic rights and the democratic state. Such members should be allowed into the civil service, where their critical views would engender debate and shake up the Establishment.[23]

Initiative Groups

Local and national organized opposition to the decree increased, once its excesses in implementation became known. Not unexpectedly, in early 1973 the DKP took the initiative in mobilizing the decree's opponents, although left groups at universities and in many communities from February 1972 on had sponsored numerous protest rallies, strikes, and action days and had issued solidarity proclamations. According to a confidential report of the *Verfassungsschutz*, the DKP requested fellow-traveling organizations, such as the German Peace Union (*Deutsche Friedens-Union*, DFU), to expand their campaign against the decree, while party functionaries were to remain in the background.

The DKP was able to gain the support of several noncommunist organizations, including the Jusos and the Liberal University Association, for a national conference held in Hamburg on May 12, 1973. The conference participants, numbering about 1,600, voted to establish a national organization, *Initiative "Weg mit den Berufsverboten"* ("Abolish the Ban on Careers"). Although participants concurred on the need for the new organization to promote solidarity with individuals subject to investigation and hearings, the noncommunist leaders at the conference called in vain for a discussion of bans on employment in communist countries.

The initiative was sponsored by an array of procommunist, left-radical, and noncommunist organizations, most of them based in universities. The DKP and DFU refrained from official sponsorship, but in the executive committee (*Arbeitsausschuss*), a number of communists held seats.[24] The left-leaning noncommunist organizations knew that communists had been the principal architects of the initiative, but they supported a united front against the decree to maximize an effective opposition. In later years, internal disputes on tactics led to frustration and the distancing of some groups, such as the Jusos, from the initiative. Nevertheless, the new organization sparked the formation throughout the Federal Republic of 120 (eventually 350) local initiative committees to promote opposition to the decree. The committees distributed a host of flyers and pamphlets, issued news releases, collected material on individual cases, and organized demonstrations and other solidarity actions. The national committee served as a coordinating center and sponsored numerous conferences.[25]

DGB Unions

The DGB unions' qualified support for the decree changed once its weaknesses became known. In November 1974, DGB chairman Heinz Oskar Vetter, contending that existing civil service laws were sufficient to keep out enemies of democracy, said, "We do not want a McCarthyism."[26] He was critical of the snooping, fear, and conformity engendered by the decree. At the Tenth Congress of the DGB in May 1975, a member of the federal executive committee called for an end to abuses in the administration of the decree. Two years later (June 8, 1977) the committee unanimously demanded an end to consideration of the political views of civil service applicants during their screening. Rather, the sole determination should be whether the applicant actively attempts to eliminate the constitution.

The teachers' union, GEW, was in accord with the DGB position. In 1974 it supported a federal government draft bill designed to end inequities in the decree. In September 1976, it accused the government and the Länder of poisoning the political atmosphere and discrediting the democratic state. The decree lacked clarity on what criteria should be used to hire applicants, producing much uncertainty and arbitrariness. The GEW demanded that stringent hiring requirements for sensitive posts be eased.[27]

Although the GEW was critical of the decree's implementation, a majority of delegates at its 1977 convention defeated a resolution introduced by the GEW's more radical Lower Saxony branch calling for an end to the decree. In the same year, the Bavarian branch issued a document in German and in English on the decree's effects. On the cover, a tombstone symbolized democracy's fate under the decree.

The Postal Workers Union supported the DGB position, but in 1974, the union's radical youth branch demanded that the decree be scrapped because of its destruction of basic rights.[28] The Railroad Workers Union and the Public Service and Transport Workers Union, whose members were also affected by the decree, backed the DGB position. On the other hand, at the 1977 convention of the left-leaning Wood and Plastic Workers Union, not involved in the controversy, delegates adopted a resolution calling for the decree to be revoked and requesting the DGB to pressure government authorities for revocation.[29]

The DGB, most of whose unions did not want to embarrass the SPD-led government on an issue that was peripheral for them, took no such action. Yet, the DGB and those public service unions whose radical members were directly affected by the decree kept up pressure on public authorities to revise the administration of the decree.

Schism in the SPD

Factionalism in the SPD intensified over the decree's implementation. The well-publicized rift reflected fundamental ideological and tactical differences between the party's left and right wings. In this instance, the left wing put priority on the promotion of fundamental rights for all citizens; the right wing put priority on national security needs. But within each wing and the more amorphous center bloc there were further differences of views.

In February 1973, eighteen left-wing SPD Bundestag deputies, joined by seven FDP deputies, issued a declaration critical of Länder that rejected applicants for their DKP membership but did not take action against NPD members ensconced in civil service positions. They also decried the applicants' lack of opportunity to practice freely some professions having civil service status.[30]

The neo-Marxist Jusos maintained their blunt opposition to the decree and in June 1973 demanded its abolition, thus going one step further than the dissident deputies, who were not yet ready to make a similar demand publicly in the Bundestag. Gert Börnsen, Juso deputy chairman, assailed conservatives and capitalists for using the decree as an instrument against left-wing critics of the economic system, including social democrats. A pluralist country must be willing to have its children educated not only by former Nazi teachers, who did not lose their jobs in the postwar period, but also by communists.

Börnsen denounced conservatives for their "creepy fairy tales" falsely depicting the "enemies of the constitution" as undermining the state. Rather, the "enemies" were dissidents who through legitimate political activity wanted to end the capitalist domination of the economy. More dangerous than their activity was that of the conservatives who attempted to limit democracy in the Federal Republic. They were as much opponents of the Basic Law as dogmatic extremists who sought to restrict the freedom to dissent.[31]

Other Juso leaders accused government officials of trying to destroy the DKP by making its members security risks, who in most instances would not be able to enter the public service. As a consequence, the party would suffer a drastic cut in membership. The Juso leaders contended that any member of a party that has not been outlawed should be able to join the public service without having to make special loyalty pledges. Because progressives voicing critical views might shake up the civil service Establishment, the economically dominant class, which is interested in a smoothly functioning public service, wants to bar their entry.

The Juso chiefs assailed the CDU/CSU's preposterous slogan "freedom or socialism," implying that the SPD's purported lack of interest in freedom meant its members might have anticonstitutional views. Had the CDU/CSU campaign succeeded, soon the SPD members would legally have been declared security risks.[32]

The Jusos also assailed SPD-governed Länder for using undemocratic means to enforce the decree. Senior SPD officials rejected the charge but were worried about CDU/CSU attempts to defame Jusos as procommunist and about the *Verfassungsschutz* putting names of Jusos (and Young Democrats) who had joined the initiatives against *Berufsverboten* or other united front organizations in the "suspect doubtful loyalty" category. This increased hostility of SPD officials to the decree, partly because it ensnared some SPD members in its net, was welcome news to the DKP, which all along had fought the decree.[33]

In order to lessen the danger of an ensnarement of Jusos, the SPD executive committee demanded in 1975 that no party member continue to work with the initiatives because of their domination by forces opposed to SPD policies. The Jusos, not seeing any harm in working with communists, did not heed the request at the time, although they began to initiate their own protest actions against the decree. They contended that the SPD must oppose the DKP politically but allow DKP members to join the civil service, where they could voice views, say on economic policies, shared by the Jusos.[34]

Earlier, at the 1973 SPD convention, party chiefs, making some concessions to the Jusos and other left-wing critics, introduced a compromise resolution calling for changes and more precision in the decree. Denial of employment cannot be based automatically on nominal membership in a radical party, on running for public office as its candidate, or on the testimony of anonymous witnesses. Instead, each case must be examined with utmost care.[35] Despite the resolution's becoming party policy, no change occurred in practice. Hence, the Jusos requested leaders to put pressure on SPD-run Länder at least to abide by that part of the resolution permitting entry into the public service of a nominal member of any legitimate party.

In May 1974, Brandt resigned as chancellor, and Helmut Schmidt, leader of the party's right wing, assumed the post. The two chiefs met with Juso leaders to resolve some of their differences on the decree and other issues, but Schmidt had little sympathy for the Jusos. Only when more moderate SPD officers raised their voices against renewed excesses of the decree did the party presidium in June 1975 reiterate its support for the 1973 resolution and ask SPD-led Länder to comply. The presidium also expressed its concern that the political Right was using terrorist actions as a subterfuge for creating a climate of opinion in which the difference between political terrorism and political radicalism was blurred deliberately.[36]

The SPD position led to a new controversy with the CDU when regional SPD leader Erhard Eppler in 1975 accused Hans Filbinger, CDU minister-president of Baden-Württemberg, of excesses in security screenings and of "fiddling with people's fates like a drunk trying to open a doorlock."[37] In reply, Filbinger accused the SPD of helping to make the DKP more legitimate and of contravening the decree's intentions. SPD leaders saw such a statement as a renewed attempt to paint their party as standing close to the enemies of the constitution.

Schism in the FDP

Factionalism in the FDP, the junior governing party in Bonn, also surfaced over the decree. The Young Democrats and several Land branches, constituting the left wing, were pitted against a more probusiness conservative majority, led by Minister of the Interior Genscher. In 1972, the Young Democrats and the Schleswig-Holstein and West Berlin branches rejected the decree as superfluous, given the existing civil service laws on political loyalty. The Young Democrats openly assailed Genscher as being coresponsible for the decree.

FDP chairman Walter Scheel in turn criticized the Young Democrats for their stab-in-the-back attitude, which could result in a weakening of the Bonn coalition. It was more important to maintain party solidarity as a means of achieving liberal goals. North Rhine-Westphalia minister of the interior Weyer, a leader of the party's right wing, argued that no DKP member could possibly be loyal to the Basic Law.

The Young Democrats, supported in later years by the party's vice chairman Martin Bangemann, maintained their opposition to the decree. They called it "the first tiny bit of fascism." To suppress communists is to move the political spectrum to the right and stifle democratization by creating an atmosphere of uncertainty and intimidation. Radical groups, because of their small number, cannot endanger the democratic system. Their members, denied employment, will become martyrs or agitators with highly plausible arguments. In short, bans on employment cannot protect democracy but will ensure its end.[38]

Despite such arguments, left-wing leaders could not convince their middle-of-the-road and right-wing colleagues to opt for revoking the decree. In a replay of the SPD factionalism, FDP government leaders made a few concessions to the left wing by calling for some reforms: uniform application of the decree, judgments based on individual cases rather than general criteria, and denial of employment only if based on facts proven in court.

Defense of the Decree

Most CDU/CSU leaders—and some conservative SPD and FDP leaders—opposed any major change in the content or administration of the decree. CDU executive members, at a meeting in August 1973, denounced the critics' demands and warned about the deliberate campaign begun by the enemies of the constitution to undermine the public service. The CDU, willing to discuss making the decree more precise but not to weaken it, hoped for a renewal of solidarity among the parties in their fight against the enemies of the FDGO.[39]

Although the CDU/CSU did not receive support from the other parties, conservative associations, such as the German Federation of Civil Servants (DBB), the German Judges League, the League for the Freedom of Science and Research, and the German Bundeswehr Association, continued to back its stand. The DBB, for instance, ever since 1973 rejected accusations from the Left that the government was using police-state methods of snooping to ferret out enemies of the constitution applying for public career posts. Rather, the government in most instances properly screened such applicants. To facilitate their entry into the service through procedural reforms would endanger democracy.[40]

A number of writers, scholars (especially Klaus Stern and other law professors), and newspaper columnists (e.g., Friedrich Karl Fromme in the *Frankfurter Allgemeine Zeitung*) supported the decree without qualification. Their arguments helped to shore up the CDU/CSU position, even though some of them were SPD adherents. They contended that freedom can be protected only if key posts in the state, the universities, and the media are not occupied by those intent on destroying the system. Even though left extremists were few, the financial assistance their organizations received from the GDR helped them mount a massive campaign against the decree. In a period of crisis, those extremists with posts in the civil service could endanger West Germany's existence through sabotage, such as blocking rails, and interrupting electricity. Hence, members of radical organizations must be kept out of the public service at all costs.[41]

Government Initiatives

Critics and defenders of the decree lobbied hard to convince the government decision makers of the merits of their views. They had an opportunity as early as September 20, 1973, when Chancellor Brandt met with the Länder minister-presidents to review the administration of the decree since its inception in early 1972. Brandt noted that the federal government intended to introduce a bill in late 1973 to provide uniformity among the Länder, lacking until then.[42] Not surprisingly, the CDU/CSU- and SPD-governed Länder held different views on the decree, but even among the latter no unanimity prevailed, as views ranged from outright opposition (Hesse, Bremen) to full support (Berlin).

Brandt also hoped that the courts could achieve more uniformity in their verdicts. Such a goal might be met if the Constitutional Court would rule on whether or not Article 33 of the Basic Law, dealing with the loyalty of civil servants, had priority over Article 21, dealing with the free formation of political parties and, by implication, rights for their members. Brandt's wish for a speedy decision could be fulfilled only if a plaintiff willing to take the case to court could be found. But the DKP had requested its members not to appeal their cases to the top court, because of the danger that the court might outlaw the party as unconstitutional.[43]

The government could not meet its deadline of late 1973 for legislative consideration of its bill because of lengthy deliberations among the Länder ministers of the interior. Finally, on March 6, 1974, the federal cabinet approved and sent to the Bundesrat a bill containing amendments to the civil service framework law. The bill called for more safeguards for applicants: individual reviews of their cases, with decisions to be based on existing law and on facts that can be evaluated in court (rather than on secret dossiers); the right to request an agency to provide reasons for a negative decision in writing; and the right to respond to reasons for denial. The bill put the burden of proof on the hiring agency to prove any disloyalty of the applicant. It omitted the controversial clause in the 1972 decree about the government's doubts of loyalty to the FDGO of applicants who were members of parties pursuing anticonstitutional goals and whose application for public service posts would in most cases justify rejection. (This clause had often been applied indiscriminately and had become the trigger for rejection.)

The CDU/CSU, intent on keeping nominal members and not just activists or officeholders of such a party out of the public service, criticized the proposed changes as a serious weakening of the decree. Therefore, in a rare parliamentary maneuver, its Baden-Württemberg and Bavarian representatives introduced into the Bundesrat a parallel bill that maintained the decree's original clause on membership.[44] As a consequence, the CDU/CSU-dominated upper chamber, representing the Länder, had to deliberate both bills.[45]

Even though the CDU/CSU had a majority of 26 to 15 in the Bundesrat, it chose on May 10, 1974, following committee debate and plenary discussion, to allow both bills to continue on their legislative odyssey. The CDU/CSU representatives could have rejected the government bill, but their negative vote would have been only advisory at this preliminary stage. The CDU/CSU representative, however, warned the government that later they would support only the opposition bill and veto the government bill.

The two bills had to be sent to the cabinet, which normally takes a position on any Bundesrat amendments to a government bill for the guidance of the Bundestag. In this instance, the cabinet, after reaffirming support of its own bill, transmitted both bills on July 31 to the Bundestag for its deliberation.[46]

During the course of cabinet and legislative deliberations, a conflict threatening the new SPD-FDP government in Hamburg erupted over the question of whether the city should hire two communists as teachers. During the coalition negotiations to form this government, following the

March 1974 election, in which the SPD had lost its majority, hard-line SPD leaders stood firm against the hiring of the two communists, while FDP negotiators, not considering the two as security risks, supported their employment. Chancellor Schmidt and FDP minister Genscher requested the warring factions to come to Bonn for a joint resolution of the conflict, but after the visit, both sides remained intransigent. Thereupon the SPD majority in the Hamburg Senate (the Land executive), over FDP opposition, voted against hiring the teachers. The senate members agreed, however, on further negotiations over the criteria to be used to bar future applicants from the service.

To prevent a similar crisis elsewhere, the SPD presidium, at a September meeting, voted to request all SPD-governed Länder to act on the decree as if the government bill had already passed. Yet, enactment was not assured. On November 15, the Bundestag, in first reading, debated both bills. In the long debate, deputies of all parties advanced the by then familiar arguments. The Hamburg crisis was not forgotten, as one FDP deputy warned her colleagues that the case of the two teachers denied employment had been more damaging to the democratic system than if they had been hired. At the conclusion of the debate, both bills were assigned to the interior, legal, defense, and budget committees but were held up when news came that the Constitutional Court would render a verdict on the decree in 1975, which might produce clarification of the constitutional issues.[47]

Constitutional Court Decision

On May 22, 1975, the Constitutional Court rendered its long-awaited landmark decision. The case concerned a law student (Heiner Sämisch) who had passed his professional examination in 1971 and had applied in March 1972 for a legal internship (*Referendarzeit*) in Schleswig-Holstein. The internship meant that he would first have to become a provisional civil servant (*Beamter auf Wiederruf*) in order to take a second examination, which in turn would enable him to become a judge, a prosecuting attorney, or a lawyer in private practice or public service. Thus the state had a monopoly on the in-service training of future lawyers, many of whom had no intention of entering the public sector. If such individuals were barred from an internship because of their political views, the state in effect barred them from their chosen profession.

The petitioner had attended forty meetings of a communist student group, "Rote Zelle Jura," while in law school. In 1972, the president of the

Schleswig-Holstein Supreme Court and the minister of justice barred his entry into the preparatory service because the student group's goals were hostile to the constitution. He appealed the ruling to the Schleswig Administrative Court. In turn, it petitioned the Constitutional Court to rule on whether or not the provision in the Schleswig-Holstein decree concerning the need for political loyalty on the part of law students entering an internship violated Article 12 of the Basic Law guaranteeing all citizens the right to choose a profession freely.

The court stated that the freedom of Länder to regulate in-service training is limited when it interferes with an individual's right to pursue his or her chosen profession. In the case of a legal internship, the Land must either waive the loyalty requirements and let any applicant who wants to practice law enter the civil service internship, or else it must let the applicant take an internship outside of the civil service. The court also noted that, under the principle of the *Rechtsstaat,* the authorities had to observe procedural safeguards. These include the right of the applicant to be informed about the evidence in his or her file and to have a fair hearing, which includes the right to be represented by a lawyer and to rebut any damaging evidence.

These liberal views were offset by the court's conservative views on the major aspects of the decree. It ruled that Article 33 of the Basic Law, concerning the loyalty of civil servants, has priority over Article 12, on the free choice of a profession. It interpreted Article 33 (section 5) to mean that the applicant, as a potential civil servant, has a duty at all times to support the FDGO actively. It noted, "The free democratic state cannot and must not put itself into the hands of its destroyers."[48]

The court viewed political loyalty, including a prognosis of future loyalty, as a key factor in an applicant's evaluation, but other factors (e.g., competence and expertise) would need to be considered. An applicant's membership in a party pursuing anticonstitutional (*verfassungsfeindlich*) aims, regardless of whether its unconstitutionality has been established by a judgment of the court, would be relevant in the assessment process.

Civil servants are expected to acknowledge the state and its constitution as worthy of defending and to show their loyalty, especially during periods of crisis or serious conflict, when the existence of the state depends on their participation. Such loyalty demands more than a "formal, correct, . . . uninterested, cool, internally distant posture vis-à-vis the state and its constitution; it demands especially from a civil servant that he distance himself unequivocally from groups and endeavors that attack, fight against, and defame the state, its constitutional organs and the existing constitutional order."[49]

The court acknowledged that persons may not be discriminated against because of their political opinions (Article 3, section 3), but in the case of the public servants, it did not interpret this clause as being an absolute prohibition. Given the history of Weimar, it would be foolish to have enemies of the FDGO subvert the Federal Republic. The court also ruled that the loyalty obligation applies to temporary and probationary civil servants, as well as to tenured civil servants. Lack of loyalty normally warrants dismissal without hearings for those lacking tenure and formal dismissal proceedings for those with tenure. Salaried employees and workers in the public service are also expected to be loyal, even though the requirements are less than for civil servants.

Although the decision was unanimous, three of the eight judges dissented on certain aspects. Two liberal judges did not consider membership in a party hostile to the constitution in itself a bar to the civil service. One of the judges contended that Article 21, dealing implicitly with the constitutional right of party members to engage in political activities, applies to civil servants; hence it has priority over articles concerning loyalty. The third judge, on the other hand, sustained the CDU/CSU position that membership in an extremist party was proof of an individual's identification with the anticonstitutional goals of that party and therefore was a decisive reason for rejecting an applicant.

The reaction of political parties and other organizations to the important court verdict varied considerably. CDU/CSU officials welcomed the constitutional argumentation as a reaffirmation of the party's position and quoted it repeatedly thereafter. Government officials generally refrained from public comments but were pleased that the court, perhaps unwittingly, had transferred the power to decide whether a party is pursuing anticonstitutional aims from the judiciary to the executive. Therefore the government could make such a decision without asking the court to ban a party as unconstitutional (*verfassungswidrig*).

Critics, including the teachers' union, warned about the danger of a government's using such blanket power irresponsibly. On the other hand, they emphasized the court's ruling of membership in an extremist party being only one criterion for selection to the public service, thus providing some flexibility to hiring agencies. The Jusos underlined the conservative nature of the court's decision—not surprising, given its tendency to uphold the status quo. The court, by emphasizing the historical duty to the state, could not be expected to rule against the 1972 decree.[50]

Parliamentary Stalemate

Prior to the Constitutional Court decision, which provided crucial legal support to the decree, the government and the CDU/CSU opposition, as noted, had introduced competing bills for parliamentary consideration. After the court decision, the Bundestag committees (all having SPD-FDP majorities) resumed their deliberations. The committee on interior affairs, as the chief committee to report to the Bundestag plenary session, supported the government bill. The committee approved the principle that membership in an extremist party was no longer to be the determining factor for civil service appointment. It added the provision enunciated by the court granting lawyers and teachers unrestricted right to an internship regardless of their loyalty to the constitution.[51]

On October 24, the Bundestag, after hours of intensive partisan debate, passed the government bill and defeated the CDU/CSU bill in second and third readings. SPD and FDP deputies underlined the liberal nature of the government bill, designed to preserve utmost legality and prevent political snooping. CDU/CSU deputies assailed the government bill as renewed proof of the SPD's failure to resist the advances of left radicals and communists.[52]

Thereupon the two bills were forwarded to the Bundesrat for another debate and vote. (Although the CDU/CSU bill had just been defeated, the Bundesrat had the right to vote on it because it affected Länder interests.) On November 28, the CDU/CSU-dominated chamber defeated the government bill and sustained the CDU/CSU bill. In the wake of this stalemate between the two chambers, the CDU/CSU-governed Länder requested the permanent mediation committee of eleven members of each house to convene and attempt to resolve the differences between the bills. On February 10, 1976, the committee failed to reach a compromise; the SPD and FDP deputies, in a majority, backed the government bill. Thereupon, in a third vote, the Bundesrat vetoed it, allowed on legislation directly affecting the Länder. The CDU/CSU bill also lay buried because it did not obtain Bundestag support.

Unable to move ahead on the legislative front, the government and the SPD-FDP-ruled Länder announced that they no longer felt bound by the 1972 decree. The dramatic announcement was more propaganda than substantive change in policy, as seen in the Bonn cabinet's approval on May 19, 1976, of new guidelines for screening applicants to the federal civil service. The guidelines corresponded to those in the aborted government bill. They reiterated procedural safeguards for applicants, underlined in the

1975 Constitutional Court decision, and emphasized that the words and actions of an individual's student or apprenticeship years, particularly if they go back a considerable time, could be used as reasons for rejection only if they were grave enough to cast doubt on an applicant's loyalty to the FDGO.[53]

The government expected the SPD-led Länder to comply with its guidelines. Their ministers of the interior set up a commission to agree upon uniform standards. But the Christian Democrats announced that in Länder and cities they controlled, the 1972 decree would remain in force without change, although they too emphasized procedural safeguards for applicants. They rejected especially the provision of the government guidelines that the state assumes its citizens' loyalty to the constitution unless it possesses facts casting serious doubt on the applicant. The Christian Democrats intended to continue making an applicant's membership in an extremist organization ground for rejection, except for important extenuating circumstances.

Conclusion

During the period from 1973 to 1976, the decree became a focus of intensive debates in the Federal Republic. Radical critics mounted a major campaign to eliminate it, and moderate critics demanded reforms to protect the rights of citizens. The Bonn and Länder governments refused to abrogate the decree, but some of the more liberal SPD-governed Länder did not enforce it too rigorously. The conservative SPD- and CDU/CSU-governed Länder, however, maintained their tough position.

Grass-roots groups, which focused their activities on individual cases, and a minority of the public had serious doubts about the fairness of the decree; they contributed to the revisionist sentiment among the policy-making elite in the federal government. This change of official position, as reflected in the Bonn guidelines of 1976, would suggest that the state's political culture bears directly on the degree of government repression of its political dissidents. If there had been unanimous support for the decree, repression would have continued. But the guidelines suggested a possible easing in the government's handling of radical applicants, partly as a result of a shift, especially among youth, in popular attitudes and values on the protection of individual rights.

The 1976 impasse on what may seem minor differences between the government guidelines and the CDU/CSU practice reflected a mounting ideological difference—a social-liberal versus a conservative weltanschauung in which anticommunism and civil liberties increasingly were viewed through different prisms. A compromise on the decree between the parties, especially in the charged political atmosphere where they were competing for electoral support, was not in the realm of possibility in the mid-1970s. Although the CDU/CSU did not retreat from its original position, despite intensive pressure by its opponents and polls indicating no overwhelming support from the public, the SPD and FDP did retreat to a more defensive position as a result of sharp criticisms from their left-wing factions, DGB trade unions, and influential persons and the media in other countries.

4

International Reactions

The West German government had not expected leading socialist officials and some conservative media in other West European countries to criticize the implementation of the 1972 decree. Put on the defensive, the government made a few changes in implementation, but not far-reaching enough to still such criticism. Although in 1977 the government easily deflected the hostile findings of the left-leaning Third International Russell Tribunal, it had more difficulty keeping established supranational organizations ranging from the United Nations to the International Labor Organization from dealing with the issue in the 1970s and 1980s. In addition, West European courts took cases on appeal from West German courts or rendered advisory opinions. In short, the decree had become an international issue.

One case that attracted attention beyond West German borders and that triggered foreign protests was that of Silvia Gingold. In the summer of 1975, this young schoolteacher, born in 1946, was denied tenure and was ousted by Hesse authorities for her DKP membership and doubtful loyalty to the state. When she appealed her case, the international press picked it up because of her unusual background. She was the granddaughter of Jewish emigrants from Poland who had settled in Frankfurt before 1933. Upon Hitler's assumption of power, they fled with their children, some of whom were KPD members, to Paris. There, hidden, they survived the occupation. Her father, as a member of the resistance, was jailed and nearly executed by the Nazis, but at the last minute was able to escape from a Gestapo prison. After the war, the family moved back to West Germany, where Silvia Gingold was born. After finishing her studies, she taught satisfactorily as a provisional civil servant for four years until her dismissal for political reasons. Ironically, at the same time that she was caught in the decree's net, her father was decorated by French president Valéry Giscard d'Estaing with the highest order of merit for his resistance work.

Gingold did not see her case as being motivated by a new anti-Semitism, although her Jewishness was emphasized in some foreign and domestic media. They criticized the SPD-led Hesse government for attacking the civil rights of a Jew, among other Germans, which smacked of an unpleasant parallel with the Nazi past. Her case, however, was little different from that of other radicals who appealed an administrative decision to the courts.

In May 1976, on an appeal by Gingold, a district administrative court ruled that the Hesse Ministry of Education must reconsider her case. The court faulted the ministry for using *Verfassungsschutz* materials, including entries about visits to the GDR, dating back to 1964, when Gingold was a high school student; for not taking the positive aspects of her personality and her excellent teaching into consideration; and for not weighing the fact that one reason she had joined the DKP was the party's symbolic heirship to communist resistance, involving her own parents, against the Nazis.

Perhaps partly because of the international attention to her case, in September 1976 the ministry, still appealing the court decision, gave her a teaching contract as a salaried employee, with less status and privileges than if she had been appointed as a civil servant. One month later, she stood as a DKP candidate for the Bundestag, which did not help her cause. In July 1977, the Hesse Administrative Court, supporting the ministry decision to give her employee status, ruled that she could not be appointed a tenured teacher with civil service status, because of her membership and activity in the DKP. She appealed the decision, but in November 1979 the Federal Administrative Court sustained the state court. As a consequence, she continued to teach as a salaried employee until 1984, when she finally received tenured civil service status.[1]

Foreign Protests

Numerous communist-dominated and noncommunist groups on several continents organized protests against the decree as a result of the Gingold and other cases. Seventeen "Initiative against *Berufsverbote*" committees were formed in other Western European countries and two in the United States and Canada. A number of persons affected by the decree traveled abroad to appear at rallies, on radio and television, and at press conferences, including one at the World Youth Festival Games in Cuba. Members of the West German Initiative against *Berufsverbote* addressed meetings throughout Western Europe and, on one trip, eight Latin American countries.

In turn, foreign socialist, communist, and liberal party leaders, including parliamentarians, spoke at international conferences and rallies in the Federal Republic to express their support for an elimination of the decree. They claimed that it violated UN, Helsinki, and other international accords and was a threat to peace in Europe.[2]

The chief criticisms of the decree came from Western European countries, including discussions in the British House of Commons and the Dutch Upper House. Before 1976, a number of media commentators had been warning for some time about West German government restrictions on civil liberties, including the repression of dissidents, reminiscent of the Nazi era. The Gingold case precipitated a chorus of protests in the foreign left-wing and establishment press. Television stations scheduled panel discussions and showed documentary films. As a result of this media exposure, the term "Berufsverbot" entered foreign vocabularies, especially in France and Scandinavia.

The most explosive criticism came from France. Socialist party chief François Mitterrand, after having corresponded with Gingold about her case, formed a "Committee for the Defense of Civil and Professional Rights in West Germany" and chided SPD chiefs for their support of the decree. Party leader Michel Rocard announced that on three previous occasions SPD officers had been told "in a friendly fashion" of his party's negative reactions. He added, "When one defends freedom, one cannot divide it."[3]

In a declaration published in *Le Monde,* senior French socialists decried the West German federal and Länder governments' intimidation of leftist citizens for their dissident views. *Le Matin* feared that West German youth would no longer have faith in political parties and would turn in despair to political extremism and terrorism.[4]

Numerous French regional *Berufsverbot* committees, on which teachers unions and the communist-dominated General Confederation of Labor (CGT) had representation, were also formed. They circulated petitions, sought to inform the French population about the decree, sent letters to German judges handling cases, and assailed the witch-hunts. Simone de Beauvoir and Jean-Paul Sartre joined the Italians Luigi Nono and Pier Paolo Pasolini in a solidarity declaration with West Germans affected by the decree.

Perhaps the most wounding criticism for West German authorities came from Prof. Alfred Grosser, a distinguished French political scientist who had emigrated from Germany in Hitler's time. On receiving the West German Publishers' Peace Prize in Frankfurt in October 1975, he said:

> What disturbs me somewhat is that a great deal is being said about the constitutional state and the free democratic order in the Federal Republic. Perhaps I am not hearing correctly. But it seems to me that there is too much emphasis being placed on "state" and "order" and not enough on the idea of the free political activity of the individual who will be constrained from developing political, autonomous thinking and acting by such terms as state and order.[5]

Grosser accused German authorities of imposing a more stringent requirement on entrants into the civil service than was true during the initial years of the Federal Republic. In the 1950s, someone who during the Nazi period had interpreted the Nuremberg Laws against Jews (1935) as normal justice could become state secretary, or someone who had justified the Gestapo could become rector or minister of education and then pledge to uphold the FDGO. He noted: "There is more and more discussion about defending basic human rights against the state. . . . The greatest danger which can threaten a democracy from within is not so much constituted by those small groups inimical to it, but rather by the conformists."[6] He decried the spirit of intolerance growing in the Federal Republic, which had led to a new wave of anti-Germanism in Western Europe.

Grosser's views, widely shared in France, were echoed years later, in February 1984, by French foreign minister Claude Cheysson. In answer to a question in the National Assembly, he averred that states normally do not interfere in the internal affairs of other states but that because of the fraternal relations between the two countries, it was permissible for the French government to call to the attention of West German authorities, as the French had done on several occasions, that the 1972 decree's implementation ran counter to French regulations and those of other European states and that it did not correspond with the French understanding of freedom.[7]

Not all French observers shared these views. Leaders from conservative parties who advocated greater European unity emphasized the need for closer French-German cooperation, which was made more difficult by the controversy surrounding the decree. They criticized Mitterrand's initiative as being based partly on his need to shore up an electoral alliance with the Communist party in order to defeat President Giscard d'Estaing at the next election and partly on his displeasure with Chancellor Schmidt's policies devoid of socialist content. They criticized Mitterrand for saying, "West Germany does not represent the type of society to which we aspire, despite the very laudable and sometimes remarkable efforts of the German Social

Democrats, who are nonetheless obliged to rely on the support" of their conservative coalition partner, the FDP.[8]

In the Netherlands, Sicco Mansholt, a former president of the European Community (EC), said that the Dutch Labor party was highly disturbed about the decree's limitations on freedom and opinion, because undemocratic tendencies in Germany sooner or later spread to other European states. In June 1976, the party council adopted a resolution denouncing the SPD for being coresponsible for the unfavorable political climate in the Federal Republic. It supported the Jusos' fight against the decree and hoped that the entire SPD would do the same. In February 1977, the Dutch party organized a mass demonstration in Utrecht, at which its top leaders condemned the decree. The SPD refused to send a representative, even though one had been invited. As in France, numerous committees to protest the decree were founded.

In Italy, seventy intellectuals published an appeal, noting the decree's parallel to American McCarthyism. Scandinavian, Belgian, and British newspapers, representing all political views, also carried stories emphasizing the trend toward the Right and authoritarianism in the Federal Republic and the danger of "ugly Germans" arising again. *The Times* (London) described a saturated, self-complacent society incapable of reforming itself, whose members were occasionally arrogant abroad. Such a society was "still more insecure and intolerant toward deviations than its neighbours."[9] The noted British economist Joan Robinson wrote to a West German Land minister of education about the worry in international academic circles concerning the decree's negative effect on developments in social science and on Germany's reputation.[10] According to the *Economist,* "Several old Nazis are sitting pretty as ambassadors, although admittedly the only constitution they are likely to endanger is their own."[11]

In this torrent of foreign criticism, the charges were sometimes exaggerated or false. Thus, for example, on a Belgian television program, left-wing commentators compared the decree to similar measures in totalitarian Chile, Iran, and Franco Spain. They said that German students could be arrested for asking political questions in class, courageous young people were haunted to death, people were barred en masse from their choice of professions, membership in a trade union was dangerous, informers were to be found everywhere, and the fascist witch-hunt was on in full force. The charges were fueled by a desire to remind foreigners that the roots of National Socialism had not been eradicated but that its parallels were visible again, to remind Germans that they still had not overcome their past and that their economic prosperity was not shared by other West Europeans, and to remind Chancellor Schmidt to stop telling French and Italian governments not to enter into popular front alliances with their Communist parties.

Negative reactions also came from Czechoslovakia, where dissidents who had signed the Charta '77 declaration expressed support for West German democrats who had been affected by *Berufsverbote*. The dissidents, equally affected by bans in their country, asked their West German counterparts for information about current cases as a means to develop mutual solidarity actions in both countries.[12]

West German Reactions

Foreign criticisms grated on raw nerves in the Federal Republic. Federal president Walter Scheel, meeting with Schmidt to express his concern, was astonished that "such a big storm struck because a small cloud appeared in an otherwise blue sky of freedom."[13] He cautioned the political decision makers, "We cannot afford for weeks and months to deal only with one problem and pretend as if there were nothing else in the world than the 'decree against radicals.' "[14]

Nevertheless, Bonn officials, aware of the need to boost the country's image, intensified their efforts to inform foreign journalists in Bonn about the "real situation" in the Federal Republic. In addition, the Foreign Office sent to its embassies abroad copies of a "catalog of arguments" dealing with the decree, as part of an offensive to publicize the government point of view. Embassy officials in Western European countries where interest in the decree was high held press conferences and gave interviews to selected media people, some of whom were invited to the Federal Republic to inform themselves of the situation. The officials talked with foreign ministers and deputies and appeared at union, school, and university gatherings. They reported to the Foreign Office in Bonn that extremist groups abroad were unwilling to engage in any discussion, because the groups were intent on waging a propaganda war.

In France, the Bonn government conducted one of its most intensive propaganda campaigns. In 1977 and 1978, Bundestag president Karl Carstens (CDU) and minister Hans-Jürgen Wischnewski (SPD) met with French officials in Paris. In addition, the German deputy press spokesman traveled twice to Paris to meet with editors of French regional newspapers, and German embassy staff distributed much official material, translated into French. The Bonn government also put full-page advertisements in West German newspapers urging tourists vacationing in France to prepare for possible questions from the French about the decree. Their answer should be that "we do not have any *Berufsverbot;* not even when someone holds extremist views. However, our civil service laws specify that opponents of the democratic state cannot be employed in the public service."[15]

Chancellor Schmidt viewed foreign reactions to the decree as motivated partly by jealousy of West Germany's economic and political strength. He acknowledged that there were still some (read CDU/CSU) Länder that kept radicals who had committed political sins during their student years out of the public service. He also acknowledged preferring to see the decree buried in the files because of the excesses committed. If West Germany had less freedom than it should have, the fault lay with the Germans' penchant for attempting to solve all problems through laws and decrees.[16]

However, Schmidt criticized Mitterrand and others for their assault on a decree that the federal government and SPD-governed Länder no longer deemed to be fully in effect. The chancellor reminded foreign leaders that the state of civil liberties in the Federal Republic compared favorably with that in other Western countries. But he also said that if the Federal Republic was serious about European integration, it must be ready to live with more foreign criticism than before.[17]

Foreign Minister Genscher (FDP) announced that Bonn would not fear any investigation by Mitterrand's committee, because West Germans enjoyed more freedoms than at any other time in German history. He criticized Mitterrand's interest in forming a popular front with communists in France, when communists in other countries, such as the GDR, were guilty of continuous violations of human rights.[18]

SPD leaders were especially irritated by Mitterrand's formation of the committee; they considered it a slap against them for having been the coarchitects of the decree. On May 31, 1976, the SPD executive committee rejected the French socialists' claim that the decree was a threat to German civil rights. That position, not based on full information, was taken without first consulting with the SPD. Therefore, it invited French party leaders to come to the Federal Republic on a fact-finding mission.

The SPD executive also prepared documentation on the decree, which its representatives presented at the June 10 Amsterdam meeting of the League of Social Democratic Parties of the European Community.[19] At the meeting, devoted primarily to a discussion of the decree, three top SPD leaders defended the party's position. They accused the CDU/CSU-governed Länder of once again having produced a "climate of intolerance" and of failing to differentiate between members of radical communist groups, demanding a dictatorship of the proletariat, and DKP members, who often distanced themselves from such a goal. This lack of differentiation led to numerous bans on public employment for persons who were not threats to the FDGO.

Foreign socialist leaders were not entirely convinced that only the CDU/CSU was guilty of excesses, remembering that Gingold had been denied a civil service position in SPD-governed Hesse. Yet, they did not want to push the SPD too hard; after all, it had been willing to change the guidelines in May 1976. Robert Pontillon, international secretary of the French Socialist party, thanked the SPD delegates for clarifying many questions and noted that his party was convinced that the SPD would continue to uphold democratic rights and principles. He criticized the CDU/CSU for its attempt to play off the SPD against the French Socialist party. Dutch Labor party chairman Ien van den Heuvel underlined how important it was for all European socialists to denounce the CDU/CSU electoral slogan "freedom or socialism." The Christian Democrats had forgotten the socialist defense of freedoms against any subjugation.[20]

Expressions of good will between German and French socialists did not last long. At a follow-up meeting in Bonn in July, French socialist chiefs urged their German colleagues to prevent excesses in the decree's implementation. SPD leaders retorted that in other countries the citizens' right to employment also was endangered. To break the impasse, both sides agreed to sponsor, at the next meeting of the EC socialist league, the formation of a watchdog committee that would continuously observe violations in West European states.[21]

While SPD officials tried to defend their position on the supranational level, they backtracked in the Federal Republic in the face of continuing foreign pressures. One SPD executive committee member admitted, "We cannot vote for liberal resolutions at SPD conventions, in other countries make believe nothing is happening, and then do the opposite in Bonn and the Länder."[22] Brandt admitted having erred in 1972 in signing the decree. In hindsight, he should have realized that bureaucratic excesses would occur and that grotesque and wrong decisions would be made. His main motivation for signing had been to prevent the Christian Democrats from taking the initiative in banning extremist parties, which would have damaged the prestige of the government in the Western world.[23]

Yet, Brandt did not let foreign critics off the hook easily. On June 23, 1976, in a speech to a UNESCO-sponsored meeting of intellectuals and politicians, he defended his country against unjustified criticisms, revived prejudices, and hasty judgments. He stated, "I regard it as idiotic to carry on as though fascism is about to break out because a schoolteacher has been rejected for a job."[24] He acknowledged violations of some liberties but reminded his audience that the Federal Republic constituted the freest state the Germans had ever known. Brandt's speech finally cleared some of the tensions between the SPD and the French Socialist party. Mitterrand told him that the formation of the French committee had rested on a misunderstanding of the West German situation.

Before Mitterrand's admission, the CDU/CSU exploited the Social Democrats' difficulties with their French colleagues. One CDU deputy demanded that the SPD distance itself from the French socialists, who with their communist ally were aiding the enemies of the constitution in West Germany. Other CDU/CSU officials were convinced that the foreign offensive was designed to facilitate a "communist infiltration" of the Federal Republic, make the German communists politically respectable, and create an anti-German atmosphere in Europe. Franz Josef Strauss called Mitterrand an "arsonist who is collaborating with the communists to take over France and is now playing with fire" in the Federal Republic. The CSU presidium characterized Mitterrand's formation of the committee as an "impertinent arrogance."[25] Gerhard Stoltenberg, CDU minister-president of Schleswig-Holstein, denounced West German left groups, including the Jusos, for their massive, concerted campaign against the decree, which triggered foreign reactions. He called on the SPD and FDP to take seriously their resolution not to work with communists.[26]

West German media reaction to foreign pressures varied according to the media's political views. The conservative *Die Welt* denounced the campaign of hatred emanating from abroad, in which one group tried to outdo the other with scare news about the reemergence of the "ugly German." Liberal newspapers, more understanding of foreign criticism, said that the accusations of reemergence were caused by deep-seated doubts about German democracy, lingering distrust of one-time militarism, and jealousy of West Germany's economic success. The Germans were troubled by the foreign response because they hoped they had overcome the shame of the Nazi era. West German television, in a program on the latest controversy, interviewed Gaston Thorn, prime minister of Luxembourg, who stated that many Europeans, looking at Germany's current economic strength and efficiency, were wondering who had won the war.[27]

An editor of *Die Zeit* asserted that West Germans did not need foreign countries or communists to hoist warning flags about liberalism declining in the Federal Republic. He denounced the "Metternichean political snooping" for producing conformism among university students who were fearful of their future careers. He argued that the legacy of an authoritarian state was the government's insistence on civil servants' loyalty, which was superfluous in a modern democratic state.[28]

The negative German reactions to foreign criticisms in turn led to more commentaries in the foreign press about the curtailment of civil liberties in West Germany. There was some puzzlement as to why the Germans reacted so negatively. After all, freedoms had been curtailed and, as one journalist put it, the "ugly Germans" were wearing new suits. No longer were they arrogant members of the master race but narrow-minded, stodgy, and bourgeois materialists. Considering their stifling of leftist dissent, it was no wonder to see one protester in Bonn carrying a sign, "Dear God, let me cower so that I can get into the public service."[29] To many foreigners, a resurgence of conformism was more dangerous than the emergence of critical radical democrats.

At the 1977 congress of the Socialist Youth International, the delegates, representing forty-four countries, expressed similar sentiments. In a resolution backing the Jusos, they warned West Germans about the dangers of an authoritarian repression and limitation of freedoms.[30] On the other hand, DGB delegates at the 1976 convention of the International Confederation of Free Trade Unions in Stockholm were able to nip in the bud a resolution, which some foreign delegates were planning to introduce, condemning the Federal Republic as a "totalitarian state."[31]

The Russell Tribunal

West German authorities were upset not only by the torrent of criticisms emanating from other West European countries but also by the Bertrand Russell Peace Foundation's announcement in 1977 that it would set up a tribunal in the Federal Republic to hold hearings on possible violations of human rights and the erosion of democratic norms. Earlier, the British-based foundation had set up well-publicized tribunals to hold hearings on U.S. intervention in Vietnam and on torture in Chile and Brazil.

On October 16, 1977, the Third International Russell Tribunal, consisting of twenty-six members, with the deliberate exclusion of West Germans, was constituted in Darmstadt. Tribunal members included the former de Gaullist deputy David Rousset, the British sociologist Steven Lukes, the American playwright Eric Bentley, the Norwegian peace researcher Johan Galtung, and, presiding, the Yugoslav writer Vladimir Dedijer.

For the first of two series of sessions, it planned to deal with the 1972 decree, investigating whether West German citizens had been denied the right to practice their chosen professions because of their political convictions. Prior to the sessions, the tribunal emphasized its independence from parties and governments, its open proceedings, and its careful examination of submitted materials. It intended to conduct five months of intensive investigations with the assistance of a five-member German advisory council, whose members sat on the jury but without voting rights.[32] The council was charged with collecting and sifting documents (five hundred cases of civil service applicants were winnowed down to twelve), raising money to defray costs, compiling a list of individual supporters and organizations, and writing the final report. Among the sponsoring organizations were the League of German Writers, the Jusos, the Humanist Union, the Socialist Bureau in Offenbach, and the Association of German Student Governing Boards (VDS).

The West German government and parties sharply criticized the tribunal before its meeting in March–April 1978, fearful that it would spark anti-German feelings in Western countries. They contended that to put possible human rights violations in the Federal Republic in the same category as the Vietnam War and torture in Latin America was unfair. They argued that the catalog of accusations against the government was evidence of finding it guilty in advance.

On November 18, 1977, Minister of the Interior Maihofer (FDP), in a Bundestag statement, asserted that since 1976 German left extremist groups, with the help of the Russell Foundation, had launched an international campaign against the Federal Republic. In June 1976, at an "anti-repression" congress in Frankfurt, the French Unified Socialist party had proposed to the German Socialist Bureau and the Communist League the creation of an international committee against *Berufsverbote*. Thereupon, two German radical groups, joined by others, met in Paris in October and November with representatives of the Russell Foundation to ask for an investigation of human rights violations in West Germany. On February 1, 1977, the foundation agreed to the establishment of a tribunal.

Maihofer characterized it as a mock tribunal. He stated that the documents justifying the charges of violations were identical to the writings of those in West Germany who supported terrorism. Indeed, groups abetting terrorism used the tribunal to promote their criminal purposes. Other groups gave a distorted portrayal of conditions in the Federal Republic, thereby creating an intellectual and political climate that helped the terrorists. Left-extremist groups sought support from democratic forces in order to end their isolation and to create a broader base for forcing through their political ideas.[33]

The tribunal's supporters in the Federal Republic denounced the government's statements as tendentious and false. They said that from the outset there was no intention of putting the Federal Republic on the same level as United States with its violations of human rights in Vietnam and as Chile and Brazil with their state terrorism. The demand to establish the tribunal had come from abroad and not from left groups in the Federal Republic. Such a demand was a legitimate expression of concern about domestic developments and would help those battling the decree at home. They contended that the government's strategy was to undermine the credibility of the tribunal before it even began to function; for instance, by labeling the decree's critics as terrorist sympathizers. There was no danger of the tribunal's falling under control of antidemocratic forces; indeed, a number of communist groups had withdrawn from their planned sponsorship.[34]

The government, remaining nervous about the tribunal's pending trial, issued a report defending its record on human rights.[35] Lawyers in the Ministry of the Interior prepared an internal secret paper, dated September 20, 1977, on how to prevent the tribunal from convening in the Federal Republic. Among the options listed were to threaten cancellation of yearly government subsidies to noncommunist groups supporting the tribunal, to bar foreign members of the tribunal from entering the country, to infiltrate the tribunal with people who would urge acquittal of the charges, and to prohibit the trial through cabinet decision.[36]

Ministry officials rejected these proposals. They kept a low profile instead, partly because the tribunal, already politically weak, kept losing support in West Germany. Several left-radical groups had withdrawn their sponsorship when the tribunal initially intended to discuss the decree in conjunction with equally controversial issues, such as the government's overreaction to terrorism. The Socialist Bureau and others convinced the tribunal to deal only with the decree in its first series of sessions and with other human rights issues in the second series (see chapter 8).

While the dispute went on, Brandt, angry that the Jusos were supporting the tribunal, called the scheduled hearings an "insulting and scandalous exercise," given the Federal Republic's ability to fight its own battles.[37] In October 1977, the SPD executive committee requested party members not to back the tribunal, to withdraw their signatures of support, and not to appear as witnesses. Failure to comply constituted grounds for loss of party membership. As a result of this extraordinary threat, the Jusos, reluctantly, distanced themselves from the tribunal. They requested it to postpone the hearings, because an objective investigation of human rights violations was impossible under the current state of terrorism and the government's tough response. The FDP put similar pressure on the Young Democrats.

The bitter struggles between supporters and opponents were more dramatic than the scheduled hearings. The tribunal met in Frankfurt from March 29 to April 4, 1978, to discuss the question "Are citizens of the Federal Republic and West Berlin being denied the right to exercise their professions because of their political views?" In an opening statement, Dedijer argued that human rights were threatened throughout the civilized world but that the Federal Republic was singled out because of Germany's history and its economic and political role in Western Europe. To defuse the charge that the tribunal was not concerned with violations of human rights in communist countries, he said that tribunal members had earlier condemned such violations.

During the hearings, tribunal members heard details about the origins and development of the decree and its legal and psychological effects, as well as reports from twelve persons who had been affected by it.[38] In preliminary and final reports, tribunal members and the German advisory council concluded that citizens were denied the right to exercise their professions in the public service because of their political views. The *Berufsverbote* represented a serious threat to human rights because of the discrimination practiced in their application. As a result, applicants often lacked possibilities for alternative employment, suffered loss of self-fulfillment and psychological damage, viewed themselves as outcasts from society, were humiliated by the hearings, and encountered long delays, uncertainties, and anxieties before receiving a decision. Sizable sectors of the population were subject to pressures to conform; others defiantly turned to acts of private or public despair, which damaged society. The *Verfassungsschutz* had gathered information about lawful political activities by German citizens. Administrative rulings were arbitrary because the concepts of loyalty and hostility to the Basic Law were vague.

Tribunal members recommended curtailing the pervasive intelligence activities that poisoned the social and political climate, disbanding Länder commissions controlling screenings, restricting special screenings to security agencies, and barring entry into the public service solely to those actively fighting the constitutional order.[39]

The reaction of the West German media to the Russell Tribunal was negative, even among newspapers normally hostile to the decree. *Die Zeit* wrote that the country does not need a tribunal for criticizing the decree's implementation; it is a problem for the Germans to cope with.[40] Other newspapers assailed the lack of objectivity of the tribunal members and the report's verdict based on only twelve, not representative, cases. *Neue Ruhr-Zeitung* called the tribunal's proceedings a "maneuver to pillory this country," "political defamation," "a farce," and accused the self-appointed judges of being incompetent. It asked how one could talk of serious violations of human rights in the Federal Republic when torture was rampant in military dictatorships and authoritarian regimes throughout the world. *Bayern-Kurier* labeled the tribunal proceedings "communist agit-prop."[41] At the root of the newspapers' negative comments may have been a rekindling of the memory of the Nuremberg war tribunal. One journalist wrote, "The international group of jurors made the mistake from the start of placing themselves in the judgment seat and putting the Federal Republic of Germany in the dock."[42] On the other hand, *Le Monde* hoped that the proceedings would further the spirit of tolerance in West Germany, which "supports rather badly any criticism." The French newspaper noted how striking it was for the West German press promptly and unanimously to label as "an anti-German campaign" any faultfinding leveled against the country.[43]

The Council of Europe

The pressure on West German authorities to abrogate the 1972 decree also originated in several supranational organizations. The impetus normally came from foreign communist representatives or organizations, as well as from West German citizens denied access to the civil service who then took their case to a supranational court.

The Council of Europe in Strasbourg dealt with the decree. Founded in 1949 to bring about greater European unity and cooperation and to promote democracy and human rights, the twenty-one-member body of primarily West European states comprises a Committee of Ministers, a Parliamentary Assembly, a European Commission of Human Rights, and a European Court of Human Rights. On May 4, 1976, in a Parliamentary Assembly session, a French communist member denounced West German authorities for creating a climate of fear and apprehension in the Federal Republic. Two German members, in a rebuttal, stated that the climate of fear was created by the terrorists and anarchists. They also contended that the 1972 decree was in accord with the Council of Europe's 1950 European Convention for the Protection of Human Rights and Fundamental Freedoms and with the UN Covenant on Civil and Political Rights, ratified by the Federal Republic in 1952 and 1973 respectively.[44] The West German government also supplied documentation on the decree to the assembly's Legal Affairs Committee, which issued a factual report without any recommendations.[45]

The Council of Europe's judicial machinery was used as a means of redress by several West German applicants to the civil service who had lost their cases in the national courts. Any citizen of a member state of the Council of Europe can request its secretary-general and the European Commission of Human Rights to take up his or her case if the member state acknowledges jurisdiction of the commission and if the plaintiff believes that the national authorities have violated the 1950 convention. The commission then sifts the requests and transmits a few cases to the European Court of Human Rights. In December 1982, the commission rejected one case dealing with the 1972 decree because plaintiff Gross, by failing to take her case to the West German Federal Constitutional Court, had not exhausted all national legal remedies.

The Glasenapp Case

On July 16, 1984, the commission transmitted two other West German cases to the court. One case concerned Julia Glasenapp of Cologne, an art teacher trainee who sought a permanent appointment in 1974 as a secondary school teacher. North Rhine-Westphalian authorities appointed her to a post but dismissed her from it a few months later for "willful deceit" after she published a letter in a communist newspaper supporting the opening of a people's kindergarten. They accused her of falsely swearing to uphold the FDGO to obtain the post and only thereafter admitting to being a sympathizer of the Maoist KPD. She appealed her dismissal to the administrative courts. On December 11, 1979, the Federal Administrative Court refused to hear her case, because the "willful deceit" charge meant that she had insufficient prospects for winning her case in court. On January 8, 1980, she lodged a complaint with the Federal Constitutional Court, arguing that there had been no willful deceit. The court rejected her complaint for the same reason as did the Administrative Court.

On November 7, 1980, she took her case against the West German government to the European Commission of Human Rights. Two years later the commission accepted her application for review because of a possible violation of Article 10 of the European Convention, guaranteeing freedom of expression. On May 11, 1984, the commission adopted by a 9 to 8 vote a report that Article 10 had been breached and forwarded her case to the European Court of Human Rights.

On October 22, 1985, the court scheduled a hearing at which a representative of the West German government urged the judges to find that the court could not deal with the merits of the case. Moreover, Glasenapp had not exhausted domestic remedies, because she had failed to allege an infringement of her freedom of expression in West German courts. That claim was made for the first time before the European commission.[46]

On August 28, 1986, the court, by 16 to 1, held that Article 10 had not been breached and dismissed her case. The judges argued that the crux of the case concerned access to civil service rather than freedom of expression. West German authorities did not violate any provision on access to a state's civil service, because none exists in the European Convention, since member states engage in varying practices. Several judges, in a joint concurring opinion, noted, however, that the 1948 Universal Declaration of Human Rights (Article 21) and the 1966 UN Covenant on Civil and Political Rights (Article 25) granted all citizens the right of equal access to the public service in their countries.

One judge, in a partially dissenting opinion, noted that Article 10 of the European Convention may apply. He wrote, "How can a drawing teacher, such as Mrs. Glasenapp, whose main task is to teach the art of drawing to young pupils, prove that she has 'constantly upheld the free democratic system?' "[47] He viewed her dismissal by the government as an action disproportionate to the aims pursued and considered the decree unnecessary in a democratic society.

The Kosiek Case

The second case considered by the European Court of Human Rights concerned Rolf Kosiek. He joined the NPD in 1965, held local and regional posts in the party, was a deputy in the Baden-Württemberg Landtag from 1968 to 1972, became a candidate for the Bundestag in 1972, and wrote two political books. In 1972, the Land Ministry of Education appointed him as a lecturer in physics with the status of probationary civil servant at Nürtingen technical college. In 1974, the ministry, after a hearing, had doubts about his constitutional loyalty, on the basis of his party activities, and gave him notice of dismissal.

In an appeal to the local administrative court, Kosiek argued that he had resigned several of his NPD posts and remained loyal to the FDGO. In 1977, the court found for the plaintiff, whereupon the ministry appealed the judgment. In 1978, the Land Administrative Court and, in 1980, the Federal Administrative Court upheld the ministry's dismissal of Kopiek. (His court appeals against dismissal had a suspensive effect, and he was able to teach until 1980.) On March 16, 1981, he applied to the Federal Constitutional Court to set aside these judgments on the ground that they contravened the Basic Law. He challenged the objectivity and relevance of the evidence and the arbitrary judgment used against him. The courts had made no attempt to establish whether the NPD violated the basic principles of the Basic Law. He contended that the party and he were not in such violation. On July 31, 1981, the Constitutional Court decided not to accept the complaint because of insufficient prospects of success.

Thereupon Kosiek took his case to the European commission, claiming, as did Glasenapp, that his dismissal was contrary to Article 10 of the European Convention. On December 16, 1982, the commission declared the application admissible, but in its advisory report of May 11, 1984, to the European Court found, by a 10 to 7 vote, that the convention had not been violated and that West German authorities had the right to restrict entry into the public service. In a hearing, the West German government representatives provided arguments similar to those in the Glasenapp case. They insisted that the case concerned issues of access to the civil service, in this instance a teaching post, and not the right of freedom of expression as the plaintiff claimed.

On August 28, 1986, the European court rendered its verdict; by a 16-1 vote it held that there was no breach of Article 10. The Land government had taken account of Kopiek's opinions and activities merely in order to determine whether he had proved himself during his probationary period. He was barred from a permanent civil service teaching post because he lacked its necessary personal qualifications.[48] West German defenders of the 1972 decree welcomed the court's decisions as further proof of the correctness of their position.

The European Community

West German critics of the decree have looked into the possibility of taking cases to the judicial organ of the European Community—the European Court of Justice (ECJ). In 1981, the German teachers' union reviewed the legal possibilities of suing the Federal Republic for its infringement of the human rights of nearly thirty communist teachers who were then threatened with dismissals, but it dropped the plan.[49] The ECJ rendered one judgment in June 1984 in the case of *Hans Moser v. Land Baden-Württemberg*. The authorities had barred Moser, a DKP member, from entry into the civil service as a probationary teacher. He brought suit in a local labor court, contending that the Land action prevented him from becoming a private teacher in another EC state, not to speak of denying him a chance to teach in the Federal Republic. Such action, he argued, was incompatible with Article

48 of the EC Treaty, which permits workers to move freely within the EC states to seek employment.

The West German local court stayed proceedings and requested a judgment from the ECJ whether the term "workers" included teachers and whether German legislation was compatible with the EC Treaty. The Bonn government, in a written communication to the ECJ, argued that because Moser was a German citizen who had never resided or worked in another EC state, the treaty did not apply. The EC Commission, on the other hand, argued that the European court should bring to the attention of the national courts matters of importance regarding EC law, implying that the 1972 decree might fall into that category.

The ECJ ruled that Article 48 did not apply to a matter, such as the 1972 decree, that is wholly internal to a member state. A person who has never resided or worked in another member state may not rely on Article 48 "to prevent the application to him of legislation of his own country, denying him access to a particular kind of vocational training." The court rejected Moser's argument that he was precluded from applying for teaching posts in other states, but it also rejected the West German government's view that it had no jurisdiction to rule on a request for a preliminary judgment.[50]

Critics of the decree have also turned to the European Parliament—another EC organ—as an additional venue to generate international debate and to put the Bonn government on the defensive. They knew that the parliament's constitutional powers within the EC framework are weak but that sympathetic members would support them. Thus, when in March 1976 thousands of demonstrators from West European countries gathered in front of the European Parliament building in Strasbourg to denounce the decree, left and liberal members of parliament received a delegation from the protesters for informal talks.

In 1980 and 1981, several West Germans who had been barred or ousted from the public service filed motions and petitions with the European Parliament to have their cases reviewed. In turn, a number of members of Parliament filed motions for resolutions contending that the decree violated Article 10 of the European Convention and provisions in the Universal Declaration of Human Rights, such as freedom of thought (Articles 18 and 19) and the right of equal access to the public service (Article 21). Although the declaration has no binding legal force, it set a common standard for the guidance of signatory states.

The Legal Affairs Committee took the motions for resolutions under advisement and in October 1982 met with a number of West German petitioners. In the meantime (a few months earlier), the committee's rapporteur, Marie-Claude Vayssade (a French socialist), had prepared a report on the 1972 decree. It notes that the European Parliament passed a resolution in 1977 calling on the EC Commission to seek an agreement between the member states to mesh their civil and political rights with EC treaties, the European Convention, and the UN Covenant on Civil and Political Rights. It also notes that the heads of state and government at an EC Council meeting in April 1978 proclaimed their determination to safeguard respect for human rights. The report points out, however, that such rights may need to be limited in the Federal Republic, where the Weimar experience and the geographic proximity to the GDR lend support to the West German government's position that the civil service should not admit or retain those who challenge the FDGO. On the other hand, the report recommends to the German authorities that they keep in mind "the principles of proportionality and adaptation of the means employed to the ends being pursued."[51] The report also recommends that West Germany enact legislation stipulating that restrictions on access should vary in accordance with the duties to be performed and should be limited to members of a prohibited party or organization or to those who participate actively in an organization pursuing anticonstitutional objectives.[52]

Political warfare between party blocs prevented approval of the carefully crafted report at a June 1983 meeting of the Legal Affairs Committee. The rightist bloc contended that parliament did not have jurisdiction, and the communist bloc viewed the report as too conciliatory toward the West German government. In November 1984, another attempt was made to produce a report, but it failed.

In October 1985, a communist member of parliament addressed a question to the EC Council concerning the decree's "flagrant violation" of international conventions. The council's president responded that the matter lay outside the EC sphere of responsibility because the EC Treaty did not cover national legislation concerning a national civil service. He reminded the member of parliament that in no country in the world is there an absolute right to public office but that if human rights were violated in a signatory state, then the European Parliament had a right to intervene.[53]

The Committee on Rules and Petitions of the European Parliament also dealt with the decree at its meeting on October 15–16, 1985, after having received twelve petitions containing the names of thirty-three Germans, of whom twenty-six were DKP members or sympathizers. The committee recommended that these individuals, who had been barred from the public service or against whom ouster proceedings had begun, "turn to the West

German courts and abide by the regulations of the federal German legislation." The committee viewed their complaints as falling outside the jurisdiction of the EC institutions. However, it urged Bonn authorities to define more precisely in national legislation what limits existed for entrance into the public service in order to avoid extensive improper applications of the decree. Only those individuals who refused to pledge loyalty to the FDGO should be barred; otherwise the *Berufsverbot* runs counter to the basic freedom of expression.[54]

The United Nations

Communist, communist-front, and leftist organizations attempted to alert members of UN organizations to alleged West German violations of human rights, but their efforts had only limited success. On June 20, 1974, the International Association of Democratic Lawyers, at the behest of the West German branch, requested UN secretary-general Kurt Waldheim to investigate the 1972 decree and its violation of UN human rights conventions and the Federal Republic Basic Law. It submitted documentation specifying that articles dealing with freedom of speech and thought had been violated, as well as Article 25 of the UN Covenant on Civil and Political Rights, dealing with the right of every citizen to have access to a public office without discrimination. Commissions on human rights of the UN Economic and Social Council and UNESCO (United Nations Educational, Scientific and Cultural Organization) discussed the association's call for action but made no recommendations.[55]

In summer 1978, the UN Human Rights Commission in New York held an inconclusive debate, sparked by documentation supplied by, among others, the communist-dominated World Peace Council, which in October 1977 had sponsored a three-day hearing in Copenhagen on the decree. The council's human rights commission had collected documentation in six West German cities in September; international lawyers and other specialists from many countries sifted through the documents and found that the ban on jobs violated human rights provisions in the Basic Law and international accords. These findings were presented at the Copenhagen hearings and transmitted to the UN commission "in order to engage world public opinion more fully in the struggle against the ban on jobs and to increase support for the victims."[56] In April 1986, the UN Human Rights Commission dealt with the decree again, during discussion of the German government's second report on the country's implementation of the UN covenant, but made no recommendations.

The International Labor Organization

Critics of the decree scored a major triumph in the International Labor Organization (ILO), a specialized agency of the United Nations, founded in 1919 to promote social justice as a basis for a lasting peace, through the improvement of conditions of labor. On January 24, 1978, the communist-dominated World Federation of Trade Unions (WFTU), with headquarters in Prague, lodged a representation with the 150-member organization, charging the West German government with failure to adhere to ILO Convention No. 111, adopted by the ILO in 1958 and subsequently ratified by 108 states, including the Federal Republic in 1961. Convention No. 111 prohibits any discrimination in employment or occupation on the basis of, among others, a person's political views, unless a person is justifiably suspected of, or engaged in, activities prejudicial to the security of the state. (A person has the right of appeal to a competent body established in accordance with national practice.)

Upon receipt of the WFTU representation, the ILO's secretariat (the International Labor Office) formed a committee to study the question. In a report of June 15, 1979, the committee supported the West German government's contention that public servants are expected to have a special loyalty to the state, as long as such a requirement conforms to the general spirit of the ILO convention. The committee referred to the Bonn 1979 guidelines, which limit the discretion of hiring authorities. In November 1979, the ILO Governing Body noted the report and ended the representation procedure.[57]

The WFTU lodged a new representation against the Bonn government, by then CDU/CSU controlled, in June 1984. It alleged that since 1979 "several hundred" cases of discriminatory measures had been taken against candidates for the public service; the Bonn government "had not made serious efforts to bring legislation and practice into conformity with the Convention."[58]

The ILO Governing Body set up a three-member committee to study the new charges. On December 18, 1984, the Bonn government rejected the allegation that it had failed to comply with the convention. It noted that from May 1975 to December 1982 there had been only 111 formal disciplinary proceedings against federal and Länder public servants for violations of loyalty to the FDGO, not all of which led to sanctions. In addition, thirty-nine public servants on probationary status were dismissed for the same reason. These totals represent but a minute fraction of all public servants.

In February 1985, the committee submitted its report, based on an examination of seventy-nine cases, to the Governing Body. The report, unfavorable to the Bonn government, stated that an individual's political activity in a legal party and electoral candidacy for a public office do not endanger public security. The Bonn representative to the ILO announced that his government was unable to accept the committee's recommendations for changes in the decree but favored a further exchange of views.

Thereupon, the Governing Body, at its June and November 1985 meetings, decided to expand the scope of its investigation by forming an official Commission of Inquiry. The commission of three distinguished members consisted of chairperson Voitto Saario, former justice of the Finnish Supreme Court, and international law professors Dietrich Schindler (Switzerland) and Gonzalo Parra-Aranguren (Venezuela). Its task was to examine whether the Federal Republic legislation and administrative practice were compatible with ILO Convention No. 111 to ensure that there was no discrimination. It was not called upon to review individual decisions taken by West German administrative or judicial authorities with a view to granting relief to the individuals concerned.

The commission requested organizations having a consultative status with the ILO (e.g., the International Confederation of Free Trade Unions), West German organizations (e.g., the Confederation of German Employers Associations), and Western and Eastern neighboring states of the Federal Republic to provide evidence and statements on behalf of the WFTU or Bonn. Thus, the GDR and Czechoslovakia sent supporting letters for the WFTU. The commission also requested the WFTU and Bonn to submit documents and statements. The WFTU, in a new documentation, said, "The Federal Constitutional Court had created a grey area with its concept of 'hostility to the Constitution' as a result of which the party concerned [i.e., DKP], its members and supporters were largely removed from constitutionally-guaranteed freedoms."[59]

The Federal Republic, in a lengthy statement, noted that the ILO was too important a body to be improperly used (read, by the WFTU) "as a weapon in the struggle against freedom, democracy and human rights and thus against the Organization's own purposes."[60] In another jab at the WFTU, the Federal Republic contended that it was a misuse of international bodies' supervising standards to appeal to them for political reasons, bypassing the highest domestic courts. Once again, it held that Convention No. 111 permits the government to impose special rights and duties on its public servants, such as keeping out "champions of totalitarian systems." Bonn must be able to protect itself in future crises by having a body of public servants ready to defend the FDGO. Even though there were currently few extremists in the public service, if one waited until their total reached a danger point, it would be too late. In its statement the government also attempted to buttress its position by citing the findings of the European Court of Human Rights in the Glasenapp and Kosiek cases.

Upon receipt of these statements, the commission met in Geneva in closed sessions on several occasions to hear witnesses, with representatives of Bonn and the WFTU present. The witnesses for the WFTU included West Germans affected by the decree; for the Bonn government, the federal disciplinary prosecutor and senior Länder officials; and for German trade unions, top officers and staff from DGB unions, DAG, and DBB. The commission also visited the Federal Republic from August 4 to 13, 1986, to interview more federal and Länder administrators, academic and union specialists, and lawyers involved in decree cases.

After hearing the witnesses and evaluating the stack of documents requested from German employers associations (favorable to the Bonn government) and trade unions (mostly critical), in March 1987 the commission submitted its findings and recommendations to the Governing Body, which subsequently took cognizance of them. In the 265-page report, reference is made to the government's observation that DKP members had deliberately refrained from exhausting domestic remedies by not taking their cases to the Federal Constitutional Court and that the DKP's aim was to fight the decree by political means rather than by recourse to the court. Yet, the court, on four occasions, declined to consider complaints on the ground of insufficient evidence.

The commission also observed that Bonn policies and practices varied considerably over the years because of the adoption of different guidelines or different responses to judicial decisions. Therefore a wide gap existed between the liberalized practices of some Länder (implicitly referring to those governed primarily by the SPD) and the stringent practices of others (i.e., those led by the CDU/CSU), as well as the conservative decisions rendered by various Länder courts and the Federal Administrative Court. The commission found that the less restrictive policies followed in some Länder caused no difficulties in the functioning of public services. Hence, it would "appear that the more stringent test adopted by other authorities established conditions that go further than is necessary for the proper functioning of the public service."[61]

The commission, in a rebuttal of the Bonn government's position that radical teachers were indoctrinating their pupils, found few cases in which such allegations were made, and none involving teachers who were DKP members. While abuse of functions may occur, disciplinary measures short of dismissal were sufficient to deal with the case. The likelihood that an abuse will occur cannot be presumed from specific political views or affiliations. The commission stated, "There can be no justification to assume that, because a teacher is active in a particular party or organization, he will behave in a manner incompatible with his obligations."[62]

The commission noted that in no case of denial of, or ouster from, a position was there an accusation of activity endangering the security of the state. It concluded that the test of political reliability of public servants should be restricted to key positions, not applied to the public service generally. The stringent practices of the Bonn government and certain Länder barring members of legally recognized parties were not in consonance with the antidiscrimination provision of Convention No. 111. The commission wrote:

> There can be no doubt that the measures taken in the Federal Republic in application of the provisions governing the duty of faithfulness to the free democratic basic order of persons in the public service have the effect of excluding those affected from such employment and of nullifying or impairing their opportunity of access to or continuance in employment. They therefore come within the ambit of the definition contained in . . . Convention No. 111.[63]

The three commission members signed the report, but one member, Parra-Aranguren, in an unprecedented dissenting vote, contended that a discrimination prohibition should not protect persons who were enemies of the FDGO. In a rejoinder, Saario and Schindler argued that it would be "contrary to the very idea of human rights and would amount to denial of human rights if persons who advocate ideas that may be in conflict with human rights would lose all rights deriving from international human rights conventions."[64]

The Bonn government had three months to respond to the report of the ILO Commission of Inquiry and to signify whether it accepted or rejected the recommendations. Should it reject them, it could request the International Court of Justice (ICJ) in The Hague to render a judgment. In its response of May 7, 1987, the government rejected the report, although diplomatically expressing its willingness to abide by the responsibilities stemming from the ILO constitution. It chided the majority on the commission for disregarding the principle that the government had an obligation to protect the FDGO and to keep out of the public service persons intent on eliminating the FDGO and human rights. The government noted that the decisions of the European Court of Human Rights (see above) confirmed its position. The government had no intention of taking the dispute to the ICJ but intended to make annual reports to the ILO bodies monitoring application of the organization's standards. Thereby it hoped to avoid being put on the ILO's "black list."[65]

The ILO could not force the Bonn government or the Länder and federal courts to accept the recommendations. When the government rejected them, it was put in the uncomfortable position of being told it was not abiding by a convention of a supranational organization or, in a broader context, of subsuming international law to national law. This view was strengthened by the government's decision not to take its case to the ICJ because it feared the court's possible negative ruling would be another blow to its position that it had a strong human rights record. The government could expect such a negative ruling because three ICJ justices, including ICJ president José María Ruda (Argentina), were also members of the ILO Committee of Experts, which fully supported the Commission of Inquiry (see below). Moreover, even though the ICJ ruling could only be in the form of a recommendation (Article 59 of the ICJ covenant and Article 33 of the ILO constitution), the government, mindful of the damage in status that would result from not abiding by a negative ruling from a prestigious court, might have had to alter or even abrogate the decree.[66] This possibility was already indicated in the report by the ILO Commission of Inquiry, which implicitly called for an end to proceedings against radicals and the rehabilitation of those who had been affected by the decree.[67]

In its defense, the Bonn government contended in press statements that the two ILO commission members (constituting the majority) could not recommend changes in the decree's implementation that would violate existing civil service legislation and provisions in the Basic Law protecting the FDGO. Its willingness to have the ILO review implementation of the decree showed its readiness to be accommodating to the ILO. After all, it did not choose to denounce Convention No. 111 or to leave the ILO, even though (not explicitly stated) it was the victim of a political move by the WFTU and the communist member states of the ILO to force a policy change.

The West German media soft-pedaled the ILO commission report, but the few comments in the establishment press showed resentment that a democratic country whose legislation protecting workers' standards is among the most advanced in the West was the first in ILO history to be the victim of a concerted communist campaign. One West German newspaper pointed out that the WFTU, which called for the ILO investigation, is the coordinating association of national union federations representing workers in states that, with few exceptions, have tighter admission requirements for the civil service and other professions than has the Federal Republic.[68]

The WFTU initiative, supported by communist states, although based primarily on human rights considerations of DKP members and other German leftists, must also be understood in the broader context of being part of a campaign against the West, which in the ILO had consistently denounced violations of workers' rights in communist states. For instance, the Western-initiated ILO investigations of Poland's crushing of the Solidarity movement led to an unfavorable report for Poland and its giving notice of withdrawal from the ILO in 1985 (the notice was rescinded in 1987). Conversely, from 1977 to 1980 the United States had withdrawn from the ILO, announcing that the organization had deteriorated into a communist propaganda front that criticized Western democracies while ignoring abuses of workers in Eastern countries.[69]

In the case of the ILO report on the Federal Republic, even though the initiative came from the communist side, the substance of the arguments against the decree was sufficiently sound that noncommunists, such as the commission members and West German opponents of the decree, supported most WFTU arguments. The West German government had to contend not only with the ILO Commission of Inquiry report but, one year later, with another critical report. In 1988, the twenty-member ILO Committee of Experts, including the FRG representative, issued a report, unanimously approved, contending that the West German government or the legislature had an obligation to make the provisions of the ILO convention effective. It urged Bonn, in consultation with the unions, to review the situation and to adopt measures to implement the convention. It hailed the decision of a German labor court that in 1987 underlined the binding nature of international law as set forth in the recommendations of the ILO Commission of Inquiry and criticized the decisions of the Federal Administrative Court that twice the same year viewed the recommendations as having no binding character.[70] As will be noted in chapter 6, the ILO reports became the focus of a renewed controversy between the proponents and opponents of the decree in the Federal Republic.

Conclusion

Bonn officials sought in vain to keep the 1972 decree out of the international arena, as communists in particular in a number of West European and other countries formed ad hoc united front groups on the issue of discrimination in the Federal Republic. The groups organized protest rallies, gathered signatures on petitions, and invited victims of the decree to provide information at rallies and on television and radio. Foreign socialist parties, churches, and unions also took independent initiatives against the decree. The term "Berufsverbot" made its mark in the European public consciousness.

West German governments, no matter what their political constellation, resented what they considered foreign interference in a domestic matter. But foreign officials insisted that the administration of the decree was a matter of great concern to them. Given Germany's history and its repression of dissent, especially during the Nazi era, the case of Silvia Gingold, a Jewish teacher denied civil service status for eight years because she was a communist, evoked painful memories in countries adjoining Germany that had been overrun by the Nazis.

When foreign pressures reached their peak in 1976, the Bonn government, then controlled by the SPD and FDP, was put on the defensive. The SPD was especially singled out for attack by its brethren socialist parties in Western Europe. In addition, the Russell Tribunal—viewed by most West Germans as a mere propaganda organ of the Left—accused the government of limiting the freedoms of political dissenters. Because the tribunal's opponents viewed it as a mock jury whose findings were predictable from the outset, it played only a negligible role in strengthening the case against the decree. More important was the report issued by the politically neutral ILO Commission of Inquiry, which found that the CDU/CSU's policies of continued support for the decree violated an ILO convention.

The Council of Europe, the EC, and the United Nations also debated the decree but, except for two European Parliament committee reports, made no recommendations. The reports supported the government's case, yet with requests for changes in the decree. The debates especially raised the awareness of international officials and parliamentarians that the Federal Republic was deeply divided by a national human rights problem. Attempts by the victims of the decree to seek legal redress in supranational courts— especially the prestigious European Court of Human Rights—all failed, however, because justices ruled that the cases they reviewed fell within the internal jurisdiction of the Federal Republic and did not violate any international treaty. Despite these positive developments for the Bonn governments, its officials during the period of SPD-FDP governance took heed of foreign pressures to liberalize further the decree's implementation, as will be seen in the chapter to follow.

5

The Aftermath,
1976–1980

If SPD or FDP policymakers in Bonn had hoped that during the parliamentary session from 1976 to 1980 the decree would become a nonissue in foreign or domestic politics, they were sadly mistaken. During this four-year period in which Helmut Schmidt was chancellor, the number of screenings increased by leaps and bounds; individual cases made the headlines; discussions arose about the psychological damage to individuals; novels, plays, and cartoons criticizing the decree helped to shape public consciousness; and pressure groups continued to debate the decree. As a result, SPD and FDP officials were willing to make further changes in its implementation in the federal civil service and in the Länder they controlled. However, CDU/CSU officials maintained their opposition to any changes.

Number Affected

Until 1979, nearly all applicants for the public service were screened automatically. According to the Federal Statistics Office, each year the service hired between 250,000 and 300,000 persons. Thus, in the eight-year period from early 1972 to late 1979, between 2 million and 2.4 million were admitted, and until 1987 about 3.5 million were screened. The *Verfassungsschutz*, which screened most of those accepted as well as those who had competed for the same positions, had files containing negative information on about 35,000. The authorities initially barred entry to 10,000 applicants, but many of the latter successfully appealed their cases to higher administrations or the courts. Ultimately between 1,102 and 2,250 were barred.

The percentage rejected varied from Land to Land, with a maximum in West Berlin of 2.3 percent (1977), but normally not higher than 0.1 to 0.5 percent. This low rejection rate was evidence, according to the critics, that the democratic state was not going to perish if those rejected had been admitted, or, according to the supporters, that the critics had overreacted to the decree's effects. In addition to the rejections, authorities dismissed 256 public servants from the service (including those denied permanent status).[1]

Whether applicants lived in SPD- or CDU/CSU-led Länder made, in most instances, little difference in their chances of being rejected for political reasons. For instance, in January 1979, authorities processed 330 cases, of which 180 were in SPD-governed Länder (especially North Rhine-Westphalia) and 150 in CDU/CSU-governed Länder (especially Baden-Württemberg, Bavaria, and Lower Saxony). In the federal service, most cases dealt with railroad and postal civil servants because the Bonn government had exclusive jurisdiction over these two branches. By 1979–80, the total number of cases being handled was slightly lower than in previous years as a consequence of fewer openings in the civil service and of greater political conformity among students.

Two-thirds of the cases being processed concerned applicants for the civil service (mostly in CDU/CSU Länder), while one-third concerned civil servants threatened with dismissal. Of those cases where a decision had already been made not to employ or to dismiss, in one-third the reason given was the individual's holding a post in an extremist party or running as its candidate for public office, in 25 percent it was membership in and active support for such a party or group, and in 15 percent it was suspected membership or support. In about four out of five instances, the extremist party was the DKP, and in most other instances it was a smaller Marxist party or group, such as MSB-Spartakus.[2] Remarkable is the small number of NPD members who applied for positions and were denied entry; the main reason was that in the 1970s few of them attended universities and wanted to become career servants.

Not all left radicals had difficulty gaining entry into the public service, because some Länder administered the decree liberally, the courts ruled in their favor, or authorities did not have enough evidence, acceptable in court, to bar them.[3] Thus, their number in the federal and Länder services increased from 1,307 at the end of 1972 to 2,360 at the end of 1980. On the other hand, the number of right radicals decreased from 1,487 in 1972 to

362 in 1980. As a consequence, in 1980 the ratio of left to right radicals was 6 to 1, compared to a slight majority of right radicals in 1972.

The decline among right radicals was caused not by mass dismissals but rather by lapses in NPD membership, resignations or retirements, and an adjustment in counting in 1974. As one illustration of the shift from right to left radicals, the number of rightist teachers fell from 127 in 1972 to 40 in 1980, while the number of leftist teachers jumped from 306 in 1972 to 932 in 1980.[4]

Individual Cases

Silvia Gingold's case attracted international attention, as seen in chapter 4, yet there were several others. One case that produced increasing doubts among SPD adherents about the decree's necessity was that of Heinrich Häberlein, who, unlike most victims, was not a communist. He had been chairman of the Bavarian section and a member of the national executive committee of the German Peace Society (*Deutsche Friedensgesellschaft*, DFG), a branch of the War Resisters International, not to be confused with the communist-dominated German Peace Union (DFU). Yet, because the DKP had two members and perhaps some sympathizers on the fourteen-member national executive committee of the DFG, the *Verfassungsschutz* put the DFG, along with the DFU, on the list of "communist-dominated" organizations. Häberlein was denied a teaching appointment in a primary school in Bavaria for lack of loyalty to the FDGO. The denial was confirmed by a local administrative court but overruled on appeal by the Bavarian Administrative Court, which ordered authorities to hire him as a teacher on probation. When authorities found out that he had signed the Krefeld Appeal against nuclear armament, they refused to give him permanent civil service status. He appealed the decision and subsequently won.[5]

Another case upsetting to the SPD was that of Edgar Vögel, who had been a member of the leftist Socialist University League (SHB) and then joined the SPD. The Bavarian Ministry of Education rejected his application to become a teacher in Munich, because the SHB had engaged in united actions with communists and because he supported the SPD long-range program (1973–85), which contained the term "class society." The ministry backtracked after a wave of protests.[6]

The case of locomotive engineer Rudi Röder made the headlines beyond Federal Republic national boundaries. His father, a communist, had been arrested by the Gestapo. Rudi Röder, too, became a communist, joining the DKP in 1968, holding party posts, and running for public office several times. In 1961, Röder began working for the federal railways, in 1970 he became a probationary civil servant, and in 1974 he was slated to receive permanent status. In hearings, examiners developed doubts about his political loyalty, and in 1976 officials were on the verge of dismissing him. Massive demonstrations, international protest resolutions, the support he received from the railways' personnel council, and a discussion in the Bonn cabinet convinced the railways authorities in 1977 to give him permanent status if he distanced himself from the DKP within two years. Having received such status, he challenged its conditional nature by becoming the party's candidate for public office in Würzburg within the two-year period. The railways authorities, at the behest of the federal disciplinary prosecutor, intended to renew dismissal proceedings but halted them when Röder decided to switch from civil service to salaried employee status.

The case aroused much attention because critics charged that it was ridiculous to dismiss railway staff who had a perfect record on the job and whose political views were immaterial to driving a locomotive. DGB president Vetter publicly supported Röder's case; he asked, "Is there a danger perhaps that with his train he will drive too far on the left?" Vetter maintained that the decree's excesses had produced fear and intimidation.[7] Referring to the Röder case, the decree's defenders retorted, among other arguments, that in a national emergency a communist could temporarily sabotage a main rail line by abandoning a locomotive on it. The critics rejected this argument; instead, they emphasized that the Nazi regime had ousted Röder's father, also a communist, from his position as a locomotive engineer.

The Röder case assumed importance not only because of this historical parallel but also because it was a test case of the government's determination to bar communist applicants to the public service and to eliminate radicals who were in the preparatory service and ready to receive permanent posts. Among them were mail carriers whom the government attempted to dismiss. Symbolic of this effort was the 1977 decision of the Ministry of Transport, Post, and Telecommunications to deny Wolfgang Repp permanent civil service status after he had served in a probationary status since 1965. Repp, a DKP member, had run as the party's candidate for local elections in 1972 and for the Hesse Landtag in 1974. But because the case aroused intensive opposition in West Germany and in other countries, he was granted career status in 1977.

One year later, the ministry initiated a get-tough policy; Repp was one of the first targets. At a hearing called on the charge that he had committed a civil service misdemeanor (*Dienstvergehen*) by holding offices in the DKP, he was threatened with discharge unless he gave up these offices and stopped his activities for the party. When he refused, ministry officials in 1979 began preliminary proceedings against him but then changed their minds and offered him a chance to give up his status as civil servant and become a salaried employee instead. As an employee he would not be subject to the stringent loyalty requirements governing civil servants. Standing on principles, once again he refused.

Thereupon, in 1983, the ministry officials started formal proceedings against him in a disciplinary court of the first instance. In March 1984, the court held that the ministry, knowing about his DKP activities, had granted permanent status; thus it had a commitment to keep him. The ministry filed an appeal in the Federal Administrative Court, which in July 1984 ruled for the ministry. The court stated that the ministry's complaint against Repp was admissible and must be heard by the Federal Disciplinary Court.

In September 1984, the minister suspended Repp with a 25 percent reduction in pay, but the disciplinary court annulled that decision. Despite the court's action, the ministry did not allow him to resume work. In June 1985, the court ruled that Repp had not undertaken political actions contrary to his duties and had not engaged in "agitatorial disloyal" activities to overthrow the FDGO forcefully. The court maintained that to be active in a legal party does not endanger the existence of the Federal Republic; if such persons were not suitable for certain posts, then more appropriate posts in the ministry could be found for them. As a result of the decision, Repp remained a mail carrier after nine years of attempts to oust him.[8]

Another case of a civil servant on permanent status faced with dismissal proceedings (the first such in West Berlin) was that of Hans Apel, who had been a teacher since 1970. The CDU-dominated district administration initiated disciplinary proceedings against him because he was an active member of the Socialist Unity party of West Berlin (SEW), the local communist party. In December 1976, the Berlin administrative court, ruling in Apel's favor, stated that he had not consciously engaged in unconstitutional activities and that he did not know his SEW membership would make him an "enemy of the constitution." The Berlin government appealed the ruling to the Superior Administrative Court, which in September 1978 overturned it. The court decided that he must be ousted for his active membership in the SEW.

Before the decision, the local Initiative against *Berufsverbote* and other organizations rallied to Apel's defense. The French Socialist party sent him a letter of support, noncommunist groups in West Berlin issued resolutions, and pupils of Apel's school went on a two-day solidarity strike. After the court's negative decision, more than ten thousand people attended a protest rally, and twenty thousand participated in a march.[9] The outside pressures had no effect on the court but made the public aware of the issue.

Implementation of the 1972 decree also was linked to the debate about terrorism in the Federal Republic in one well-publicized case. In June 1977, thirteen university professors in Lower Saxony, as well as thirty-five professors and other professionals in other Länder, reprinted with little commentary the text of an obituary written by a leftist student, under the pseudonym "Mescalero," who had expressed "clandestine joy" about the assassination of federal prosecutor general Siegfried Buback. (The latter had been assigned to prosecute the Baader-Meinhof members.) The left-wing professors rejected terrorist acts such as Buback's assassination, for which there was no justification, but viewed publication and wider dissemination of the controversial eulogy, which also had been quoted out of context, as a test of the freedom to publish. In response, Land minister of education Eduard Pestel (CDU) requested the professors to declare their loyalty to the constitution and to the state; refusal would lead to ouster proceedings. As a matter of principle, Peter Brückner and another professor refused to sign a pledge of loyalty.

Brückner, teaching in the psychology department of Hanover Technical University, had been accused before the "Mescalero" affair of providing shelter to Ulrike Meinhof when she was hiding from the police. He had also been the author of a pamphlet on the controversial Buback obituary. His refusal to sign the pledge of loyalty led to a ministry order suspending him from teaching and cutting his salary. Administrative court decisions in 1978 and 1981 approved this action. The judges ruled that since 1977 he had accused police officials of inhumane and terrorist acts, labeled the state as repressive, and did not distance himself enough from Red Army Faction terrorists. The Superior Administrative Court concurred on the suspension but not on salary cuts. It ordered further study of his writings to see whether he had violated a duty of loyalty to the FDGO. With Brückner's death in 1982 the case was closed, but it had roused concern in left academic circles that conservative government officials were seeking to limit academic freedom and intimidate and harass radical university professors.[10]

Most civil service cases involved left radicals, but on occasion right radicals fell under the decree, such as Jurgen Schützinger, who in 1970 had joined the police force in Baden-Württemberg. Active in the NPD, he swiftly rose in its ranks, becoming the party's candidate for the Landtag and

Bundestag as well as for mayor of his home town. (He did not win.) The party selected him as Land chairman at the age of twenty-four.

When told by his superiors that he would be discharged as civil servant on probationary status for his political activities, he claimed that he was not active while on duty. In his appeal to an administrative court, he maintained that not only he but the NPD also supported the FDGO. Yet, the court rejected his pleas, contending that Schützinger's activity as NPD Land chairman was a considerable dereliction of duty and his fealty to the FDGO mere lip service. As a consequence of the court verdict, the Land Ministry of the Interior suspended him without pay. Once more, Schützinger appealed the government decision. In 1980 the Land Administrative Court, expressing serious misgivings about the reasoning of the local court's decision, ruled that for the time being Schützinger would remain in the service.[11]

The police officer's case also had become a political football. FDP leaders, in opposition to the CDU government of Baden-Württemberg, declared that the government was seeking his dismissal in order to remove leftists more easily from the public service. Stating that no one should be removed for political views, they noted the irony that in theory a successful candidate for public office of a constitutionally legitimate party (read NPD or DKP) would participate in lawmaking but, if ousted from his job, would be shut out from the implementation of laws. CDU leaders denied making any discrimination between left- and right-wing radicals. In the meantime, the SPD, less supportive of the NPD members than was the FDP, issued a release containing the names of twenty-seven NPD members, of whom ten were civil servants in CSU-controlled Bavaria and the rest in CDU-governed Länder, against whom no dismissal proceedings were pending.[12]

The cases just reviewed, as well as many others, point to the sharply differing court verdicts rendered when individuals appealed a negative administrative decision. As noted earlier, while some courts, especially labor courts, viewed mere membership in a radical party as permissible, others viewed it as ground for nonhiring or dismissal. Such differing verdicts increased the plaintiffs' uncertainty and anxiety as to what was and was not constitutional. They lived in an unenviable Kafkaesque world.

Psychological Effects

Even defenders of the decree acknowledged that administrators, in their penchant for perfectionism, had committed excesses in enforcing it. But the defenders also assailed critics who, they claimed, exaggerated the decree's negative effects, thereby in a self-fulfilling prophecy creating political withdrawal among some youth and lessening their interest in the public service. If an applicant had a "clean" political record, there was no reason for worry.[13]

To obtain more scientific data on the decree's effects on applicants as well as on those not directly affected, several organizations conducted studies. In 1976, the German Society for Behavior Therapy, with six thousand members, of whom 80 percent worked for the state, formed a commission to prepare a report on the social, economic, and psychological effects of the decree. In response to a questionnaire, members stated that the decree had created a climate of intimidation and mistrust, even affecting the relationship between psychologists and their clients. For many victims of the decree, the social and economic consequences were insecurity concerning jobs; unemployment or lack of unemployment insurance, leading to financial difficulties; stigmatization as a radical, with a poorer chance for future employment; or lack of contact with colleagues. The psychological consequences were often severe, ranging from anger, resignation, disappointment, powerlessness, or depression to "stepping out" of the system and into a private world. A number of victims, however, were aroused enough by the perceived unfairness of proceedings to fight back.

The report reprinted the text of a letter that Heinrich Häberlein, whose case was discussed above, wrote to a friend about the emotional turmoil he had suffered. He recounted the effects of the stack of radical leaflets the examiner had brought to his exhausting five-hour hearing. Häberlein, as an editor from 1970 to 1976, had signed the leaflets, never realizing that they would be used in evidence against him. He presumed that either there had been an informer in the DFG group or he had been under surveillance for many years. Ever since the hearing, not knowing whether or not there had been an informer, he began to distrust everyone in the group. In such an Orwellian "Big Brother 1984" atmosphere, he was less frank, even though he had nothing to conceal, and more suspicious of others. He had also become more nervous and started smoking heavily again. He wrote: "Outwardly, I try to remain the same fellow, to keep my personality. But inwardly, there is something nicked, something broken, something worn. I begin doubting myself, my self-confidence has somewhat gone . . . I have had discussions with my parents for months. Every time I come home for a visit, I ask myself, what do they think of me now? Do they consider me an enemy of the constitution?" But his father, a minister in a small conservative community where the residents believe that all the decree's victims were halfway terrorists, supported him.[14]

The report also emphasized the negative consequences of the decree on individuals not directly affected by it. In an atmosphere more characteristic of authoritarianism than of democracy, many feared that if they were typed as radicals, their chance of entering the public service or remaining in it would be endangered. Hence they were prudent in conversations and behavior; as one respondent put it, "The pair of scissors in my head already works." Some did not dare participate in demonstrations any longer, enter left-wing bookstores, throw leftist printed materials into wastepaper baskets, put stickers against *Berufsverbote* or nuclear plants on their cars, sign Amnesty International and other petitions, or associate with communists. In one instance, a church employee was threatened with the loss of his job because he had supported a victim of the decree. A number of university students purged their research papers of quotations from books printed in the GDR or from the works of Marx and Engels. Still others switched their major from a social science to a "safer," less political subject.[15] According to another survey, many students, aged eighteen to twenty-two, saw what normally would be considered legitimate activities as too risky. Thus 84 percent would not dare regularly borrow leftist literature from the city library; 57 percent would not wear a "Stop Strauss" (CSU chief) button; and 44 percent would not join a citizens initiative group against the construction of a superhighway through a settled area.[16] This fear at times became neurotic; students avoided topics in conversations, thereby producing a "coalition of silence." A minority became angry and escalated the political vocabulary—for instance, calling opponents "foes." Such an atmosphere created a feeling that whoever was "not for me was against me."[17]

Typical of the fear generated by the decree was one instance in which Bonn students milled around a table discussing whether or not they should sign petitions protesting it. When a Swedish photographer in all innocence started taking photographs of the students, a fight nearly ensued because they did not want their pictures taken.[18]

In the late 1970s, many students throughout the Federal Republic became less engaged politically or, among law students especially, more conservative. A number of them, disillusioned, viewed the earlier struggles as having failed to produce significant changes in the universities and in society at large. They blamed the decree and the antiterrorism measures for contributing to the resignation and conformity then prevalent among the 1968 generation. Peter Glotz, SPD official, estimates that at least half of the 900,000 university students were affected by the climate of fear.[19]

On the other hand, a nucleus of thirty to one hundred students at many universities remained in the vanguard of the movement calling for an end to the decree. After graduation, some sought civil service posts. Among them were women who, according to one, "fought against their *Berufsverbot* more intensely than many men who were frozen in their anxiety. . . . And that probably comes from the fact that women generally have to fight more than men in order to realize their plans. You have to be a bit better than the men."[20]

The self-assertiveness of these women, however, sometimes led to conflicts with their male partners. One author notes that "*Berufsverbot* inhibits effective social participation of women who have developed radical democratic and leftist political perspectives. It encourages others to think in terms of the status quo and to accept prescribed government alternatives with regard to women's politics as well."[21]

In high schools, numbers of pupils joined the struggle against the decree. For instance, in 1980, at a meeting in a Bonn school auditorium called in support of a teacher affected by the decree, a pupil said: "No teacher will be able to tell me what I should think. I cannot be manipulated." He had no fears of signing a petition in support of the teacher.[22]

Yet among the university teaching and nonteaching staffs, the decree had an intimidating effect, because from 1972 to 1980 at least 178 of them were involved in nationwide loyalty investigations and hearings. In replies to a questionnaire sent out by the teachers' union (GEW) to its members in North Rhine-Westphalian universities, 54 percent of 417 respondents wrote that the decree made them more fearful; 16 percent, that they had evidence, presumably made known to them at hearings, that informants were taking notes of their political statements in seminars and lectures; and 13 percent, that they had given up taking political positions.[23] Respondents who no longer were active politically justified their new position by contending that they have "less hope to change anything," that "their own existence was endangered," and "what was the use of it all?"[24]

Commenting on college lecturers' being more cautious and exercising self-censorship in their political comments in class, Professor Narr wrote: "One holds judgements back, is silent, does not participate, drifts out of society and conforms, often without even recognizing it; self-censorship, no longer operating consciously, invades the very concepts we use. Should one use the concept 'capitalist society' in one's work? Isn't it better to speak of 'modern industrial society'? Under no circumstances should one write the words 'class struggle.'"[25]

As a consequence, dialogue was stymied, differences of opinion were squelched, and learning and research were confined to a narrow spectrum. By producing a climate of fear, some of the decree's supporters may have achieved one of their objectives: to cut back political radicalism and enhance conformism. Potential applicants to the civil service think twice before engaging in radical activities, knowing that their chances of then gaining positions are small.

Media

Whether the climate of fear had an effect on the nation's television and radio programs as well as on the press is difficult to determine. Although the director of the West German radio network prohibited his staff from using the term "Berufsverbot" because of its tendentious connotation, the networks carried many symposia on the decree. In 1978, one Baden-Baden commentator, Franz Alt, told his viewers that he had written his party chief, Helmut Kohl, about a letter sent in 1975 by Czech Communist party authorities to a young Catholic in Prague barring his entry into the teaching profession because of his church activities. On the same day Alt had received a copy of a letter sent by the Ministry of Education in Baden-Württemberg to a teacher, which informed him that he would not receive tenure because of his DKP affiliation. Alt concluded that intolerance in both systems was lamentable.[26]

Newspapers opposed to the decree printed a host of critical articles, photos, and cartoons. In one photo of a demonstration, a man carried a placard inscribed with the message "Jesus today would have also received *Berufsverbot*—Christians demand an end to *Berufsverbote*."[27] One cartoon showed parents ready to go out for the evening telling their two children that if they do not behave, the radicals will come and get them. In another cartoon, a male school official told a female teacher, on probationary status, "Your ancestor fought in the peasants' war against the princes, in 1848 your great-granduncle stood on the barricades, and you want to enter the civil service as a teacher? You have absolutely no chance, girl!"[28]

The graphic designer Staeck drew a satiric public poster that became a big hit. It read, "Public Notice, re Radical Decree. The population is once again notified that former membership in the NSDAP, SA, SD [security service], SS . . . does not bar employment in the public service. Signed: Land Commissioner for Loyalty." Staeck became irritated when asked repeatedly whether this notice really existed.[29]

Theater and Novels

Several theater companies produced plays touching on the decree that were shown in a number of cities and towns to audiences totaling in the thousands. One play, put on by the Hesse State Theater in Wiesbaden, entitled *Freedom Dies by the Centimeter,* dealt with case E., in which the speaker declaims, "Ladies and gentlemen, the most important question for us as well as for the authorities is, How do you recognize an enemy of the constitution? The difficulty is that so far one has not even given any thought as to what a friend of the constitution really looks like."[30]

In another satirical play, *Many Thanks, We Will Let You Know,* a senior civil servant says, "One must be much more efficient. One must throw out all the leftist professors, then there will be no more leftist teachers who could produce leftist students."[31] Another play, put on in Frankfurt, which dealt with two teachers who were DKP members, caused a major political controversy in the city council. CDU councillors questioned whether tax monies should be used to subsidize a play that "represented DKP interests," and they demanded its ban. They argued that it gave the DKP a platform to inveigh against the Hesse minister of education, who wanted to keep radicals out of the public service. The council did not support the CDU request.[32]

Novelists, poets, and artists contributed their talent to the campaign against the decree. Peter Schneider's novel *Already You Are a Constitutional Enemy: The Unexpected Expansion of the Personnel File of the Teacher Kleff* became especially well known in radical circles. In Kafkaesque fashion, Schneider tells of the ordeal facing Kleff, who after seven years of probation as a teacher receives an official letter informing him that doubts have arisen as to his loyalty to the FDGO. As a consequence, he becomes oversensitive, paranoid, and uncertain about himself. He partly accepts the accusation, saying, "I asked myself occasionally whether I really was, without in fact knowing it, an enemy of the Basic Law."[33]

His friend tells him that one stops thinking at a point where one's fear begins, and in the end one no longer knows what one thinks, because of either cowardice or conviction. Kleff starts to keep a file on himself that parallels the file kept on him by the bureaucrats. He does this for therapeutic motives but also to counter their strategy and to use as a weapon in his defense at the hearings.

After one month of uncertainty, Kleff is informed that the charge against him rests on one memorandum he wrote to colleagues, opposing the suspension of three pupils for having distributed radical leaflets in front of the school. Kleff, having advocated the right of resistance against unjust laws, refuses to change his position and fails to receive the tenured job. Readers of Schneider's novel could empathize with its documentary reality, epitomized in Kleff's assertion at the end that he remained dismissed because he offered resistance against his illegitimate dismissal.[34]

Organizations

From 1976 to 1980, critics of the decree maintained a steady pressure on government policymakers either to change or to rescind it; defenders, to keep it unchanged. The Initiative against *Berufsverbote* scheduled a series of protest actions for one week in November 1976 and over seventy demonstrations from then until January 28, 1977, the fifth anniversary of the decree. In February alone, nearly two hundred protest actions, rallies, demonstrations, and film showings were held. In addition, there were theater performances and an outpouring of songs, essays, and placards. In November 1977, the initiative organized a two-day international protest rally in Oldenburg, attended by hundreds of delegates from local initiatives and many representatives from other countries. In June 1980, another international conference was held in Hamburg to call for an end to the hearings and the snooping and for the annulment of the decree.[35]

In the meantime, in February 1979, the Jusos, less eager to associate themselves with the initiatives, formed an "Initiative for Democratic and Social Rights" with other noncommunist youth organizations. In the same year, a number of well-known professors founded a nationwide organization, known as the Committee for Basic Rights and Democracy. The new organization, which may be compared to the American Civil Liberties Union, had the support of about sixty academics, journalists, and union cadre members, many in the left wing of the SPD. One of its working groups was to study the effects of the decree on individuals and the degree of liberalization in its implementation. In May 1980, it issued a report contending that no significant liberalization had taken place.[36]

DGB unions supported a change in the decree. In May 1978, the DGB federal board urged the government to restrict the dismissal of public servants to those who had actively attempted to overthrow the FDGO. The GEW leadership called for an end to the screenings, which produce fear and conformity—dangerous consequences for democracy.[37]

The conservative German Teachers Association, on the other hand, maintained its steadfast support of the decree, although admitting that some excesses had been committed and recommending minor procedural changes in its administration. It denounced the radicals' hysterical statements concerning the necessary surveillance.[38]

The churches were split on their positions toward the decree. The Central Committee of German Catholics, in support, rejected the proposal that certain civil service groups, especially teachers, be exempt from pledging loyalty to the FDGO and supported instead the CDU/CSU strict interpretation of the decree. The League of German Catholic Youth in Bavaria took the same position.[39]

Protestant churches were less supportive of the decree. In 1976, a council of the Fifth Synod of the Protestant Church of Germany issued a report that criticized the "excessive security measures suffocating freedom." It called on administrators to distinguish carefully between persons holding radical views concerning injustice and those pursuing unconstitutional goals. Screenings should be restricted to applicants for security posts or to individuals about whom there is serious doubt of loyalty. The *Verfassungsschutz* should not collect materials just to keep radicals out of public service. In short, government officials should be more tolerant of dissidents.[40]

The Klose Plan

The continuing discussion about the decree among organizations was reflected within the SPD. The Jusos and the Association of Social Democratic Jurists continued to insist that the decree violated constitutional provisions and should be annulled. The Jusos proposed that the three categories of civil servants, salaried employees, and workers in the public service be eliminated, to be replaced by one service to which entry would not be barred to members of any legitimate party. They requested the SPD organs to discuss their proposals and recommended that potential SPD candidates for public office be queried on their attitude toward the decree.

Although the Jusos' proposals were not accepted by the party, the SPD mayor of Hamburg, Hans-Ulrich Klose, initiated changes in the decree's implementation in his city. Ironically, Hamburg had unilaterally introduced the decree in 1971 prior to national action in 1972, but by 1975, Klose, who once had been a hard-liner on this question, called for a review. According to some reports, his "liberated" daughter and the arrival of a new journalist on his staff convinced him to change his mind.[41] In addition, the FDP, in a governing coalition with the SPD from 1974 to 1978, put pressure on him to make changes. In response, the mayor, concerned about the decree's excesses, declared in September 1978 that he would rather hire 20 DKP teachers than make 200,000 young people insecure through state surveillance.[42]

But before 1978, Klose's proposal for changes had been blocked by conservative SPD city officials heading the administrative and civil service offices, who maintained their strict screening practices. In October 1978, Klose, however, had enough support in his party (the left wing had made gains in a local election) and support in the FDP to receive backing in the Hamburg Senate for his latest proposal. The Klose plan, enacted into law, assumed that all applicants and civil servants would uphold the FDGO unless they actively sought its destruction. Hiring agencies would no longer make inquiries of the *Verfassungsschutz* of all persons seeking entry into the public service, except for applicants for judge, prosecuting attorney, the police, the professional army, and other sensitive and responsible posts. Implicitly, membership or function in a legal party would not be sufficient reason for rejection of applicants for nonsensitive posts. If public servants during their probationary period and while on duty engaged in anticonstitutional propaganda or one-sided ideological influence or approved the use of force to achieve political goals, hearings would be held to determine whether their employment should be terminated. Such negative information about them, however, would have to have come to the attention of the hiring agency without asking the *Verfassungsschutz* for information.[43]

A few national SPD officers were critical of the plan's substance or its timing. Chancellor Schmidt publicly expressed concern that some of the changes might not be constitutional, while others criticized its being published one week before a crucial Hesse Landtag election, in which the SPD feared it might lose votes as a result of the controversial Klose plan. Indeed, the CDU in Hesse made the plan a last-minute campaign issue. CDU chief Alfred Dregger said that the SPD sought a free route for communist teachers into the classrooms. He asked Minister-President Holger Börner (SPD), in vain, for a pledge to bar such teachers in all Hesse schools. Despite the CDU's offensive, the SPD won the Hesse election.[44]

In Hamburg, the CDU also used the plan in its campaign against the SPD. It organized a citizens action committee of concerned parents to protest the hiring of "red" schoolteachers as part of the "Communist Plan." The committee began a six-week signature campaign and asked respondents to check off on a mock ballot support for the statement "I am opposed to the Klose plan. Communists and neofascists must not become civil servants in our state and teachers of our children," or support for the converse statement "Communists and neofascists should become civil servants of our state and should become teachers of our children."[45]

The CDU action did have the effect of generating a debate among the public and in the media on the alleged politicization of the schools. Most communist teachers refrained from injecting propaganda into their teaching because they knew that the pupils would tell their parents, who in turn would protest to school authorities. The teachers would not risk being fired when their job was at stake. Thus it was not surprising that, when up for tenure, they received high praise from parents and parents' councils for their excellent teaching. There were, of course, exceptions in which some teachers introduced communist propaganda into their classes and were fired; their cases were used by the Christian Democrats to make sweeping accusations against all communist teachers.

The Koschnick Plan

The debate in the SPD over Klose's Hamburg plan was paralleled by a discussion as to whether the party should revise its position and propose a just and fair nationwide plan applicable to the Bonn government and the Länder it controlled. In February 1978, Brandt and the executive committee requested Hans Koschnick, deputy party chairman and mayor of Bremen, to analyze the existing practices and to draft revised guidelines for the government's consideration.

Koschnick held talks with the legal experts of the Bundestag Fraktion of the SPD, members of the government, representatives of the Länder ministries of the interior and education, and specialists in the public service unions. He then drafted a report, which he cleared with FDP officials in Bonn and the Länder. In summer 1978, it was circulated for comment in the SPD, and in December, accepted unanimously by a special party convention at Cologne.

Koschnick's plan resembled the Klose plan, except for the tougher provision that the off-duty behavior of a public servant, rather than just the on-duty behavior, would also be a criterion for determining the individual's loyalty to the FDGO. As in the Klose plan, screenings were to be restricted to individuals seeking responsible and sensitive posts.[46]

Although the Jusos reluctantly supported the Koschnick plan because it at least liberalized the screening procedures, they reiterated their demand for the annulling of the decree and for an overhaul of civil service laws.[47] SPD leaders again rejected their demands as too far-reaching but were eager to make liberal reforms for political reasons. They did not want to be accused by the decree's critics in the Federal Republic and other countries of favoring continued restrictions on civil liberties in 1979, when elections to the European Parliament were scheduled. Brandt reportedly wanted to become its first president and head of its socialist bloc, but such ambitions could not be realized if the other socialist parties maintained their opposition to the decree. In addition, the SPD was eager to court leftist voters in pending Landtag elections. Conservative SPD politicians, however, feared that the CDU/CSU's strong criticism of the Koschnick plan as being the prelude to further infiltration of communists into the public service might convince moderate voters to turn away from the SPD and vote CDU/CSU.[48]

The FDP Position

The internal schism in the SPD over the decree was mirrored in the FDP. The Young Democrats maintained their principled opposition, contending in 1978 that a "creeping McCarthyism" was taking place in the Federal Republic and that the parties should not be surprised if the democratic engagement of youth disappears in the face of the authorities' disregard for the constitutional right to freedom of opinion. They charged that the judicial system was still filled with old Nazis who were "blind in the right eye" and therefore battling the Left almost exclusively.[49]

Senior FDP leaders were less hostile to the decree but demanded changes in its administration. Fraktion chief Wolfgang Mischnick called for liberalized screenings that would not endanger domestic security. Inquiries should be restricted to those on a short list of applicants who were the top contenders for a position. Incriminating evidence in the *Verfassungsschutz* files should be reviewed periodically and destroyed if outdated.[50]

At its Mainz convention in November 1978, the FDP passed a resolution, after some debate, demanding that automatic screenings be stopped and that inquiries to the *Verfassungsschutz* be limited to applicants about whom negative facts were known to the hiring authority just prior to their being accepted into the public service. Once such persons are hired, any damaging facts that had been submitted by the *Verfassungsschutz* must be removed from their personnel file. Radical behavior up to their eighteenth birthday should not be considered during the screening.[51]

The CDU/CSU Position

Not unexpectedly, in 1978 the CDU/CSU denounced the SPD and FDP proposals for changes. In a Bundestag budget debate in January, CDU leader Dregger insisted that a routine request for information from the *Verfassungsschutz* best protected the state; security agents could not take their jobs seriously if the government requested their help only in exceptional circumstances. A CSU deputy accused Minister of the Interior Maihofer (FDP) of endangering national security by allowing communists into the state service. Maihofer responded that routine requests were a "bureaucratic hangover" of the decree. By abandoning them, the *Verfassungsschutz* would stop being the target of unjustified mistrust.[52]

In an attempt to win over public opinion, CDU and CSU leaders accused the SPD and FDP of supporting—partly opportunistically, to attract young voters—a national and international campaign waged by left-wing socialists and communists. The SPD's emphasis on solidarity with Marxists rather than with democrats was also proof that the new Marxist-oriented youth, which does not see communists as foes of a democratic order, was playing an increasingly active role in the party's cadres.[53]

In October 1978, CDU delegates at their national convention rejected government plans to change the decree's administration and insisted on maintenance of the status quo. Party officials also hinted that they might request the Constitutional Court to rule on a new government plan, then being drafted, that would facilitate the entry of communists into the public service.[54]

On November 17, the CDU/CSU Fraktion, in an official question to the government, asked whether it was aware of the need for civil servants to distance themselves from extremist parties and whether it was true that the so-called *Berufsverbote* campaign was initiated, and continued to be steered, by the DKP.[55] Needless to say, such a question, following the practice of opposition parties in all parliamentary systems, was put to embarrass the government, which in turn gave an answer supporting its case.

Bonn Guidelines, 1979

The sparring of the political parties was the opening round for the government's promulgation of new guidelines in early 1979. Earlier, SPD and FDP cabinet members, at a meeting on October 25, 1978, requested the new minister of the interior, Gerhart Baum (FDP), to prepare a report based on the Koschnick plan. He formed a committee of experts in his ministry, which, with the support of the Ministry of Justice, checked on the constitutional aspects of proposed changes. Baum wanted to make sure that if the CDU/CSU challenged the guidelines' constitutionality in court, the government would win the case. The committee of experts took cognizance of the Chancellery's internal study, which showed federal ministries using different screening procedures. For instance, the Ministry of the Interior requested information about all applicants from the *Verfassungsschutz,* while other ministries restricted inquiries to only those applicants with doubtful loyalty or who had applied for sensitive posts.

On November 1, the cabinet discussed a draft of the new guidelines submitted by Baum and accepted the draft provisionally one week later. But it postponed final approval until the FDP arrived at a position at its November convention. Schmidt, eager to dampen the emotional discussion within the SPD and FDP about the decree in order to secure swift cabinet approval, forbade cabinet members to express themselves publicly as long as the cabinet had not yet taken a final position on the then most controversial domestic problem.

The chancellor was worried about pending Länder elections in Schleswig-Holstein and West Berlin, in which the Christian Democrats might convince voters that the Bonn government could not reach an accord on the decree and could not depend on the SPD and FDP, which were internally split on the issue. Therefore, Schmidt told his cabinet colleagues that the government must act independently of any decisions reached at party conventions. But they insisted that the guidelines reflect convention resolutions.[56]

Foreign policy considerations also may have played a role in the chancellor's decision to get speedy cabinet approval for the guidelines. According to one press report, USSR general-secretary Leonid Brezhnev, while on a visit to Bonn, put pressure on Brandt and SPD foreign policy specialist Egon Bahr to end the defamation of communists in public employment in the Federal Republic if Soviet-German ties were to be maintained.[57]

Finally, on January 17, 1979, the cabinet, after a nine-hour discussion, approved the new guidelines, effective April 1. The guidelines, which revised the 1976 ones, applied only to applicants to the federal service. They stipulated that hiring would proceed on the presumption of the loyalty of an applicant, who would no longer need to prove it. The hiring authorities would stop checking routinely with the *Verfassungsschutz* and would make inquiry only when there is concrete evidence about an applicant's lack of loyalty during the preparatory and provisional status periods, or when the agency definitely intends to hire a person and there are new questions about his or her loyalty. If an applicant is appointed in spite of incriminating information from the *Verfassungsschutz*, the agency must remove such information from the applicant's file.[58]

In justification of the new guidelines, the government referred to its 1976 policy declaration for the four-year legislative session. In the declaration, Chancellor Schmidt had stated that the decree's procedures had given rise to doubts about the liberality of the Federal Republic concerning the exercise of people's basic rights. In keeping with Constitutional Court rulings and the principle of fairness, all must be done to prevent the emergence of general distrust. In further justification, the government also admitted that the practice of routine inquiries had been the wrong reaction to the threat of extremism and had sparked misgiving in the younger generation. The government did not intend to bar applicants on general criteria such as party membership.

This liberalization was intended to make a sharper distinction between unconstitutional parties or groups, engaged in "active, warlike, aggressive conduct" against the FDGO, whose members would not be admitted into the public service, and parties deemed by administrative decisions to be "hostile to the constitution," such as the DKP, whose members had a chance to be admitted if they were not actively fighting the FDGO.[59] Yet, the cabinet did not accept the recommendations made at SPD and FDP conventions to include the provision that the only ground for rejection of an applicant be demonstrated activity against the FDGO. Worried about the CDU/CSU, it contended that such a provision would run counter to the 1975 decision of the Constitutional Court, which had reaffirmed the need for civil servants to support actively the FDGO.[60] The cabinet also did not accept the provision in the Koschnick plan restricting screenings to responsible and sensitive posts.

The Aftermath

The reactions to the new guidelines among interested parties and organizations and in the media ranged from qualified approval to rejection. The Jusos and moderate newspapers, which supported the liberalization, complained, however, that the government had not spelled out clearly the new criteria, such as "actual evidence" of disloyalty, for denying jobs to applicants, but they welcomed the end of mass screenings.[61]

Conservative organizations, such as the CDU/CSU, the Central Committee of German Catholics, the DBB, the German Teachers Association, the League for the Freedom of Science and Research, and the German Judges League, rejected the guidelines and argued in most instances for retention of routine inquiries. Some conceded that mistakes had occurred but insisted that this was no reason for dropping the inquiries. Several stated that the hiring agencies normally do not have information on applicants' unconstitutional activities. If, under the new guidelines, they cannot make inquiries with the *Verfassungsschutz*, they will begin their own snooping on a haphazard basis. As a consequence, hiring practices will reflect a hit-and-miss approach, which is discriminatory.[62]

On January 25, 1979, Christian Democratic deputies, led by CDU Fraktion chairman Kohl, engaged in a marathon debate with government deputies in the Bundestag. They accused the cabinet of failing to defend the nation's freedom against its enemies. By abandoning routine inquiries, the cabinet had given the green light to radicals to enter the public service freely. Its guidelines were unconstitutional, because hiring authorities would be forced to violate their official duty to keep out the state's enemies. The deputies, hinting at a constitutional challenge, contended that the new screening procedures, shutting out the *Verfassungsschutz* in most instances, raise questions about the agencies' ability to spot extremists during the preparatory service, especially if they "lie low." Only by chance would an administrator, say, by picking up an extremist flyer signed by an applicant, gain information about an applicant's doubtful loyalty. The deputies accused the SPD and FDP of having given up on the constitutional principle of militant democracy and on the need for a consensus of democratic political forces.

In response, Minister Baum argued that not even the CDU/CSU Länder had developed a consensus on the decree's implementation. The routine inquiries had become unnecessary and had weakened rather than strengthened democracy. Because young people were afraid to become politically active, the guidelines would be a step forward in raising their hopes for a more liberal state. Baum emphasized the guidelines' heavy reliance on the Constitutional Court's decision of 1975.[63]

On February 2, Baum met with the Länder ministers of the interior, and two weeks later Schmidt met with the Länder minister-presidents to explain to them the federal guidelines and gain their support. As expected, the SPD-FDP-governed Länder promised to follow suit (some already had adopted the guidelines), while the CDU/CSU-governed Länder intended to continue making routine inquiries. Thus, the intent of the 1972 decree to provide for uniformity among the federation and Länder was aborted once again.

Despite the official unchanged CDU/CSU position, in practice the decree was not administered uniformly in the Länder it governed. In some, only applicants who were on a short list and had a chance to be hired were screened. In Rhineland-Palatinate, Baden-Württemberg, and Bavaria, youthful activities were normally disregarded if the applicants distanced themselves from earlier political views.[64] Lower Saxony did not screen teaching and judicial apprentices or applicants for the lower-level civil service. Schleswig-Holstein retained its extensive screening, but the Saar dropped its automatic security checks.

Although all SPD-governed Länder adopted the guidelines, they too administered them differently. In some Länder, such as Berlin and North Rhine-Westphalia, the authorities continued to keep out or to oust radicals. Thus, in 1980, North Rhine-Westphalia scheduled numerous hearings, many for civil servants being considered for permanent status.[65] In addition, critics charged that some administrators were circumventing the ban on automatic screenings by their informal and long-standing links with colleagues in the *Verfassungsschutz,* who supplied them surreptitiously and at times without being asked with derogatory information, such as lists of radicals who were candidates for public office or secret versions of the agency's yearly reports describing the activities of radical groups. Sometimes an administrator asked a colleague in another agency for information about an applicant, acted on the basis of a denunciation, or, as happened in Berlin, cancelled a position rather than hire a radical.[66]

In some SPD-ruled Länder, such as Hesse, the authorities were more liberal in administering the decree. They did not attempt to discharge radicals as long as they refrained from political activities on the job. For example, in 1980 in Hesse, 248 public servants were members of left-radical organizations (of whom nearly 70 percent were in the DKP), and 23 were members of right-radical organizations. The preponderance of leftists was even higher among teachers—161 to 2 rightists. Among radicals in the Hesse public service, about half were civil servants, nearly half were salaried employees, and only a few were workers. A third of the civil servants held offices within their parties, and several were candidates for public office. While the number of radicals in the Hesse service seems high, the federal government and the other Länder, including those governed by the CDU/CSU, also had numerous radicals on their payrolls.[67] In many instances, the Länder tried to keep them out, but they won their cases in court, or information about their membership surfaced long after they had received appointments.

Controversy in Bonn

Although the 1979 guidelines seemed to presage liberalization in the offing for applicants to the federal civil service, a tougher policy emerged for radical civil servants with permanent status. Hans Rudolf Claussen, the federal disciplinary prosecutor (*Bundesdisziplinaranwalt*), was partly responsible for this policy. In office since 1954, he was charged by the minister of the interior to bring indictments in the Federal Disciplinary Court (first instance) and Federal Administrative Court (second instance) against career servants accused by any federal ministry of having violated the civil service laws, including the 1972 decree.

Claussen, a political conservative but not a member of any party, had been critical of government policy since 1972 because permanent public servants were not fired when shown to be extremists. Until the late 1970s the federal ministries had been reluctant to take action, given the long and complex formal discharge proceedings and given that the threshold of what constitutes grounds for discharge had never been clear. Remaining unresolved was whether or not membership in a legal but extremist party was sufficient cause for dismissal. Claussen's interpretation, not shared by all judges, was that membership in the DKP, for instance, meant support for its goals—hence evidence of an offense and ground for dismissal.

In 1978 and 1979, before the cabinet began discussion of the new guidelines, Minister of Transport, Post, and Telecommunications Kurt Gscheidle (SPD), in office since 1974, had started, in cooperation with Claussen, formal ouster proceedings against nine public servants and had scheduled preliminary hearings against about forty others in the railroad and postal services, where many leftists were concentrated.[68] The minister stated that in the nine cases, the individuals had been active in the DKP and became candidates for public office. As civil servants, they lacked political loyalty and therefore had committed an offense. Gscheidle also warned the probationary civil servants in his ministry that they would have to refrain from active engagement in extremist parties and organizations if they expected to get permanent status.[69]

The CDU/CSU criticized Gscheidle's failure to proceed against all extremists but supported his and Claussen's get-tough policy against some of them.[70] The SPD and FDP also criticized Gscheidle, but for the opposite reason—he and Claussen should not have taken action to discharge civil servants at a time when a new liberalization policy for applicants was being planned. Twenty-three left-wing SPD members of the European Parliament castigated Gscheidle for his policies and said they would raise the issue at the 1979 SPD convention.[71] The Jusos requested Schmidt to dismiss him as minister for failing to follow SPD directives or to stand up against Claussen. Schmidt, in a show of solidarity with Gscheidle, took no action.[72]

While the SPD and FDP held their conventions in late 1979, Gscheidle retreated from his tough position, which in turn led to increased tension between him and Claussen. As a result, SPD convention delegates called, in vain, on Minister Baum to fire Claussen, whom one SPD deputy characterized (two years later) as "a relic from feudal times rather than an institution of democracy."[73] The deputy objected strongly to Claussen's failure to consider individual cases on their merits and to ask whether the accused had actively fought against the FDGO. Claussen retorted that it was his job to assemble all facts in the dossiers of the accused and let the disciplinary courts decide the cases.

Claussen's firm policy was reinforced by a 1980 decision of the Federal Disciplinary Court in the case of Hans Jürgen Langmann, a railroad conductor. The court ordered the dismissal of Langmann as a public servant with permanent status for his membership in the DKP. The critics charged that the decision was a new escalation in the strategy of intimidation against radical political activities.[74]

Public Opinion

From 1976 to 1980, the public remained aware of the national and international discussions centering on the decree. Seventy-three percent of respondents in an Infratest poll of June–July 1978 had heard of the discussions, a large majority for a political theme. The degree of support for the decree varied from year to year and according to the phrasing of the questions by different polling institutes. In the Infratest poll, 33 percent of respondents favored keeping extremists out of the public service, while 41 percent favored screening applicants only for sensitive posts, and 22 percent opposed any restrictions on entry into the service on political grounds (4 percent had no opinion or did not respond).[75]

In answer to a question about restricting screenings to sensitive posts as called for in the Koschnick plan, 48 percent were in favor, 22 percent opposed, and 28 percent had no opinion (2 percent did not respond). Among those in support were 37 percent of CDU/CSU, 60 percent of SPD, and 61 percent of FDP respondents. Thus not all CDU/CSU adherents backed their party's position, as was commonly assumed; even the SPD and FDP could not count on full support among their adherents.[76]

The Infratest results indicated strong support for a change in the decree toward greater liberalization; however, a Bielefeld Emnid-Institute survey taken three months later indicated much greater opposition to any change. The chief reason for the discrepancy may lie in the nature of the Bielefeld question, which, in the spirit of the CDU/CSU argument that the Klose plan in Hamburg was an invitation for communists to stream into the civil service, asked respondents whether the civil service should hire communists. In reply, 75 percent said no, 20 percent said yes, and 5 percent gave no answer. The greatest opposition (86 percent) to the entry of communists centered in Bavaria and Baden-Württemberg, and the least (60 percent) in Berlin, Bremen, and Hamburg. As in the Infratest, attitudinal differences between generations were visible; 86 percent of the respondents between fifty and sixty-four years old opposed the entry of communists, compared with only 48 percent of those between fourteen and nineteen years of age (40 percent of the latter approved their entry and 12 percent were undecided).[77]

The Allensbach Institute polled a sample of the population over the years on a number of questions related to the decree. In March 1979, when asked which administrative issues were most salient, 41 percent listed keeping radicals out of the public service, while even more respondents listed the fight against terrorism and crime, keeping a lid on taxes, and data protection. When asked which party does the best job in keeping radicals out of the public service, 30 percent said the CDU/CSU, 8 percent the SPD, and 8 percent the FDP.[78]

In a November 1978 poll, 70 percent favored screening communists and NPD members and, if loyal, admitting them into the civil service; 21 percent were opposed to any screenings and *Berufsverbote*; and 9 percent were undecided.[79]

In December 1978, the Allensbach Institute sought to find out the amount of support for the proposed government guidelines to eliminate most screenings. The institute found that 45 percent were in favor, 37 percent opted for retaining automatic screenings, 10 percent opposed any screenings, and 8 percent were undecided. However, when asked in 1982 if a DKP member should be appointed as a judge, 64 percent said no, and 13 percent yes.[80]

Despite variations in the results of the three polling organizations, attitudinal patterns emerged during the 1976–80 period. Most respondents favored either automatic screenings of all applicants or only of those who applied for responsible or sensitive posts, such as police officers. A shift to greater support for restricted screenings shows that the critics' arguments of excesses in the decree's administration had been effective. Yet, the demand of radical critics for a complete elimination of the decree was acceptable to only one in five respondents. The polls do not indicate why the percentage was so low, but it may be surmised that the political culture of anticommunism and the fear of an overthrow of the democratic system played a significant part. The popular conception that the CDU/CSU did the best job in keeping communists out of the public service did not fully correspond to the facts; as noted earlier, many SPD and FDP administrators were as vigilant as the toughest CDU/CSU administrators in this task.

Conclusion

The high visibility of the issue was a reflection of the large number of loyalty screenings, the controversy surrounding the cases of career servants' being dismissed from their posts, the adverse psychological effects on individuals, the role of the media and the arts, and SPD and FDP efforts to shape new federal government guidelines. It was also a reflection of the deep schism in the body politic between three groups: (1) the conservative bloc, defending the decree at all costs; (2) the social-liberal bloc, retreating from its earlier unconditional support of the decree, as a result of the growing fear and conformity among youth, administrative excesses, and foreign pressures; and (3) the left-radical bloc, unsuccessfully demanding an elimination of the decree. Given the fundamental ideological differences between the three blocs, no resolution to the conflict was in sight, although the governing parties continued their schizoid policies producing both some liberalization and continued repression at the same time.

6

The Aftermath, the 1980s

In the 1980s, interparty and intraparty schisms over the 1972 decree did not abate, public opinion still regarded it as salient, and critics concerned about the state of liberties in the Federal Republic were indignant about dismissals of career servants. Yet, the high-pitched and emotion-laden debates of the 1970s had tapered off, and the number of screened individuals declined. In the national election campaigns of the 1980s, the issue did not play a major role. (Even in 1976 it had only been of minor importance as a campaign issue.)

What were the causes for this decline? Had liberalization occurred in the Länder and in Bonn? Did the downfall of the SPD-FDP federal government and its replacement by a conservative CDU/CSU-FDP government in 1982 signify a change in policy? For some answers, let us look first at the political, economic, and social climate of the 1980s and then at developments in the Länder and in Bonn.

The New Climate

In the late 1970s, a number of Initiatives against *Berufsverbote* committees became inactive or were dissolved. As a consequence, the mass rallies, demonstrations, petitions, and other forms of protest against the decree almost became relics of the past. In addition, some young people who would ordinarily have entered the university and then sought entry into the public service opted instead for an alternative life-style. They renounced traditional politics, work, and social patterns and emphasized instead the need for greater democratization in all spheres. Many of them joined the Greens and citizens initiatives and took part in the massive protests against nuclear power and armament and environmental pollution. These demonstrations, organized by the new social movements, drew greater numbers of participants than those against the decree because the problems were seen as more threatening to the average citizen.

At the universities, a new generation of leftist students, who in earlier years would have formed the core of protesters against the decree, organized or joined the new protest movements. They were no longer interested in engaging in sectarian warfare between radical groups on campuses. As a consequence, many groups vanished, and the universities became more quiescent politically (as they did in other countries). The lack of campus political issues was also caused by tougher university restrictions and student fears of not getting jobs upon graduation. Many students became more conformist; some more conservative.

But the chances even of such students getting positions as civil servants were limited, given budgetary restraints, hiring freezes, and cuts through attrition in personnel, especially in rail and postal services and in the schools. Only 10 to 30 percent of students from each graduating class received civil service positions, compared with about 66 percent in the 1970s. For that small number of vacancies, radical students, including those in the peace and ecology movements, had little chance of being hired, and thus many did not even apply.[1] Others, as noted, had lost interest in the civil service as a career. The result was a drop in the number of applicants rejected for political reasons.

In the period 1979–81, however, federal, state, and local administrators still handled about four hundred cases, including those of civil servants subject to dismissal and cases on appeal making their way through the courts. Hence, critics in the early 1980s charged that the government's liberalization policy stemming from its 1979 guidelines was an illusion. Although the Bonn government stopped making automatic inquiries with the *Verfassungsschutz* (from 1979 to 1985, it requested information in relatively few cases), it continued to dismiss permanent civil servants or initiate preliminary disciplinary proceedings.[2]

It claimed not to have rejected a single applicant for lack of political loyalty from 1980 to 1985,[3] omitting the fact that it denied some radicals positions by cloaking the rejection in terms of budgetary cuts. Failure to tell the truth created frustration among applicants, who did not know why they were denied a job. They could guess, however, when at first there was great interest in their application but then rejection, or when another applicant was hired who had applied later for the same position, or when authorities did not notify them of subsequent vacancies.

SPD-governed Länder

The SPD-governed Länder accepted the 1979 federal guidelines, checking with the *Verfassungsschutz* only about applicants for whom the appointing authority had negative information. Most of the Länder no longer kept out those who were members of the DKP or other radical parties.[4] In 1983, Bremen went one step further and restricted its checks to applicants seeking high or sensitive positions.[5]

In Bremen, Hamburg, North Rhine-Westphalia, and Hesse, authorities shelved preliminary investigations that had been started before 1979 and hired applicants or kept civil servants. In Hesse, the Landtag also passed a resolution that opposed the retention of the decree in any form, but the government did not respond. Chairmen of the Landtag SPD Fraktionen in the Saar, Bavaria, Lower Saxony, Schleswig-Holstein, and Rhineland-Palatinate announced that should they become minister-presidents in their Länder (in many cases unlikely), they would declare the decree defunct and end all screenings.[6]

Their promises were turned into reality in the Saar, where the CDU government, following defeat in the 1985 Landtag election, was replaced by an SPD government. On June 25, 1985, the new SPD minister-president, Oskar Lafontaine, then a leader of the party's left wing, declared that the cabinet had lifted the decree entirely, the first Land to take this dramatic action. In justification, Lafontaine contended that the decree had seriously damaged the reputation of the Federal Republic by creating a "climate of fear of political snooping."[7] He noted that since 1972 the Saar had hardly made use of the decree, having screened only one applicant and rejecting none. To lift the decree would facilitate more tolerance in political discourse.

In support of Lafontaine, the Saar minister of the interior stated that there was no reason why active DKP and NPD members should not become, for instance, mail carriers or teachers if they performed their jobs satisfactorily. The existing civil service law, demanding civil servants to have a special loyalty to the FDGO, was sufficient to bar the real enemies of the constitution.

CDU and CSU officials reacted sharply to the Saar announcement. They contended that the Saar was distancing itself from the Basic Law in a "scandalous manner." Unless the Saar reversed its decision, the CDU/CSU might take the case to the Constitutional Court. They criticized the Saar for having failed to clear its new policy with the Länder conference of minister-presidents of the interior, as was the custom, and requested a discussion at the next meeting. They also accused the Saar of undermining the public service and allowing a Trojan horse into its midst, drawing the analogy to Weimar, when the Nazis easily entered the civil service.

Lafontaine characterized the CDU/CSU comments as party polemics. He reminded the Christian Democrats that under their governments since 1949, Nazis had gained high government offices and judgeships. He assured the opposition that under the new policy the Saar would remain politically stable.[8]

Liberal newspapers lauded the Saar policy as an important symbolic step, even though in practice the previous policy had differed little. They warned, however, that the consequence was a wider schism between the governing and opposition parties. One conservative newspaper asked rhetorically why the Saar would permit enemies of the FDGO into its career service and then try to oust them if they were proven to be anticonstitutional. Would Lafontaine have raised the gate if right radicals (now few) had been as numerous as left radicals? The newspaper viewed the Saar's decision to allow NPD members into the civil service as a bitter pill for the SPD to swallow.[9]

CDU/CSU-governed Länder

The CDU/CSU-governed Länder, with the exception of West Berlin, refused to follow in the footsteps of SPD-ruled Länder, which had abolished making routine loyalty inquiries with the *Verfassungsschutz*. In the case of West Berlin, the SPD, still in power in 1979, followed the guidelines; when the CDU won the 1981 election and assumed the reins of government, it did not reinstate routine inquiries. But it warned judges and prosecuting attorneys to stop taking public stands on political and military issues.[10]

Bavaria, however, maintained its uncompromising position and applied the decree more vigorously than most other states, occasionally even excluding left-wing SPD members and conscientious objectors from its public service. The conservative climate was such that when applicants won their cases after years of litigation in the courts, some were so discouraged that they changed profession or moved to another Land rather than working for the Bavarian government. A few proceedings took eight years to settle, primarily because the government often appealed lower and state court decisions to the Federal Administrative Court, even when in comparable cases the court had decided for the applicant. According to one report, the Bavarian authorities lost their appeals to bar defendants in 87 percent of all court cases. The legal costs of such proceedings ran into the millions of DM.[11]

Although Bavarian minister of the interior Gerold Tandler admitted in the 1980 Land *Verfassungsschutz* report that political extremism did not constitute a serious danger, the authorities viewed criticism of the decree as part of an international communist conspiracy against the FDGO.[12] Thus, the government rejected an ILO attempt during its 1986 investigation (see chapter 4) to gain information about the Land's execution of the decree. CSU chiefs told their CDU colleagues in Bonn that the federal government should not have given the ILO information about how the decree is applied to the federal civil service, because the investigation constitutes a defamation of the country.

In April 1983, the Bavarian government issued a regulation further limiting civil servants' political activities, which included a provision forbidding them to criticize constitutional bodies in "mean, agitational, and instigative ways." The opposition parties labeled the regulation a "muzzle decree" that sought to curb the civil liberties of one group of citizens.[13]

In Lower Saxony, in the wake of a Federal Administrative Court decision of 1981, upholding the dismissal of a civil servant in the postal service (see discussion of the Hans Peter case below), the Ministry of the Interior initiated disciplinary proceedings against at least sixteen DKP teachers and other civil servants who had been candidates for public offices in local elections. In the Landtag, the SPD, FDP, and Greens assailed the move.[14] The government also warned the rest of its 120,000 civil servants that they risked disciplinary proceedings if they were to become DKP candidates for public office.

Leftist teachers were the objects of attention by other Länder. In 1982, in Baden-Württemberg, the government warned 100 teachers to stop urging the public to attend a show protesting the decree and put reprimand notes to this effect into their personnel files. Similar action was almost taken in 1983 against 166 teachers who had signed newspaper advertisements for peace and against war education. Administrators warned them of further disciplinary measures if they did not desist. The Land GEW, in a solidarity action, handed the minister of education protest petitions containing the signatures of 14,000 teachers. The minister backed down.[15]

Newspapers carried reports of disciplinary measures taken against teachers in other parts of the Federal Republic who had taken part in demonstrations, signed publications and flyers, supported political actions by students, or criticized their superiors. The GEW warned administrators that these were legitimate activities; teachers should not be harassed and intimidated. Moreover, the GEW said, administrators should stop using ridiculous reasons (e.g., visiting relatives in the GDR) to reject applicants who wanted to become teachers.[16]

While some CDU/CSU Länder governments took a hard line against radicals, including noncommunists who participated in the peace movement of the early 1980s, others screened fewer applicants or attempted to oust fewer civil servants.[17]

Federal Government Actions

Until 1982, the CDU/CSU, in opposition in the Bundestag, requested the SPD-FDP government to stop allowing radicals into the civil service and to dismiss those already in it. In 1982, the government, in response, asserted that it had begun dismissal proceedings against twenty-eight out of a total of fifty-six right extremists and seventy-nine left extremists.[18]

These actions constituted a stepped-up drive to get rid of radicals in the civil service, especially in the postal and railroad branches. They ran counter to the spirit of the 1979 federal guidelines, which produced only 98 inquiries to the *Verfassungsschutz* about the loyalty of 130,000 applicants and no rejections of them in the 1979–81 period.[19] This contradictory practice was caused by Minister Gscheidle's insistence that radicals must be dismissed for their DKP membership and activity. Once again, as in the period before 1980, left-wing SPD deputies of the European Parliament protested that Gscheidle, by not halting the practice, which did not abide by SPD convention resolutions and the intent of the guidelines, encouraged the Länder to take similar actions. The deputies reminded the minister that a change of policy on his part would produce more sympathy for the SPD among alienated youth.[20]

In the aftermath of the 1980 national election, resulting in a renewed SPD-FDP coalition, Volker Hauff (SPD), heading the newly created Ministry of Transportation, was more sympathetic than Gscheidle, who remained minister of post and telecommunications, to the plight of left and right radicals against whom disciplinary proceedings had been started.[21] Hauff, after consulting with ministry and railroad administrators, offered to put eight railroad civil servants who were subject to dismissal into the salaried employees category, in which the requirement for constitutional loyalty was not as high as in the civil service. The accused personnel reluctantly agreed to this proposal because it meant remaining in the public service and performing the same tasks, even though the status and benefits of salaried employees were lower than those of civil servants.[22]

Gscheidle, who finally became more flexible on the loyalty issue in 1981, checked to see if Hauff's action could be duplicated in his ministry. He was willing to transfer sixteen postal civil servants (of whom eleven were DKP members and five NPD) into salaried employee status but noted that three were working in top-level security posts and would have to be reassigned. It was not yet clear then whether the civil servants would have accepted such a transfer, because they were inclined to stand on the principle that as loyal citizens they had a right to remain civil servants. In any case, the CDU/CSU denounced both ministers for intending to violate federal disciplinary orders and keep extremists in the public service. As a result of the ministers' "horse trade" with the DKP, the judicial authorities would no longer have such cases on their docket and be able to render decisions on possible dismissals.[23]

The Peter Case

Despite Gscheidle's increasingly liberal attitude, he did not stop the cases of several postal servants initiated during his earlier period in office. One case that achieved great publicity in the Federal Republic and elsewhere was that of Hans Peter, who had worked in a telecommunication exchange in Stuttgart since 1951. Peter joined the DKP in 1969 and became a candidate for the Landtag and for a town council thereafter. He had visited the GDR twice and also had been a member of the DKP district executive committee from 1975 to 1978. At the time, such activities were not to the liking of Gscheidle, who, with the support of prosecutor Claussen, in 1977 set disciplinary proceedings into motion—apparently the first time an attempt was made under the 1972 decree to oust a permanent civil servant for disloyalty. In February 1979, after six preliminary hearings and after he was transferred to a position where no security was involved, Peter's case was handed to the Federal Disciplinary Court, which began its own investigation.

In March 1980, the government, at Peter's trial, charged that he had committed a service violation, owing to his lack of political loyalty. Peter maintained that he was loyal, because the DKP was not an enemy of the constitution; hence he saw no need to distance himself from the party.[24]

The court found in his favor because he had fulfilled his duties in an exemplary manner and because his superiors did not contend that he had violated his service duties by being a party member.

In June 1980, Claussen appealed the decision, after the authorities had offered a salaried employee position to Peter, who turned it down on the ground that he was not a security risk, spy, or saboteur. On October 29, 1981, the Federal Administrative Court, in a landmark verdict, supported the government decision to dismiss Peter because of his membership in a cadre party that demanded maximum loyalty of its members—regardless of whether they were active in it or stood as its candidates for public office— and because he would be a security risk in time of crisis.[25]

Minister of the Interior Baum (FDP) was critical of the verdict, which was bound to have a great influence on the practice of authorities and on other court decisions. He stated that if the court had relied more on the 1975 decision of the Constitutional Court, the outcome would have been a victory for Peter. Baum hoped that the Constitutional Court would reconsider the question of membership in a party hostile to the constitution, but the court could render a decision only if Peter was willing to appeal. The DKP apparently urged him not to appeal because it did not want to take the chance of being declared unconstitutional. Mayor Koschnick (SPD) of Bremen requested the Center for European Legal Practice at the University of Bremen to study whether or not the Federal Administrative Court's decision contravened the European Human Rights Convention, guaranteeing freedom of expression and prohibiting discrimination. The center found that it was a violation.[26] Despite this criticism and finding, the verdict stood, and Peter lost his job.

The Meister Case

The second case in the Ministry of Post and Telecommunications that received much publicity was that of Hans Meister, whose background was typical of some of the accused civil servants. Son of a worker's family, he refused military service because of his Christian-pacifist convictions. He served as a conscientious objector and participated in the marches against nuclear weapons and the emergency laws. As a member of the Club Voltaire in Stuttgart, a center for radical youth, he became a communist. In 1971, he joined the DKP and eventually served on the Land DKP executive committee. In 1980, he was a candidate for the Bundestag and in 1982 for mayor of Stuttgart.[27]

In 1959, prior to his political activities, he had joined the postal service, soon becoming a functionary of the Postal Workers Union. Because of his DKP work, he did not receive promotions on the job, even though he was recognized for his technical qualifications. In May 1977, the Stuttgart postal administration invited him to a hearing because of doubts about his constitutional loyalty; in early 1978, it transferred him to a less sensitive post and initiated a preliminary disciplinary action against him. At the time, Minister Gscheidle still was of the opinion that a civil servant who was an active member of the DKP should be dismissed.

In July 1979, the ministry began formal disciplinary proceedings against Meister but by the end of the year suspended them because it had no evidence that he was disloyal to the constitution. More telling for this reversal was Gscheidle's sensitivity to protests from the SPD about his tough stance and calls for his resignation. Claussen, disagreeing with Gscheidle's reversal, reopened the case in 1980. Thereupon, Gscheidle offered to transfer Meister to salaried employee status, but Meister refused.

In November 1982, the Federal Disciplinary Court ruled that Meister's political activities had not violated the duty to be loyal to the FDGO. Claussen appealed the ruling; on May 10, 1984, the Federal Administrative Court held, as it had in the Peter case, that he must be dismissed from the service for his DKP activities. Once again, the courts disagreed in their interpretations of the same set of facts.[28]

Prior to the verdict, Meister's defense lawyers put much weight on ILO Convention No. 111, at the time the subject of great dispute, and Articles 10 and 11 of the European Human Rights Convention, which prohibit discrimination on the basis of political activity and guarantee freedom of expression. The lawyers admitted that international covenants do not take priority over the constitution, but according to the Federal Republic Constitutional Court and judicial literature, the constitution should conform to international law. As long as the Federal Administrative Court had flexibility, the judges should take the option coinciding with the international law obligations of the Federal Republic. The lawyers requested a postponement of the proceedings until the ILO had finished its investigation. The judges denied the request, contending that the pending ILO report would not produce a legal act binding on the Federal Republic.[29]

The Baum Bill

From the time the SPD-FDP government received its last electoral mandate in 1980 until it was replaced by a CDU/CSU government in October 1982, the cabinet ministers became increasingly critical of Claussen's moves to remove civil servants such as Peter and Meister. In 1980, the FDP, which had made gains in the election, partly from youth attracted by its liberal stance on civil liberties, urged the cabinet to further liberalize the decree for those in the civil service. It proposed that the decree cover only those in positions of responsibility (e.g., senior civil servants) and exempt minor public employees (e.g., most postal and railroad staff). The party's stand was shared by the SPD, which in 1977 had criticized the Bundeswehr's dismissal of a cook who in his youth had joined a communist-front youth organization. In support of him, one SPD deputy in the Bundestag asked, "Did the cook go too heavily on the cherry and raspberry desserts, the beets or the red peppers?"[30]

In a more serious vein, the two parties, in discussing a new government program after the 1980 election, concurred on the need to draft legislation based on the FDP proposal. Chancellor Schmidt, in the government declaration, underlined the need for proportionality, although reiterating the ritual statement that extremists were not wanted in the public service.[31]

The government's decision to change the decree through legislation was not acted upon until after the Federal Administrative Court's ruling in October 1981 to dismiss Peter. The cabinet rejected the alternative proposal of Hans-Jochen Vogel, erstwhile SPD minister of justice, to challenge the court's ruling in the Constitutional Court on the ground, among others, that it did not conform with Article 10 of the European Human Rights Convention. Cabinet members warned that if the government lost the appeal, any freedom of action to liberalize the decree would be lost.

In January 1982, Baum and Minister of Justice Jürgen Schmude (SPD) received cabinet approval to draft a bill to change the decree for civil servants—the 1979 guidelines had already changed it for applicants. The bill envisaged civil servants' falling under different loyalty criteria on the basis of their jobs. Under the rubric of proportionality, the seriousness of a service offense on the job would be determined by the duties performed— less, say, for an army cook than for a senior civil servant. If the weight and evidence of the offense were serious enough, the civil servant would be subject to dismissal proceedings.

To maximize freedom of expression and conform with Article 10, the bill also envisaged allowing civil servants during their off-duty hours full political freedoms, including the right to be active and hold office in an extremist but legal party. During their on-duty hours, they would be expected to abide by the loyalty provisions of the civil service laws. Thus, a teacher would not be allowed to propagandize in class but could do so elsewhere after school hours. Baum, in justification, contended that civil servants off-duty were citizens above all and should enjoy the same constitutional rights of expression as others; he warned, however, that if the political activities infringed on job-time performance, they would count against the civil servant in any legal proceeding.[32]

Baum also claimed that the decree's execution "had weakened rather than strengthened the democratic substance of this Republic." The Federal Republic had lost prestige among other West European democracies through its "too perfectionist and bureaucratic rigidity," which does not correspond to the spirit of the liberal Basic Law.[33] Baum's planning chief stated that the ministry for years had hoped that the hunt against extremists, as in the McCarthy era in the United States, would soon be over, with regret for what happened.[34]

Prior to cabinet approval, the CDU/CSU mounted a major campaign against the bill. It accused Baum and Schmude of preparing a bill that did not correspond to the Constitutional Court decision of 1975, which said that every civil servant, regardless of function, had a duty to be loyal. It argued that, for instance, in a crisis, a railroad engineer, even though not classified as a top civil servant, had important responsibilities of transporting Bundeswehr or police units as well as military freight. One CDU leader noted that railroad engineers could commit sabotage against the state, recalling a KPD flyer of 1923 requesting them to sabotage the rolling stock.

A CDU deputy asked tellingly whether an extremist civil servant who during his off-duty time gave thought to overthrowing the societal order would give up his intention upon entering his office, in the same manner as giving his hat to a checkroom attendant. Other CDU/CSU deputies accused the ministers of creating a "privileged caste of civil servants," referring to communists and neo-Nazis who would not be expelled from the service but who were intent on creating a Jacobinic state. Instead of being sheltered, the extremists should be dismissed.[35]

A number of SPD leaders, in response to the CDU/CSU verbal assaults, defended the government bill. The new minister of post and telecommunications, Hans Matthöfer (SPD), replacing Gscheidle in 1982, foresaw the end of dismissal proceedings, while Minister of Transportation Hauff envisaged an end to the transfer of radicals from civil service to salaried employee status.

Not all cabinet members supported the bill. Two conservative FDP ministers (Josef Ertl and Otto Graf Lambsdorff) had doubts about the constitutionality of differentiating job function, as did Federal president Karl Carstens (CDU), whose signature would be needed if Parliament were to give its approval. When Carstens told Schmidt about his doubts, the chancellor requested Baum and Schmude to convince the president of the bill's constitutionality. The effort did not succeed, especially when Baum announced that the bill would not require the assent of the CDU/CSU-dominated Bundesrat.[36] The CDU/CSU insisted, however, that because the bill would amend several clauses of the civil service framework law, the Länder would need to change their laws to conform with it. As a consequence, the Bundesrat must vote. The party threatened that unless the cabinet submitted the bill to both houses, it would ask the Constitutional Court to rule on the dispute and on the legislation. On June 16, 1982, the cabinet approved Baum's bill but, yielding to the CDU/CSU, agreed to submit it to both houses.

On August 27, the chancellor transmitted it to the Bundesrat president with a request for a vote by the deadline, October 8. In defense of the bill, Schmidt contended that its passage would necessitate few changes in the civil service laws. But in the meantime the government fell, because of differences over economic policy between SPD and FDP. The latter promptly joined a coalition government with the CDU/CSU under the chancellorship of Helmut Kohl. Some FDP ministers remained in the cabinet, but not Baum, who had opposed a break with the SPD.

During the coalition negotiations between the CDU/CSU and the FDP before the formation of the cabinet on October 1, the FDP yielded ground to the CDU/CSU on a number of civil liberties issues, including the Christian Democrats' insistence that the Baum bill be withdrawn from further consideration. The decision came too late for the Bundesrat to take it off the October 8 session agenda. However, given the CDU/CSU–FDP majority in both houses, it never had a chance of parliamentary approval in the first place unless there had been concessions to the Christian Democrats. Remaining firm in opposition to the bill, they defeated it in the Bundesrat. They claimed once again that the Constitutional Court did not allow any differentiation in job function, that the bill represented a danger to the FDGO, and that a person's loyalty was not divisible between duty and nonduty hours.[37]

The CDU/CSU-FDP Government

When Friedrich Zimmermann (CSU) became minister of the interior in the new cabinet, critics of the decree feared that as a tough law-and-order conservative, he would insist on revoking the 1979 guidelines, which had eliminated the automatic screening of applicants to the federal civil service. Even though the CDU/CSU had opposed the guidelines at the time, Zimmermann did not touch them, primarily because the FDP ministers insisted on their retention.[38] As will be seen, however, discharge proceedings against extremists in the civil service continued at an increased rate.

On October 27, 1982, the SPD, in opposition in the Bundestag, introduced a bill corresponding to the defunct Baum bill, knowing well that it had no chance of passage.[39] But the party hoped thereby to generate another discussion on the issue and to project an image of being the progressive party.

After the March 1983 election, the CDU/CSU and FDP gained a majority and formed another government, with SPD and Greens in opposition. (For the first time, the Greens had gained more than the minimum 5 percent needed for Bundestag representation.) During the coalition negotiations between the CDU/CSU and the FDP, Zimmermann was requested—as he had been following the October 1982 negotiations—to prepare a report on the 1972 decree's implementation and policy recommendations for the future. But none has ever been published, apparently because Minister of Justice Hans Adolf Engelhard (FDP) opposed any change toward a tougher policy.[40]

Each federal ministry made its own decision whether or not to dismiss radicals. Most ministries did not need to prosecute radicals because nearly all their decision-making staff were in the upper levels of the civil service, where left radicals had rarely sought employment. The few radicals in the ministries were unlikely to be fired, given the lack of automatic screenings of most career servants in nonsensitive posts. Only if radicals were denounced or ran for public office would their names become known to the authorities, and action might be taken.[41]

The Ministry of Transportation, responsible for the federal railways, processed few cases, partly because its DKP members, unlike those in the Ministry of Post and Telecommunications, had been willing to transfer to salaried employee status. The Ministry of Finance began proceedings against a few customs officials. The Ministry of Post and Telecommunications, however, initiated large-scale actions against DKP members who were working in its telecommunications network (classified as sensitive by NATO's 1981 guidelines) or who had become politically visible by running for public office on the DKP ticket.

Postal Minister Christian Schwarz-Schilling (CDU) ordered new screenings and transfers into lower-paying unskilled jobs for at least 40 suspected radicals (most of them workers or employees in telecommunications), preliminary discharge proceedings against 6 individuals, and the continuation of formal proceedings against 5 others.[42] Even though 11 individuals threatened with discharge were only a fraction of the 530,000 on the ministry's payroll, and even though a number of cases had been initiated by the SPD-FDP government, the critics, by then including an increasing number of DGB unions, strongly objected to the purge of persons who had always performed well on the job.

The Bastian Case

One of the ministry's well-publicized cases was that of Herbert Bastian, who in 1959 had become a mail carrier in Marburg; twelve years later he received permanent status. As in the cases of Peter and Meister, he was active in the DKP, gaining a seat on the Marburg city council. In 1979, in preliminary hearings, he stated that his superiors had been supportive, giving him time off to fulfill his duties as city councillor.

In 1984, as a result of the Meister verdict and the tough policy of the Kohl government, Bastian's superior indicated to him that if he wanted to remain in the public service, he would have to give up his post as councillor and refrain from all DKP activities. Bastian in turn brought a charge against his superior of attempting to intimidate him and of violating a city ordinance that states that no councillor can be restrained from carrying out his mandate. A ministry official retorted that the proceedings were legal because they were directed against Bastian in his capacity as postal civil servant.[43]

In August 1984, Bastian was suspended from his job, but in November the Federal Disciplinary Court held up the disciplinary proceedings when it discovered that serious legal errors (proceedings had been secret, personnel councils had not been heard) were made by the ministry in this and other cases. Eventually the court resumed its investigation and hearings and in 1987 ordered the dismissal of Bastian from the postal service. In 1988, a number of Bundestag deputies, union officials, and other prominent persons requested Federal president von Weizsäcker to issue a pardon for Bastian.

Bastian's case raised constitutional issues concerning the carrying out of his mandate as a councillor. As early as 1979, a number of professors at Hesse universities accused the ministry of violating the Hesse constitution and a law stipulating that no one can be prevented from seeking, or holding, a seat in a municipal council or the Landtag.[44]

In January 1985, the SPD, FDP, and Greens, in a majority in the Hesse Landtag, passed a resolution closely corresponding to the position of the professors. The SPD mayor of Marburg wrote to Minister Schwarz-Schilling that Bastian's participation in city affairs was an expression of the democratic will.[45]

Pravda attacked the minister for being the first one in the conservative cabinet, aided by court verdicts, to begin a witch-hunt against Bastian and others in the postal service. The DKP denounced trials against its members who were being punished for being candidates for public office. The party maintained that free elections had become a farce.[46]

The head of the German Postal Workers Union (DPG), Kurt van Haaren, wrote to Schwarz-Schilling urging a case-by-case study of each accused rather than an undifferentiated action. The Hesse branch of the union found scandalous one of the minister's statements, in which he contended that DKP membership was as serious a violation of duty as employing a civil servant who stole money. SPD deputies disagreed with the ministry's argument that the removal of the few radicals would secure an orderly service. West European countries would not react well to the dismissals, seeing in them once again a demonstration of an authoritarian will. The opposition parties, Initiatives against *Berufsverbote*, and the DPG also sponsored a number of protest meetings.[47]

In response to the criticisms, ministry officials contended that it was normal practice under any government to suspend or dismiss civil servants when they had committed serious service violations. The officials also announced that the government no longer would consider as right extremists NPD candidates for public office who leave their party.

In reply, an SPD deputy found the new position on the NPD puzzling, because leaving a party did not mean that the persons had necessarily changed their views. Rather it meant that they had left the party for opportunistic reasons—to keep their jobs.[48] In October 1984, another SPD deputy asked the ministry if it was willing to transfer civil servants involved in disciplinary proceedings to the salaried-employee category. A senior official responded negatively, although he promised that some social welfare benefits would be available to such individuals if they lost their jobs.[49] The gulf between opponents and proponents of the decree remained as wide as ever.

Renewed Controversy, 1984–87

The Greens, upset by the Bastian and other postal cases and in favor of annulling the decree, took the offensive in the Bundestag. In October 1984, in a major query (*Grosse Anfrage*) to the government, they requested it to answer a series of questions concerning *Berufsverbote*.[50] In July 1985, eight months later, Zimmermann finally responded in writing. He objected to the Greens' use of the term "Berufsverbot" as polemical and false. He noted that the number of applicants for federal positions rejected for political reasons before 1980 had been minimal.[51] From 1980 to 1984 none had been rejected, while only 5 civil servants and employees out of a June 1983 total of 1,182,000 on the federal payroll (including workers) had been discharged for political reasons.[52] Zimmermann revealed that the federal ministries would continue their selective screenings of applicants. Critics charged him with the use of incorrect figures concerning the number affected by the decree, with minimizing the controversy still surrounding it, and with not answering many questions correctly or fully.[53]

On January 30, 1986, the Bundestag held a long debate based on the Greens' major query of October 1984 and a resolution to annul the decree and on an SPD resolution to resuscitate the defeated Baum bill. A deputy of the Greens criticized the continuing practice in two CDU/CSU Länder of preventing radicals from becoming teachers or lawyers by barring them from the training service. He pleaded for support of the Greens' resolution to end once and for all the loyalty screenings, the job ban, and the decree and to rehabilitate those adversely affected by the decree.

An SPD deputy remarked that democracy will not be endangered by a small number of extremists in the service but will be by conformism, cowardly silence, opportunism, and blind obedience, as well as by economic crisis, mass unemployment, an increasing gap between the privileged wealthy and the hopeless poor, and the demonization of alleged or real domestic and foreign foes. He called for a halt to all disciplinary proceedings.

In response, a CDU deputy contended that neo-Nazis and communists remained foes of the constitution. No sensible person, he stated, would want to see neo-Nazis as teachers, state prosecuting attorneys, or judges. Communists saw as their model the GDR and the Soviet Union, which were both guilty of human rights violations. These party members seek to gain their goals through revolutionary force and terror. An FDP deputy also defended the decree but admitted that intolerance and overeagerness had been shown in individual decisions. He called for administrative restraint and noted that in a number of Länder and municipalities, low-level and middle-level civil servants had not been screened, but no danger to the service had resulted. Not unexpectedly, the CDU/CSU and FDP majority of deputies defeated the Greens' resolution to scrap the decree and the SPD resolution to limit its application.[54]

The debate showed that the positions of the CDU/CSU and the SPD had not changed from the late 1970s on. The FDP, which had supported the aborted Baum bill, remained ambivalent about the decree since 1982, when it switched coalition partners in Bonn. The Greens, making their debut in the Bundestag, took the most negative position of all the parties. Yet, because the Bundestag served as a forum for debates to influence public opinion, no one party spokesperson expected to convince the deputies of other parties to change their positions.

In 1987, on the occasion of the fifteenth anniversary of the decree, the Greens welcomed the decision in SPD-ruled Länder not to initiate new cases of *Berufsverbot* and to drop charges against persons whose cases had been started years earlier, when the policies had been more stringent. The Greens announced that they intended to continue to support those affected by the decree as administered by CDU/CSU authorities in Bonn and the Länder.[55]

In 1987, the publication of the ILO report criticizing the execution of the decree (see chapter 4) produced another round of debate among the parties and interested organizations. SPD deputies criticized the government's rejection of the report as a renunciation of international law, which should be strengthened and not weakened. They asked the government what consequences it would draw from the report's conclusion that its practices and those of CDU/CSU-led Länder were not in consonance with ILO Convention No. 111 calling for nondiscrimination in employment and occupation. Should not the government abide by the recommendation to assume the loyalty of all applicants unless it had evidence to the contrary and to differentiate among job functions held by the civil servants? In response, a CDU/CSU deputy reiterated the imperative of civil servants' loyalty to the FDGO.[56]

In Lower Saxony, SPD chief Gerhard Schröder hailed the ILO report and requested the CDU-led government to suspend immediately all loyalty cases and to reinstate those dismissed. In Baden-Württemberg, the DGB Land chairman made the same request, citing the ILO report's reference to the cases of three teachers in the Land against whom disciplinary proceedings had been started. In May 1987, the DGB, supporting the ILO report, stated that the Federal and Länder governments (CDU/CSU) cannot justify barring or ousting persons for their political views or membership and activity in a party accused of unconstitutional goals. Disciplinary measures should be taken only against those proven to have acted against the FDGO.[57]

The deputy chairman of the DPG asserted that the best response to the ILO report would be to revoke the decree rather than make changes. He asked for the suspension of all proceedings against DPG members and the reinstatement of discharged civil servants. Communists should be fought politically rather than by jeopardizing their livelihood.[58] Christian Democratic officials in Bonn and the Länder, not acceding to such demands, reminded labor leaders that in earlier years, when the SPD was in power, they supported (more or less) the decree.[59]

Conclusion

In the 1980s, the controversy over the decree abated, despite the critics' renewed demands for changes in its execution or for its revocation. The controversy abated partly because less economic growth meant fewer civil service jobs, which in turn meant fewer radical applicants seeking government employment. A trend toward political and social conservatism in the nation's political culture also produced fewer young radicals eager to change the system through public agencies considered too resistant to pressures from the Left.

The trend toward conservatism was not universal, however, as seen by the SPD-FDP's veering partially away from its earlier tough policies toward extremists. Under the liberalized 1979 guidelines, the Schmidt government and the SPD-led Länder governments ended the automatic screening of applicants to the public service. Yet, at the same time, the Bonn government did not stop ouster proceedings against permanent civil servants begun prior to 1980. Perhaps to make up for its tarnished image in these cases, Minister Baum prepared a bill to restrict loyalty investigations to officials in responsible or sensitive posts, but the fall of the government in 1982 and the opposition of the CDU/CSU to a further liberalization of the decree doomed the bill in the Bundesrat.

The CDU/CSU's assumption of power in coalition with the less liberal FDP in 1982 meant that there was no chance for a further easing of the decree in Bonn or in the Länder they controlled. Indeed, no one expected the wide gap between, say, CSU-ruled Bavaria and SPD-ruled Saar (which had revoked the decree) to be bridged. To the credit of the FDP minister of justice in the Kohl government, after 1982 the cabinet did not reintroduce automatic screenings of applicants for the federal service, as practiced in most CDU/CSU-led Länder. The Ministry of Post and Telecommunications, however, renewed its drive to get rid of radicals in its service.

The presence in the Bundestag and Landtage of one set of new political actors—the Greens—who resolutely demanded the lifting of the decree, ensured that the discussion would not end too swiftly. The ILO report issued in Geneva pushed the federal government further into a defensive position, especially when the SPD, the Greens, and the unions supported its conclusions.

7

Civil Service Loyalty in Other Countries

The 1972 decree played a significant role in the domestic policies of successive West German governments, constantly testing their will to restrict the degree of freedom granted to radicals. For a wider perspective on the subject of communists' and neofascists' being admitted into or fired from the public service, this chapter focuses on practices in other West European countries and especially in the United States, where the loyalty question also played an important role in the postwar period. A comparative survey should reveal whether the 1972 decree was unique in Western democracies or was typical of transnational repressive moves against political dissidents.[1] This survey will not deal with the position of public servants in the former communist states of the Eastern bloc, whose ideology called for loyalty to and propagation of Marxism and the building of a socialist state. Such a comparison would have little meaning, given the vanishing differences between the FRG system and those of the East (although it might also show a parallel in the banning and ouster of political dissidents—communists in West Germany and anticommunists in the erstwhile Eastern communist states).

Great Britain

The lack of a written constitution results in British practice resting strongly on tradition and common law, codified in many instances by parliamentary acts. Hence, individual rights and freedoms are not guaranteed formally in one basic document and have no precedent over other legislation. Yet, the rights of British citizens are quite real. Thus a number of laws—such as the Trade Union and Labour Relations Act of 1974, which regulates the dismissal of public servants and others—do provide some protection to individuals. Moreover, citizens enjoy freedoms as long as Parliament does not enact legislative restrictions.

Civil servants, also named servants of the Crown, comprise fewer categories of personnel than in West Germany and exclude police agents, fire fighters, teachers, and local administrators, who are all salaried employees. Civil servants, who work primarily in the ministries, are under the control of the Civil Service Department; they are expected to remain politically neutral during their on-duty hours.

Applicants to the civil service are not queried concerning their political views and do not take a loyalty oath. Rather, they are normally screened and accepted on professional qualifications, based on written tests and interviews, and receive permanent status after one or two years. If an applicant is not accepted, no reason need be given. In 1948, in the wake of some spy scandals, the prime minister announced that communists, fascists, and their sympathizers would not be employed in posts where the security of the nation was at stake. Each ministry would determine which positions fell under that category and transfer civil servants deemed to be security risks into nonsensitive jobs.

In 1952, the government began a "positive vetting" (screening) procedure, which includes an investigation of political views and character defects, for sensitive positions, the diplomatic corps, and top civil service posts. By the end of 1953, the government had screened about 17,000 out of over 1 million civil servants, selecting those representing a degree of security risk. As a consequence, 148 were suspended. Of these 28 were reinstated once their loyalty had been demonstrated, 69 were transferred to nonsecret work, 19 resigned, 9 went on special leave pending decisions, and 23 were dismissed because they were suitable only to do secret work.[2]

In November 1955, years after the escape of the British diplomats Guy Burgess and Donald Maclean to the Soviet Union, for whom they had spied, the government requested a Conference of Privy Councillors to review security procedures and to recommend any additional measures. In 1956, the conference issued a report, which became the basis for new procedures one year later. A civil servant employed in a security post who was or recently had been a member of the British communist or fascist parties or who had been sympathetic to communism or fascism, associated with communists or fascists or their sympathizers, or was susceptible to communist or fascist pressures was deemed a security risk. In such an instance, the civil servant's loyalty to the state would be decided on the merits of the case. A minister who had jurisdiction over the civil servant would first rule whether there was a prima facie case. If there was, the civil servant could not be given any details that might disclose the sources of the evidence of guilt. The minister might reconsider his or her ruling if the civil servant sent convincing written evidence of loyalty. If the minister lets stand a ruling of doubtful loyalty, the civil servant may request the minister to refer the case to an advisory tribunal of three members.

Under revised procedures of 1962, the civil servant may be accompanied to the tribunal's hearing by a friend or staff official (but not by a lawyer), but such an individual can be present only during the civil servant's opening statement. The civil servant is not entitled to be informed of the evidence in his or her case and cannot cross-examine any witnesses. The civil servant does have the right to ask third parties to testify as to his or her record, reliability, and character.

Upon conclusion of the hearing, the advisers inform the minister whether they support the prima facie ruling. If they do not or have no firm views, they must assess the evidence in detail. The civil servant will not be informed of their advice to the minister, who can accept or reject it. Between 1962 and 1964, only one person was dismissed and one barred from secret work as a result of the new security procedures.

The government also screens employees of private firms engaged in secret defense work. The minister must receive from the firm a list of all employees who have access to secrets in their work and then on the basis of intelligence information decides which individuals shall be denied access because they are considered security risks. After 1956, such individuals had the opportunity to appear before the advisory tribunal, which then advises the minister whether dismissal or transfer to a nonsensitive job is warranted in each case.[3] The government's justification for its security procedures was enunciated in 1956 by the Conference of Privy Councillors: "It is right to continue the practice of tilting the balance in favour of offering greater protection to the security of the State rather than in the direction of safeguarding the rights of the individual."[4]

Some civil libertarians have been critical of the government's failure to provide legal rights to civil servants or employees in defense industries, such as the right to have their lawyers present at the tribunal's hearings or to have recourse to a court. The critics also have objected to the government's dismissal of soldiers on security grounds without giving them adequate legal protection and to the procedural aspects of screenings of persons seeking secret employment. In the latter instance, the Ministry of Supply on occasion has expected university teachers to answer detailed questions, including information about political affiliations, concerning their colleagues and students. Intelligence officials, with the support of the Ministry of Education, have requested similar information at times from schoolmasters about their pupils.[5]

Applicants for university teaching posts, who are hired directly by the universities, have not been subject to political screenings by state authorities. Applicants for high school teaching posts have been screened; occasionally an extreme leftist or rightist applicant has not been hired. Conversely, some teachers have been dismissed if they discriminated against pupils who did not share their political views. The Council for Academic Freedom and Democracy has checked into such cases and has recommended, when appropriate, an appeal to an industrial tribunal, which then serves as an administrative review body.

Despite criticisms of some aspects of the British loyalty-security program, on the whole it has been administered fairly and reasonably. One American observer, noting that no moral stigma is attached to negative personnel decisions based on political extremist views of civil servants, writes, "Such a program of austerity as to dogma and ideology lends no aid and comfort to the witch hunters and fanatics who seek to turn Communists into a class of economic and social outlaws."[6]

France

The French tradition of human rights, based on the 1789 Revolution, is anchored in the many constitutions that the country has had since then. Thus, the preamble to the 1946 constitution contains a provision that no one can be discriminated against in work or position on account of origin, political views, or religion. Freedom of opinion for civil servants is cited specifically in several articles. The civil service statute of 1959, based on a 1946 statute, prohibits mention of political, philosophical, or religious views in the personnel files of civil servants.

The principle of equal opportunity for all guarantees citizens the right to apply for any civil service position if they fulfill the educational and other nonpolitical qualifications. They cannot be excluded for political reasons, even if they belong to extremist left or right parties. In several cases, the Council of State (the highest administrative court) has found for appellants who claimed discrimination against them in hiring or being fired. One important case concerned Barel and four other university students in Paris who wanted to take a competitive examination to enter the prestigious *École Nationale Administrative,* from which they could expect to receive important administrative posts in the civil service. In 1953, a state secretary denied them the right to take the examination because they presented a risk—they were members of a communist organization, and Barel was also chairman of a leftist student federation. The students took their case to the Council of State, which in 1954 asked the state secretary—in vain—to let council members see the files of the applicants. When he gave no detailed reason for his decision to bar them from the examination, the council ordered him to reverse it, on the ground that discrimination against applicants cannot be permitted.[7]

Although in this case the Council of State overruled a discriminatory practice, newspapers reported numerous instances of discrimination against left unionists and communists. Trade unions repeatedly denounced government agencies for requesting the police to investigate the political and union views of applicants to the public service. Some ministries, such as Foreign Affairs and Interior and its subsidiaries, the prefectures and police, have not hired left and right radicals, while Defense has excluded them as career soldiers, usually on the pretext that they did not score high enough in the competitive examinations. On the other hand, the Ministry of Education has hired thousands of communists to become teachers (including some university professors), as long as they retained objectivity in their teaching.[8] Once communists are in the public service and become members of the communist-dominated trade union federation (CGT), some are discriminated against, perhaps for not showing enough restraint in voicing their political views.

Public servants do not pledge loyalty to the state, although they are expected to be loyal to it. They also must abide by the constitution and the laws and remain politically neutral in their positions. Because the communist and other radical parties of the Left and Right are legal and, unlike those in the Federal Republic, gain some electoral support, the French do not categorize such parties as being hostile to the constitution. Thus, the 1972 decree would be unimaginable in France. Legislative proposals to bar Communist party members or adherents of its front organizations from the public service have never mustered a majority in Parliament, partly because most public servants have seen in the proposals a threat to their own democratic rights.[9]

Italy

There are strong parallels and a few differences between France and Italy in their views of the political loyalty of civil servants. In Italy, newly hired civil servants must pledge loyalty to the Republic and its constitution and laws and must fulfill the duties of the office. A constitutional provision prohibits discrimination in hiring public servants. Most applicants to the public service can belong to any legal party (including the neofascist party) or hold any political views. They are to be selected solely on the basis of their entrance examination performance, but (as noted below) there is a way to circumvent this requirement. Top civil servants, diplomats, judges, police agents, and soldiers are constitutionally not allowed to belong to a political party, although implementing orders have been issued only for the police. Thus, given the strength of the Communist party, it is not surprising that the party is well represented in the public service, including judges who belong to an ultraleft group "Democratic Magistracy."

Government administrators can keep out applicants if they do not meet the criterion of "good conduct," which signifies that an individual has not been convicted in court and has behaved satisfactorily. Normally, the mayor of the town in which the applicant resides will issue a certificate of good conduct after the police or other town personnel have made inquiries of the applicant's neighbors. If authorities exclude an applicant from a competitive examination, reasons must be given, but normally communists and fascists have not been barred from most civil service posts. The vagueness of the criterion of "good conduct," however, gives administrators some leeway not to hire an applicant on a provisional or permanent status.[10]

Sweden

As expected, Sweden's tradition of tolerance and political moderation is mirrored in the way the country treats the question of political extremism and the civil service. Civil servants do not pledge any special loyalty to the state but are expected to be loyal and nonpartisan in their tasks. The political views of applicants to the civil service and those in the service are not relevant to employment, a reflection of the fact that parties can be formed at will and cannot be prohibited. In the few instances where administrators have asked applicants to low-level posts about their political views, an ombudsman has ruled that such inquiries were inadmissible. Party views of prospective personnel are, however, taken into consideration for a few top posts and the security service. Such applicants are screened by the security section of the national police.[11]

Comparison of West European Practices

This brief survey of how a few West European countries deal with civil servants' loyalty to the state needs to be supplemented by a broader thematic comparison between the West German practice and the practices of other West European states, including the ones covered above. Two major comparative studies have indicated marked differences and a few similarities.[12]

The European Human Rights Convention prohibits discrimination on political grounds in the hiring of civil servants and guarantees freedom of expression for all citizens. Several countries, such as France, Italy, Austria, and the Netherlands, constitutionally guarantee entry into civil service positions for all top qualified applicants for which there are openings, although in practice in Belgium and Austria the top positions are distributed on a party-proportional system. Civil servants, who compose a smaller percentage of all public employees than in the Federal Republic, are expected in all countries to be loyal to the state. Yet, only in Belgium, Italy, Netherlands, Greece, and Switzerland—in addition to the Federal Republic—are there specific loyalty provisions in the statutes, which require such pledges or oaths of loyalty as a precondition for hiring.

Most states view security screenings for sensitive posts as more effective than pledges of loyalty. Belgium, Austria, Switzerland, and Italy do not have any official screenings, but it may be assumed that in these countries authorities keep applicants who are politically suspect out of such posts through less formal means, such as secret data collection by the police or intelligence services. In small countries, such as Austria, Denmark, Ireland, and Switzerland, agencies do not systematically gather information about individuals, but in some instances the local police are asked to assist. The rationale for this haphazard procedure is that it is difficult for political extremists in such countries to function anonymously. Norway and Sweden have established strict controls over data gathering.

In no country other than West Germany are applicants for teaching posts screened. In 1976, Joop den Uyl, Dutch prime minister, said on West German television, "I think no one in the Netherlands will be worried if there is a communist in the school. That is quite normal."[13] On the other hand, only in West Germany, Netherlands, and Italy must authorities reveal the reasons for nonemployment, and only in West Germany, Italy, and Belgium will an administrative court hear appeals of applicants who were not hired. Dismissals from the service for political reasons were rare in all West European countries other than the Federal Republic in the late 1970s and early 1980s. In Belgium, a civil servant could be dismissed if proven to have engaged in an anticonstitutional activity; in France, if proven to have shown no political restraint; in Britain, if there was a violation of loyalty; in Sweden and Switzerland, only if there was a clear violation of duty.

The United States

There have been many similarities in practice regarding civil service loyalty between the Federal Republic and the United States. The chief reason for the repression of dissidents in both states has been the policymakers' anticommunism and fear of communists, even though the Communist parties have never attracted much support after 1945. But the entrenched government and corporate interests viewed them as threats or used them as pretexts for maximizing ideological conformity and minimizing dissent.

In the United States, policies repressing dissidents go far back in history. The Alien and Sedition Act of 1798, for instance, authorized the president to arrest or deport any alien considered dangerous to the country. The Espionage Act of 1918 made it a crime to obstruct the draft or interfere with the war effort. Under this act, socialist leader Eugene Debs was sent to prison on a charge of sedition. The post–World War I era witnessed a wave of anticommunist and antiradical hysteria on the part of the federal and state governments, with the former rounding up and deporting "Red" aliens and the latter passing a spate of acts against sedition and even a few against flying red flags. Yet, the era was also marked by successful litigation in courts against some repressive laws. In 1938, Rep. Martin Dies of Texas, worried about the worldwide communist movement (but less about fascism), received legislative support to set up the forerunner of the House Un-American Activities Committee, which got permanent status in 1945 and, in the succeeding decades, contributed its share to the Cold War zeitgeist.[14]

In 1939, Congress passed the Hatch Act, which, among several provisions, made it unlawful for a federal government employee to engage in partisan activities or to be a member "in any political party or organization which advocates the overthrow of our constitutional form of government."[15] In 1941, the FBI was empowered to inquire into subversive activities among government employees. In 1947, with the advent of the Cold War, the Republican party accused Pres. Harry Truman of being soft on communism, despite his tough stance against the Soviet Union. J. Edgar Hoover, FBI chief, warned the president about the "Red Menace." As a result, Truman promulgated a landmark executive order establishing a loyalty program, which denied federal employment to those deemed "disloyal" to the U.S. government. (There is a striking parallel here to the issuance of the West German 1972 decree by Brandt and the minister-presidents after the CDU/CSU charged him with being soft on communism.)

On the basis of the program, all prospective civil servants or those already in government employment were to undergo loyalty investigations on the basis of information compiled by the FBI, the Civil Service Commission, military intelligence, the House Un-American Activities Committee, and local police agencies. When derogatory information was unearthed, a full field investigation was conducted by the FBI or the commission. If deemed necessary, a commission hearing board would be convened to review the case of a civil servant. Individuals had the right to appeal an adverse decision before a Loyalty Review Board set up by the commission.

An adverse loyalty finding was made if there was "reasonable ground" that the person was "disloyal." But the executive order did not define disloyalty, other than listing six types of activities that the agencies might consider: (1) sabotage, espionage, and related activities; (2) treason or sedition; (3) advocacy of illegal overthrow of the government; (4) disclosure of confidential information; (5) service with a foreign government in preference to the interests of the United States; and (6) membership in, or affiliation or "sympathetic association" with, an organization designated by the attorney general as totalitarian, fascist, communist, or subversive.[16]

As in the Federal Republic, the first five categories were already grounds for criminal prosecution under existing laws; the sixth category, dealing with subversive organizations, referred to beliefs and association rather than specific activity. One critic noted, "It is clear that the real purpose of the loyalty program was to attempt to determine whether or not 'disloyal' *thoughts* were being entertained in employees' or applicants' heads, which *might* at some future time lead to disloyal action."[17]

The loyalty program's provisions for public employees working in "sensitive" agencies (the Atomic Energy Agency, Departments of Defense and State, the Central Intelligence Agency, the Economic Cooperation Administration, and the Voice of America), employing 800,000 people, were more strict than for other government agencies. Congress from 1947 on authorized the heads of the sensitive agencies to dismiss employees summarily and to bar new applicants whenever they saw it "necessary or advisable" in the interest of national security. A dismissed employee could appeal to the Civil Service Commission for transfer to a nonsensitive agency.[18]

Many serious abuses developed under the loyalty program, comparable to those in West Germany in the 1970s. Because much information was gathered by confidential informants, the charges against individuals were often vague and erroneous. Those accused of grave allegations could not determine who their accusers were or confront and cross-examine them. The failure to set a time limit on alleged subversive activities might mean that an applicant or civil servant who sympathized with a radical group decades earlier might still be denied employment or be ousted from the civil service. Given the variations in procedures among hearing boards, civil servants could be cleared by one agency but face a hearing if transferred to another. As in West Germany, at hearings examiners asked inane and irrelevant questions such as "There is a suspicion in the record that you are in sympathy with the underprivileged. Is this true?"[19]

The loyalty program received a significant degree of support among conservatives but was strongly criticized by civil libertarians. Among them was the essayist E. B. White, who wrote a letter in 1947 to the *New York Herald Tribune* reproaching its defense of the Hollywood blacklist of writers and directors.

> I am a member of a party of one, and I live in an age of fear. Nothing lately has unsettled my party and raised my fears so much as your editorial, on Thanksgiving Day, suggesting that employees should be required to state their beliefs in order to hold their jobs. The idea is inconsistent with our constitutional theory and has been stubbornly opposed by watchful men since the early days of the Republic. I can only assume that your editorial writer, in a hurry to get home for Thanksgiving, tripped over the First Amendment and thought it was the office cat.[20]

In the course of time, critics of the loyalty program not only rejected loyalty oaths but warned that the possible result of the state's use of a mass of informers and FBI agents to pry into people's private lives and to compile secret dossiers would be the growth of a police state. One consequence would be the stifling of political dissent, as individuals, and especially government employees, would be reluctant to join radical organizations that might be targeted as subversive.

Nevertheless, Congress pressed forward its own anticommunist crusade. In 1947, the House Un-American Activities Committee declared its intention to expose and ferret out government-employed communists and communist sympathizers who were bent on destroying the American way of life. In early 1950, Sen. Joseph McCarthy began his anticommunist crusade.[21] It contributed to the hysteria about the highly publicized espionage cases and about alleged communists and fellow travelers infiltrating key government departments and defense industries, holding jobs as teachers and professors, and being active in the media, especially the motion picture industry. As a result, in 1950, Congress passed, over President Truman's veto, the Internal Security (McCarran) Act, which defined communist and communist-action organizations. It required them to register and disclose their membership lists and barred their members from government or defense industry employment. In 1954, Congress passed the Communist Control Act, which further defined communism as a conspiracy directed by a foreign power against the security and internal order of the United States.

Truman's loyalty program, supplemented by congressional acts and investigations, provided the base for a massive loyalty check of government employees or potential employees. From 1947 to 1952, government agents checked 4.3 million loyalty forms—2.5 million of applicants to the civil service and 1.8 million of those on government payrolls. More than 22,000 cases were referred to loyalty boards for review, of which nearly 14,000 were cleared by favorable decisions. Of the other 8,000 cases, 414 were denied employment or removed on loyalty grounds, and the remainder were discontinued because individuals had left the service or had withdrawn their applications (5,234 cases) or because the cases were still being adjudicated.[22] Once again, there are striking parallels between the United States and West Germany in their prodigious efforts to keep political extremists from, or to root out the relatively few in, the civil service.

Although the U.S. loyalty program showed tangible results (including the firing of many innocent persons), the lack of uniform standards, excesses in its administration, and the existence of three parallel subsidiary programs convinced Pres. Dwight Eisenhower that it needed overhauling. In 1953, he issued Executive Order 10450, which established a new and more stringent uniform loyalty program. The order stipulated that employment or retention in employment in the federal service must be "clearly consistent with the interests of national security." By making "national security" rather than "loyalty" the cornerstone of the program, agencies and departments could summarily dismiss those persons who did not meet the new standard. Hence, cases could be reopened in which a full field investigation by an increasingly powerful FBI (or other agencies) had already been undertaken during the Truman period.

The new order abolished the Loyalty Review Board and gave departments and agencies the authority to review cases directly. The Civil Service Commission maintained a file on all persons refused, or dismissed from, employment. As a result of the broad powers given executive officials, the number of cases of nonhiring or ousters of "subversives" rose dramatically during the Eisenhower administration. According to the commission, almost seven thousand federal employees had been dismissed or had resigned. Vice President Richard Nixon proudly announced that the administration was "kicking the communists and fellow-travelers and security risks out of government . . . by the thousands."[23]

Defenders of the loyalty programs, such as J. Edgar Hoover, contended that "a government job is a matter of privilege and not of right." Some cited the opinion of Supreme Court justice Oliver Wendell Holmes, who, before becoming a defender of free speech, held in one municipal employment case that "the petitioner may have a constitutional right to talk politics, but he has no constitutional right to be a policeman. . . . The city may impose any reasonable condition upon holding offices within its control."[24]

The critics admitted that no one has a constitutional right to be a government employee and that the government can make reasonable restrictions concerning employment. They said, however, that to deprive a person arbitrarily of an opportunity to gain such employment, especially given the lack of a clear and present danger to the country, transgresses the important right of equal opportunity. Some cited the Supreme Court ruling in 1945 that to proscribe anyone from serving the government is "punishment, and of a most serious type."[25]

The federal loyalty program was duplicated by the states, supplementing already-existing criminal syndicalism and antisedition laws. Thirty-two states had loyalty oaths for teachers, and twenty-eight barred "subversives" from public employment. The pervasive loyalty screenings spilled over into defense industries and other private companies (as in the Federal Republic). Even the American Bar Association adopted a loyalty oath for its members; Indiana required it of barbers, junk dealers, and professional wrestlers; and Texas required it of every schoolbook author.[26] The American Civil Liberties Union barred communists and fascists from serving on its governing councils and staff and did not welcome them as members.

Thus, the star-chamber proceedings of the McCarthy senatorial hearings and government loyalty investigations engendered a repressive atmosphere that wrecked the professional lives of thousands and helped to create a mood of conformity and fear at the height of the Cold War. This was especially true among civil servants, who became less outspoken and more timid and whose morale was affected, and among university students who intended to pursue a public career. As in the Federal Republic, the loyalty investigations contributed to the decline in the number of students who became activists, joined student organizations, or signed petitions.

In reviewing this period of American history, Walter Millis aptly wrote: "The pursuit of the communist heresy in our midst had become in itself a heresy against the basic principles of American life. In the tenth year of the international cold war, the cold war at home was raising more perils to the

American system than any still to be apprehended from international communism or the Soviet Union."[27]

The Supreme Court had contributed to the illiberal atmosphere through its decisions supporting loyalty oaths, investigations of associations, disbarment of lawyers, and other restrictive measures, although Justices Hugo Black, William O. Douglas, and Earl Warren dissented vigorously. But from 1956 on, the Court rendered more liberal verdicts. In the 1956 *Young* decision, it limited the federal loyalty-security program to sensitive positions. In the 1957 *Service* decision, it ruled that the dismissal of a civil servant had violated the substantive and procedural rules of the department concerned. In the 1957 *Yates* decision, the Court reversed the convictions under the Smith Act (1940) of leading Communist party officials whom it had found guilty in 1951 (*Dennis* decision) of conspiring to teach and advocate the violent overthrow of the government. In *Yates,* it asserted that whereas advocacy of action to overthrow the government by force and violence would have justified conviction, advocacy of mere belief did not. (Justices Black and Douglas opposed conviction for either variety of advocacy.)[28]

Although the Supreme Court decisions contributed to a more liberal climate on civil liberties in the late 1950s, other factors also helped to staunch McCarthyism. The decline of the Cold War, public awareness of the gross injustices produced by McCarthy and the loyalty programs, and the realization that the minuscule Communist party did not represent an immediate threat to national security all played a role in expanding the sphere of individual freedoms.

Yet, the score for civil liberties in the United States since the 1950s is not as high as many observers had hoped. Most requirements of loyalty oaths and screenings of federal and state government employees have remained. As noted above, up to 1952 over 4 million people were screened. But the figures pale in comparison with the loyalty screenings of those who worked in defense and other industries. According to one study, by 1957 an estimated one-fifth of the nation's labor force, or 13.5 million persons, had been screened or checked for loyalty as a condition of employment. At least ten thousand persons had been ousted for political reasons; as in the Federal Republic, they had to shift to less rewarding and less challenging jobs.[29] Others who were retained did not get salary increases or promotions and were treated as second-class citizens.

In addition, civil liberties have been curtailed for radical groups and individuals who are vigorous critics of the administration's foreign policies but who constitute no threat to internal security. Radicals continue to be harassed by the FBI, which has used illegal means of surveillance against them. Such harassment increases the sphere of authoritarian controls.

Conclusion

The parallels between the U.S. and West German loyalty programs for its public employees are strong, including the similar political climate in which they flourished. They peaked in intensity at different times—in the United States in the 1950s and in West Germany in the 1970s—but in each country restricted individual liberties of some of its citizens. There were differences too, such as strong legal safeguards available to West German applicants, which was less true in the United States.

Other West European countries, some with sizable communist parties, have not been overconcerned with the loyalty of civil servants. This is one reason why the CDU/CSU has urged Christian Democratic and other conservative parties to introduce their own decree against radicals in their countries. Its efforts so far have been unsuccessful, because the other states have assumed that their public servants will be loyal to the state and have worried less about allowing radicals who might undermine the constitutional order into their civil service system. Hence, these civil servants need not be more loyal to the state than is the average citizen, as they must be in the Federal Republic. Even though few are turned away from nonsensitive posts, all countries deny radicals entry into sensitive posts, most without giving reasons. This procedural secrecy, less pronounced in West Germany, creates a gray zone of uncertainty for applicants. Most countries have no provisions allowing them to appeal unfavorable decision in the courts.

Despite these negative aspects, other West European countries have been more liberal than the Federal Republic in allowing radicals into the public service. Yet, as daily newspaper reports show, their score on civil liberties violations in general (e.g., the British Northern Ireland problem), and their treatment of minorities and foreigners in particular, is hardly better, if not worse, than that of West Germany. It lies outside the scope of this study to explore such violations in countries other than West Germany (to be examined in the next chapter). Suffice it to say that causes for repression are multifaceted and vary from one state to another dependent on historical and cultural makeup, the existence of religious and ethnic minorities, the strength of a civil liberties tradition, and other factors.

8

Civil Liberties in the Federal Republic

This volume has focused on the 1972 decree as a case study of the attempt by West German governments to preserve the political, economic, and social status quo by keeping political radicals out of its public service and removing some of those already in it. Restricting our inquiry in this chapter primarily to the most important developments in the broad civil liberties sector—ranging from private employment to the census controversy—in the 1970s and 1980s, we must ask if the attempt at system maintenance through the 1972 decree was an isolated repressive move against dissidents or part of a wider pattern of suppression, first, of efforts by left and right radicals to gain more strength in the Federal Republic, and second, of efforts by concerned citizens to stop the growth of an increasingly powerful state whose executive, legislative and judicial branches are seen as imperiling or restricting the civil liberties of its population.

Repression in the Private Sector

The answer is clear: a pattern of discrimination against left radicals in particular has been widespread, especially during the periods of turmoil in the 1970s. Such discrimination has not been restricted to the public sector; taking their cues from government actions sanctioned by the 1972 decree, many private-sector employers did not hire young radical activists or tried to purge those already on their payrolls.

One survey of eighty personnel chiefs of the largest West German firms found that for their upper-level job openings they preferred to hire university graduates who were sympathetic to the business community rather than to Marxist dialectics. Thus, students who had graduated from one of the universities noted for radical studies (Berlin, Bremen, Frankfurt, Heidelberg, and Marburg) had little chance. This practice was unfair to all applicants, including the conservative students, who often had no choice as to the university where they could study.[1]

The Hamburg Steel Works typified a company screening applicants for blue-collar as well as upper-level vacancies. Names were sent to the Hamburg *Verfassungsschutz* for a check on whether the applicant had engaged in any previous radical and union activities. If damaging information existed, the applicant was not hired, and the information was forwarded to other employers in the metal industry.[2] In Schleswig-Holstein, the *Verfassungsschutz* maintained contact with twenty firms to provide them with data on applicants. The data, mostly collected in schools, universities, and youth organizations, led to blacklisting of a number of radicals or to DKP employees' being inhibited in their political activities.[3]

Other publicized examples included the *Stuttgarter Zeitung*'s dismissal of one of its employees for becoming a DKP candidate for public office. In another case, the Federal Labor Court in 1972 supported the dismissal of an employee who in his spare time had distributed a DKP flyer assailing his bank and banks in general.[4] When the *Verfassungsschutz* also began to monitor the results of shop-council elections throughout the Federal Republic to see whether radical workers had won, Eugen Loderer, chairman of the Metal Workers Union, protested to Minister of the Interior Baum that the "outrageous" action was intimidating to unionists, who could take care of their own affairs.[5]

Private schools were hardly more liberal than their public counterparts in hiring radicals. One communist teacher, dismissed from the public school for his membership in a small communist party, applied to fifty private schools for a position. All rejected him except one Catholic private school, which hired him but discharged him one week later when it received a warning from the CDU-controlled Ministry of Education in Baden-Württemberg that the school's public subsidy would be canceled and its legal status would be withdrawn if he was kept on the payroll.[6]

In CDU-ruled Rhineland-Palatinate, the Catholic Bureau in Mainz and the diocesan authorities permitted the Ministry of Education to screen applicants for teaching posts in its private schools. The screenings also covered part-time teachers who gave Catholic religious lessons in public schools. A bishop in Münster did not permit a teacher of religion who had been a Marxist to be on the staff of a Catholic school. In Protestant churches, some ministers lost their positions for making alleged radical statements in their sermons.[7]

Although these cases of discrimination against left radicals in the primarily private sector, ranging from industry and schools to the churches, provide further proof of repression, most radicals found employment sooner or later. But many had to change profession or accept a lower-paying job. The psychological effect of not being hired in, or of being dismissed from, one's preferred profession, followed in some instances by blacklisting, often on the basis of information in a *Verfassungsschutz* dossier to which the individual had no access or means of defense, was most damaging.

Terrorism

As noted in chapter 2, from 1968 on, a wave of mainly left-wing terrorism produced further repression against left radicals who were not directly involved. Although the terrorism did not compare with that of Weimar, when 376 political assassinations took place between 1918 and 1922, it resulted in one decade in 28 assassinations, 93 persons injured, 15 hostages taken, as well as numerous bombings, arson, bank robberies, and burglaries of weapons and explosives.[8]

These terrorist acts were perpetrated at first by one small SDS faction of desperate individuals who, enraged by police violence against student demonstrators in Berlin in 1967 and 1968, were intent on producing societal upheavals by illegal acts, including assassinations of representatives of the government and business communities whom they identified as "agents of imperialism." The terrorists, members of the Baader-Meinhof group, later known as the Red Army Faction (RAF), as well as other small rival groups, had no hope of gaining the support of the majority of radicals. Most terrorists were caught and sentenced to prison terms. From 1970 to 1978, 215 persons were convicted of terrorism, 94 were under investigation, and 42 were still being hunted.[9]

Yet, because terrorism arose initially out of the left movement and because terrorists did receive assistance in the late 1970s from several hundred leftist sympathizers, conservative leaders and newspapers exaggerated the linkage. They tarred communists and SPD left-wingers as terrorist sympathizers, and pastors Martin Niemöller, Helmut Golwitzer, and SPD chairman Brandt as "spiritual instigators" of terrorism.[10] For instance, CDU theoretician Kurt Biedenkopf told a party meeting in September 1977: "Not only the terrorists are guilty. Those responsible for the situation we are in are the so-called liberals and left-wing intellectuals, whose only thought is to create insecurity in the population and to destroy the freedom-loving instincts in our society."[11] Franz Josef Strauss used the terrorism threat as an occasion to assail the governing parties: "SPD and FDP let criminals and political gangsters take over this government."[12]

These statements against the Left, the SPD, and the FDP were designed to create an illiberal atmosphere among the public, which would then be receptive to undoing the domestic reforms of the social-liberal governments—including an expansion of civil liberties—and to voting CDU/CSU. One leftist writer noted, "Terror can only destroy the in-roads of those progressive groups who had partially succeeded in entering the civil service and educational institutions to offer new alternative ways of thinking to the younger generation."[13]

The setback to the progress made by leftist forces in the public sphere had of course other causes as well—economic stagnation, fewer jobs, resignation and apathy, less interest in public affairs and progressive causes—but terrorism and the subsequent antiterrorist legislation were important factors. Carl Amery, a leftist intellectual, estimated that terrorism set back West German progress toward democracy by at least ten years.[14]

Antiterrorist Legislation

Any democratic government must of course protect itself against terrorists who are not inhibited in the use of violence to seek its overthrow. In the Federal Republic, criminal statutes have always provided an array of penalties for those caught by the police on information supplied by intelligence services. But during the height of terrorist activities, the SPD-FDP government contended that existing statutes did not suffice to curb terrorism.

Aware of the favorable reception the public gave to CDU/CSU calls for law and order but also intent on projecting an image of toughness, the government asked Parliament to pass new legislation. Precipitating this request was an accusation against twenty left-wing lawyers of having aided jailed terrorists by passing communications to those on the outside and by other acts violating the Code of Criminal Procedure and an accusation against sixty lawyers of having "slandered the state" or shown "disrespect for the court" in their defense of members of the Baader-Meinhof group. Parliament from 1974 to 1978 passed a number of amendments to the code, such as Section 138a, which grants the government the power to bar lawyers from defending certain clients if there is suspicion that the lawyers have misused communication with those jailed "for the purpose of endangering the security of a house of detention." Other revisions allow a lawyer to defend only one client in a case, restrict lawyers from making "irrelevant" statements in court, permit a judge to see written notes between a lawyer and a client if the latter is accused of terrorism, and grant authorities the right to monitor telephone and telegraph calls of lawyers suspected of supporting a criminal organization.[15]

In September 1977, in the aftermath of the kidnapping of Hanns-Martin Schleyer, the president of the employers association, and prior to his murder in October, the federal and Länder ministers of justice ordered the isolation of about a hundred prisoners accused of supporting, or being members of, a terrorist organization. They could no longer receive newspapers, listen to the radio, send or receive letters, and talk to or correspond with their lawyers.[16] This practice was swiftly legalized by Parliament, which enacted the Contact Ban Law, popularly known as the solitary confinement law. It grants authorities the right to bar prisoners accused of or guilty of terrorism from having any contact with one another, with their lawyers, or with the outside world for thirty days—and is renewable.

The governing parties during the Bundestag vote on the law could not gain the support of all their members—a rare occurrence. Breaking party discipline, four left-wing SPD deputies voted against the bill, while sixteen other SPD and FDP deputies abstained. The four SPD dissidents stated that they could not in good conscience vote for legislation that would limit the civil liberties of any individual. Thus, they said they were upholding the FDGO. Manfred Coppik, one of the four deputies, asserted: "Anyone who still says, 'What's it got to do with me? I am not mixed up with terrorists,' must be told clearly that under the new law no one, however innocent, can be sure of not being imprisoned as a result of denunciation and vanishing into a prison for weeks and months without contact with a lawyer or even with his relatives. In terms of the rule of law, I consider this intolerable."[17]

In an angry reply, Herbert Wehner, SPD Fraktion chief, characterized the dissenting votes of the party's deputies as a grave breach of Fraktion discipline. He noted that the great majority of the Fraktion had supported the Federal Republic. Fifteen dissidents, in a written reply to Wehner, argued that they were acting in the best interests of the country. Thereupon, nearly two hundred SPD deputies signed a letter of support for Wehner, whom they praised for having upheld the principles of democracy in the Bundestag.[18]

Opponents of the Contact Ban Law challenged its constitutionality in the Federal Constitutional Court but lost out. Former members of the Baader-Meinhof group also contended in an appeal to the European Commission of Human Rights that their isolation in prison cells had violated their rights under the European Human Rights Convention. The commission did not support their position.[19]

In 1978, new antiterrorist legislation authorized the police to ask persons in public buildings and public transport for identification, even if there was no suspicion of their having committed a crime. Failure to show identification could mean being held for up to twelve hours, during which persons would be fingerprinted, photographed, and have other means used to establish their identities. The police also received authorization to search all apartments in a building in which a terrorist might be hiding, to engage in wiretapping, and to stop and search motorists at control points set up in "dangerous" areas. To cope with the increased police activity, the number of federal border guards had risen in earlier years, from 22,673 in 1969 to 28,901 in 1976 (a 27.5 percent increase), and the number of police agents from 132,386 in 1969 to 176,267 in 1976 (a 33.1 percent increase). To maintain internal security, the police force also received new technological equipment, became more heavily armed, and was authorized to use machine guns and hand grenades if necessary.[20]

The new antiterrorist legislation giving the police more powers did not go unchallenged in the Bundestag. In February 1978, the CDU/CSU voted against the bill because it was not tough enough, and four left-wing SPD deputies voted against it because it was too stringent and was likely to violate civil liberties. The bill passed with only a slim majority but was blocked by the CDU/CSU-dominated Bundesrat. This time, the left-wing SPD deputies' votes were needed in the Bundestag to override the veto. They reluctantly voted for the bill to prevent the fall of the SPD-FDP government, which would then be replaced by a more conservative Christian Democratic government intent on taking tougher actions against terrorists.[21]

A number of SPD leaders, including Chancellor Schmidt, viewed the actions of the dissident SPD deputies as being close to treason, especially when the survival of the government was at stake. Some right-wing SPD deputies wanted the party to oust the dissidents for breaking party discipline in the Bundestag. But the dissidents felt that conservative SPD deputies should heed their warnings to stop supporting bills that seriously infringed on civil liberties. The dissidents noted that the original government bill had called for longer periods of detention and had given the police the power to comb an entire neighborhood without search warrants, until legislative leaders realized that the majority of deputies would not support such a bill.[22]

Nor did the majority support CDU/CSU legislative proposals to give the police the right to shoot to kill, rather than wound or incapacitate, suspected terrorists and to wiretap districts where terrorists might be hiding. The failure of some CDU/CSU proposals did not mean that a liberal atmosphere emerged. On the contrary, in the months following October 1977 a virtual national emergency existed; the police stopped and searched hundreds of thousands of motorists at control points and appealed to the population to report suspicious persons who suddenly changed their addresses, cut their hair or made other cosmetic changes, or who mailed suspect publications.[23]

Government officials discussed further legalization of emergency procedures, such as entering the names of demonstrators into the computerized intelligence files and, once again, allowing police searches of entire neighborhoods in case of a terrorist action. With the nation on practically an emergency footing, the media and the political parties helped to create a law-and-order atmosphere. Society became polarized, as young men with long hair were suspected of being "waterboys of terrorism." According to the conservative *Die Welt,* those who spoke against "capitalism," including left-wing Social Democrats, were guilty of creating a "sliding transition" to the kidnapping of business leaders.[24]

Thus, as noted, radical democrats and left-wing intellectuals who opposed terrorism on moral principles and because of the dangers to civil liberties that it posed were identified by conservatives as spiritual instigators or sympathizers of terrorism. In response, Nobel Prize novelist Heinrich Böll, who was one of the democrats singled out, said, "We have simply had it. Until now they have been trying to intimidate us with blanks, but it won't be long before they start using real ammunition. We must start fighting right now to preserve what little remains of the *Rechtsstaat.*"[25] The liberal weekly *Die Zeit,* in agreement, wrote, "If the opposition [CDU/CSU] had its way, our whole life would change, and the *Rechtsstaat,* which we are trying to defend, would cease to exist."[26]

Yet, the blame for restrictions on the rights of individuals must also be placed on the SPD-FDP government, which through its hastily drafted legislation contributed to the erosion of civil liberties. Such a policy made it more likely that the police and intelligence agencies would commit abuses, as was shown in the 1975 illegal entry and wiretapping of the residence of a leading atomic scientist, Klaus Traube. The government lost its case in court when the wiretap records exonerated Traube from the charge of having had conspiratorial links with terrorists. Despite his court victory, however, he was discharged from his position as a top manager of the nuclear development firm Interatom, after the police had accused him of having close links with one of the lawyers defending members of the Baader-Meinhof group, having been a Communist party member at age seventeen, and having an "unusual" private life (he was divorced).[27] The liberal media not only publicized the Traube affair but also, at the height of the terrorist scare, criticized the police for using excessive and brutal force on a number of occasions, killing at least one innocent person as a result of a mistaken identity.[28]

During the last two years of the SPD-FDP government (1980–82), the Free Democrats increasingly objected to some of the precipitous antiterrorist legislation that they had supported in the 1970s. During the formation of the SPD-FDP government in 1980, the SPD promised them that it would back amendments ensuring suspects legal protection during the investigation of a terrorist crime. But the SPD, eager to identify itself with a strong state, opposed the abrogation of the Contact Ban Law.

In the 1980s, terrorist group actions became less frequent, partly because of the arrest of most of their leaders. Yet, after Chancellor Kohl took office in 1982, Minister of the Interior Zimmermann called for a tightening of security laws. FDP ministers initially opposed his plan but subsequently made compromises.

This tightening occurred, for instance, in the aftermath of the RAF assassination of a Foreign Office senior career official (Gerold von Braunmühl) in October 1986, when the Bundestag passed another package of antiterrorist laws. One law granted terrorists a chance to turn state's witness against their colleagues and receive reduced sentences or amnesty—a provision that had been dropped from an earlier bill when the FDP refused to endorse it.

Other laws called for longer prison sentences for members of, or assistants to, a terrorist group and for persons found guilty of attacks on transportation carriers and public utilities. Still other laws made instruction in violent methods a criminal offense, expanded the powers of the federal prosecutor in terrorist cases, and gave the police access to the data banks of the Federal Motor Vehicle Office for the purpose of tracking down terrorists. The laws received the support of the CDU/CSU and most FDP deputies (three abstained), but deputies of the SPD and the Greens voted against them because the laws were broader than necessary.[29] Civil libertarians were also opposed to possible infringements on individual rights.

In 1986, one incident lightened the seriousness of events. The CDU government in Lower Saxony, as supportive of law and order as Bonn and other Länder, was embarrassed by the disclosure during the election campaign that it had authorized a police antiterrorist squad to dynamite a hole in the wall of the Celle jail where terrorists were housed and then had blamed the action on terrorists on the outside who intended to free their colleagues.

Even though the opposition parties made political capital out of this incident, the fight against terrorism was one in which no party (other than the Greens) wanted to be trumped by any other. Therefore, the parties swiftly passed new laws to promote internal security. According to critics, these were mostly unnecessary and did not improve it but, on the contrary, increased the fears of citizens.

Such fear is graphically described by Heinrich Häberlein, who had been implicated in the 1972 decree (see chapter 5). In April 1978, in a letter to a friend, he wrote:

> About nine months ago—that was last summer—I sat at my desk at the window, from where I can see the street, and I saw a police car stop in front of the house. The policemen stayed in their car for a while, then got out and walked a bit to and fro. I got terribly afraid; I thought: now I'll also get entangled in the hunt for terrorists. In such a situation, you imagine the most horrible things. A Munich incident came to my mind, where someone was simply shot through the door and killed because he didn't open fast enough.
>
> I thought of a house search and of preliminary arrest. Rapidly, I searched through my mind: What could be held against me? Had I illegally posted bills recently? Had I taken part in a public demonstration, which ran into trouble? Did I have any connection with people accused of being sympathizers of terrorists?
>
> The policemen rang the bell and came up the stairs. I was quite distraught and at first could not even listen to what one of them was saying. I forced myself to be calm, but as I said—I was afraid. Then it transpired that some weeks ago, when I had been in Zurich, I had run through a red traffic light. The policemen had simply come to hand me a warning ticket from their Swiss colleagues.
>
> For a long time afterwards I sat there and my whole body shook. Now you know I am rather robust. One of my friends keeps saying I have the hide of an elephant. After such an experience, however, you feel quite washed-out.[30]

Censorship

In January 1976, at the height of the terrorist scare, the Bundestag unanimously approved Paragraph 88a, the Law for the Protection of Communal Peace (also known as the Anticonstitutional Advocacy Law), which amended the existing criminal law statute, effective May 1. The minister of justice in justification contended that it would curb violence and "its verbal preliminaries." It provides for a maximum three-year jail sentence for those who produce, distribute, publicly display, and advertise materials that recommend unlawful violent acts—such as disturbing the peace in special (e.g., armed) cases, murder, manslaughter, robbery, extortion, arson, and the use of explosives.[31]

When Paragraph 88a was coupled with Paragraph 129 of the criminal law concerning a person's support for, or membership in, a criminal organization, which would be punished with a sentence of up to five years, censorship, primarily of books that might aid the terrorist cause, was legally justified. Thus authorities assumed that store owners who displayed and sold books written by members of terrorist organizations were supporting a "criminal organization." On August 18, 1976, the police at dawn searched the private homes of bookstore owners and managers in seven cities, as well as ten bookstores and a book distribution center. They confiscated numerous volumes that they considered subversive—but which could be found in most university libraries.[32]

In an earlier case, under a different criminal statute, a Berlin court had ordered the seizure of a political manifesto written by the Red Army Faction, published by a Berlin underground press and subsequently by a left-wing publishing house. The police confiscated all copies at the printer and in the stores and even attempted in some cases to find out who had bought them. On another occasion, copies of a German volume about the Haymarket affair in Chicago were seized in West German stores on the ground that they contained descriptions "of how explosives can be produced with the help of dynamite."[33]

In other instances, bookstores and publishing companies throughout the Federal Republic that belong to a leftist trade association were searched, with occasional fines and jail sentences for their owners. The harassment extended to truck drivers prosecuted for transporting "dangerous" left-radical volumes from warehouses to dealers. The authorities insisted that the drivers should have known the content of the books they were carrying.[34]

One newspaper reported that *Verfassungsschutz* informants had checked on the names of borrowers of suspect volumes in public libraries.[35] Such scare tactics and intimidation had the intended effect of making radicals more cautious and other youth more conformist, limiting freedom of expression for authors and restricting the printing and selling of some books. A few prominent intellectuals, such as Heinrich Böll, raised their voices in protest. Böll's novel *The Lost Honor of Katharina Blum,* which deals with a police and press campaign harassing an apolitical woman who had fallen in love with an alleged radical lawbreaker and helped him escape, reflected

Böll's ordeal and own fear for his safety. When a play based on the book was to be staged in Würzburg, the city authorities ordered its cancellation, stating that the political climate was not "peaceful" enough for its performance. Karl Carstens (later to become president of the Federal Republic) and other CDU chiefs urged the population not to buy or read the book and suggested that it should be put on a special index, if not banned altogether.

After the kidnapping of Schleyer, forty armed policemen of a special antiterrorist unit raided the Cologne apartment of Böll's son—a publisher, who was not involved in politics—and found nothing, after an anonymous telephone caller told police he had seen armed men enter the building. When the Bavarian radio the next day interviewed the elder Böll, he said that he doubted a raid would have taken place if the son of Franz Josef Strauss had been similarly involved. The Bavarian radio banned the interview as inflammatory and only aired it a week later, when it was accompanied by an editorial commentary.[36]

The Federal Border Guard, from 1976 on, registered the names of West German travelers leaving the country by air or land who were carrying any of 287 legal leftist publications or who were members of any of 239 leftist organizations. The lists of names were then transmitted to the *Verfassungsschutz*. In May 1978, when a liberal newspaper disclosed this and other constitutionally doubtful practices (listing the names of travelers between twenty and thirty-five years old who crossed the border several times from October 1977 on as possible contact persons for terrorists), Minister of the Interior Maihofer claimed not to have had any knowledge of such actions. He ordered the names on the lists to be erased immediately.

Left-wing SPD and FDP critics and several lawyers pointed out that the Federal Border Guard was enjoined by law from engaging in police activities; the government had thus broken the law by allowing it to serve as an unofficial arm of the intelligence service. Moreover, the compilation of lists of leftist journals, newspapers, and literature was an "unscrupulous limitation of freedom of thought."[37] In 1981, under pressure of the critics, the government rescinded the controversial Paragraph 88a granting it the right to curb materials inciting to violence. It realized that existing legislation would give it sufficient powers to meet its goals.

Censorship, self-censorship, or attempted censorship also extended to television, radio, and theater. The Saar television canceled a showing of Lina Wertmüller's film *Love and Anarchy*—the title alone caused concern among officials. On one West German television show, the script included the questions "But who started the violence [in the Federal Republic]? Did Ohnesorg shoot the policeman, or did the policeman shoot Ohnesorg first?" (The latter is correct. Benno Ohnesorg was killed in Berlin during a June 1967 student demonstration against the visit of the Shah of Iran. Ohnesorg's death precipitated subsequent terrorist acts.) The author of the television script was requested to eliminate the questions. When he refused, the network canceled the show. In Munich, Julian Beck, the American director of the Living Theater, was arrested for slandering the Federal Republic by accusing it of torture in connection with the treatment of terrorists in prisons.[38]

In an attempt to suppress some left-radical views, conservative city administrators, for instance, threatened to cut off state funds and subsidies or not make public space available to amateur theater groups that intended to stage plays deemed to be too incendiary. In broadcasting, one radio commentator (Hannes Heer), at the Third International Russell Tribunal (see below), spoke of the difficulties of reporting on the mass protests against the construction of a nuclear power plant at Brokdorf because the administrative council of North German Radio, at the request of its CDU members, had decided to examine all reporting on the power plant to ensure its "balance." This action came on the heels of a sharp protest by Minister-President Gerhard Stoltenberg (CDU) concerning a critical film about Brokdorf shown on television.

Heer also called attention to radio and television networks' prohibiting the broadcasting of a song that mocks the FDGO, another song for its "no-atomic-power" message, and a discussion of a DGB-published book, *In Our Factories,* for its "agitational" tone.[39] These examples of censorship or intimidation inducing self-censorship in the literary and artistic communities were government attempts to silence not only those who might be assisting terrorists but also radical critics of the system. The overreaction on the part of zealous administrators was counterproductive because it damaged the reputation of the Federal Republic as a bastion of democracy.

Their actions reinforced the critics' view that the Establishment was only too ready to repress dissident views in the name of fighting terrorism. In response, the authorities stated that they had the right to censor materials that would promote terrorism; they supported, for instance, the excision by the reputable German publisher Luchterhand of a section on how to make explosives in the German edition of Regis Debray's novel *The Loner.*[40] According to the authorities, such actions were necessary to safeguard the democratic system in the face of a serious terrorist threat.

Demonstrations

While terrorism and the censorship revolving around its axis continued to some extent in the 1980s, the focus of controversy turned to the new social movements, which protested an array of government policies ranging from the construction of nuclear plants and airport runways (at the expense of forests) to the deployment of U.S. intermediate-range missiles. Most demonstrations sponsored by ecology, peace, and antinuclear energy groups remained peaceful, on the premise that nonviolence is the best tactic, but some turned confrontational and violent when a small group of demonstrators did not abide by the premise or reacted to police brutality. Once the police or *Verfassungsschutz* agents began to film the demonstrators to identify radical leaders or to have evidence on participants using violence, a number of demonstrators began to wear masks to hide their identity.

Until 1982, the CDU/CSU put pressure, in vain, on the SPD-FDP governments to support legislation prohibiting the wearing of masks (except at carnival time). After the 1983 election, when the CDU/CSU-FDP scored a victory, Strauss insisted that Chancellor Kohl, in his coalition negotiations with the FDP, must gain some concessions from the FDP on civil liberties issues—especially given Strauss's agreement not to be given a cabinet post. The FDP reluctantly accepted modification of a pending contested demonstration bill, especially when the CDU/CSU agreed to relax the Contact Ban Law by allowing a bipartisan authority to provide legal support for terrorist prisoners.

In June 1985, the Bundestag passed the demonstration bill, which prohibited the wearing of masks and clothing intended to prevent authorities from identifying the wearer and prohibited the carrying of "protective" weapons (slingshots, stones, and so forth) to counter police measures at public gatherings or demonstrations. The bill made it a criminal offense, with a maximum one-year sentence or a fine, for a person to refuse a police order to remove a mask or weapon or to refuse to disperse if a demonstration turns violent. On the other hand, peaceful protesters were guaranteed the right to demonstrate, even if authorities had reason to anticipate that individual protesters or a small group might instigate violent incidents. In the same month, the Federal Constitutional Court ruled unconstitutional a ban that local authorities had imposed in 1981 on a planned march at the construction site of the Brokdorf nuclear power plant.[41]

In November 1987, a small demonstration took place at the Frankfurt airport, marking the sixth anniversary of the police razing of a shantytown that had been put up as a protest against the proposed new runway. The gathering turned violent when the riot police tried to disperse the crowd. Thereupon, an unknown demonstrator killed two policemen. The police eventually arrested and charged a sympathizer of the anarchist group "Autonome" with the murders and held one accomplice. The Autonome members have no links to terrorists but have turned against a society that has not provided them with jobs or much hope for the future. Many travel from one demonstration to another, where they march in a "Black Bloc" (another name given to them), wearing ski masks, black helmets, and black clothes. They are ready to do battle with the hated police, symbolic to them of agents of the omnipotent state. The *Verfassungsschutz* estimates that of the approximately three to nine thousand members and supporters, from fifteen hundred to two thousand are militants who are ready to use force.[42]

The shootings of the police at the airport, the first time ever that such an incident occurred in a political demonstration, precipitated calls by Zimmermann and other CDU/CSU ministers for still sterner legislative measures against violent participants. Some demanded the right of police to use rubber bullets. They contended that demonstrations had become increasingly violent; the record showed that 139 policemen had been injured in 1984, and 818 two years later. FDP ministers, who in the past had asserted that existing laws were sufficient to curb violent demonstrators and yet protect civil liberties, were willing to discuss tougher legislation, especially after an emergency party convention in December gave them such authority by a vote of 210 to 185. (A majority of the FDP executive committee and the Bundestag Fraktion voted against the resolution.) The SPD and Greens rejected the proposed new laws, while distancing themselves from violence. SPD leader Vogel denounced the militants for bringing peaceful marchers into discredit and called on organizers of marches to isolate the militants and not allow them to hide in demonstrations. A deputy of the Greens declared that the law prohibiting masks had not prevented the killings; in this instance the assailant apparently had not worn one. The deputy called for dialogue with the Autonomen to convince the militants to stop using force.[43]

In a cabinet session of December 2, Zimmermann demanded that the law banning face masks be changed from a misdemeanor (the chief reason why police did not try to enforce it) to a felony as one way for the police to be less handicapped in their fight against militants. He also called for the reintroduction of an old Land breach-of-peace law and the issuance of measures to include better equipment for the police and the formation of more combat police units (*Einsatzreserven*). Continued disputes between CDU, CSU, and FDP ministers on specific changes delayed cabinet approval of a new bill until May 1988. It penalizes individuals who call for the use of force against state agents; increases penalties for taking hostages, stealing weapons and explosives, and seriously interrupting public services; obliges demonstration organizers to coordinate plans with the authorities; heightens penalties for wearing face masks and carrying weapons at outdoor meetings and demonstrations; penalizes calls for persons to join forbidden or dissolved assemblies; and provides for relief to terrorists who turn state's evidence.[44]

In March 1989, the Bundestag committees on legal and domestic affairs approved the cabinet bill, in which the CDU/CSU committee members made some concessions to FDP members. The revised bill allows the police to record demonstrations on film and sound only when the protesters pose a substantial danger to public safety and order. Such records must be immediately destroyed unless they are needed for the "prosecution of a criminal offense" by a participant. In spring 1989, the bill received Bundestag approval, with the SPD, Greens, and several FDP deputies in opposition.[45]

The *Verfassungsschutz*

Although the police and the Federal Criminal Investigation Bureau (*Bundeskriminalamt*) were the chief agencies fighting terrorists and militant demonstrators, the *Verfassungsschutz* was also involved, even though its primary functions are to track foreign spies in the Federal Republic and to keep a watch and disseminate information on left- and right-extremist organizations and their members (see chapter 3). Critics of the 1972 decree warned that the *Verfassungsschutz* had expanded out of proportion to any actual threat to the state. In 1972, it installed an integrated data system, which is also at the disposal of other intelligence services, collecting information over the years on more than 2 million citizens, many of them tagged as being loyalty risks. It also has access to computerized records of public libraries, universities, and the personnel departments of the public services and governments of the Länder. It makes and stores films of all demonstrations, including trade-union sponsored ones, and does not destroy films of those demonstrations that remained peaceful. Although the *Verfassungsschutz* is nominally accountable to the ministries of the interior, the federal and Länder parliaments have little direct control over it.[46]

The critics have also charged that the *Verfassungsschutz* has too many people on its payroll who are former Nazis and current CDU/CSU members, accounting for its strong anticommunism. It has been involved in scandals, including the defection of a senior official (Hans Joachim Tiedge), who fled to the GDR because of personal problems. It has compiled dossiers on some Green and possibly left-wing SPD deputies because of their alleged connections with terrorists.[47] After 1982, Zimmermann and *Verfassungsschutz* president Heribert Hellenbroich began a campaign to defame peace-movement adherents as constitutional enemies who were led astray by communists paid by the East and to criticize the Protestant church for participating in the movement.[48] Rebutting the critics, government and *Verfassungsschutz* officials have underscored the agency's fidelity to the democratic state and its strictly legal operations.

Data Banks

Civil libertarians have been concerned about the proliferation of data banks in the intelligence services, police, and criminal investigation bureaus. Intelligence agents can draw on Länder and city data banks, which contain up to 400 entries per citizen; university data banks that can provide the names of suspect students, such as those enrolled in social science seminars; Länder and university library records that reveal the reading habits of borrowers (forbidden in Hesse); government personnel record centers and Länder educational computer banks that contain the results of psychological tests and IQ profiles; and data banks of agencies dealing with social welfare, social insurance, foreigners, finance, resident registration, and motor vehicles.[49]

This battery of computer banks provides the government with increased facilities for data gathering on every resident in the Federal Republic. At the height of the terrorist scare and thereafter, the intelligence agencies justified the need for massive data gathering as an important means of protecting the constitutional order and the internal security of the country. While most citizens did not take issue with these goals, they were worried about the misuse of data and the names of innocent persons stored in intelligence computer systems. According to 1986 security legislation, the police are required to transmit to the Federal Intelligence Service (*Bundesnachrichtendienst*) in Munich any information that might be used in the foreign and security aspects of intelligence. The police thereby could relay massive amounts of data to prevent any charge that they were withholding information. In turn, intelligence services can require law enforcement agencies to send data without justifying their request.

The legislation contains a number of safeguards. The authorities may not set up joint computer files, and the intelligence services may not have joint computers. If intelligence authorities refuse to divulge to an individual the information they possess on him or her, they must allow data protection officials access to the file. Data on juveniles under sixteen may be stored in paper files but may not be computerized. Such data can be exchanged with other agencies only to prevent an act of violence. Finally, authorities that relay data from their computer files to other authorities must automatically notify them when data turns out to be inaccurate or incomplete.[50] But despite these safeguards, excesses in data collection and dissemination have occurred. Moreover, there is no provision in the legislation as to what facts may be collected—itself an invitation for further excesses.

From April 1987 on, after years of controversy, the government began to issue computer-readable, forgery-proof identity cards to every citizen and, beginning in January 1988, replaced expired passports with new ones to conform with an EC standardization requirement. Although the information on the cards and passports is limited to name, date of birth, nationality, and country of issue, authorities can rapidly gain more information about individuals from the multitude of data banks in public agencies and from control points set up at borders and near demonstrations and meetings of radical groups. Information about individuals gathered at these control points can, under law, be stored for up to nine months under certain circumstances, thereby increasing the chance that names of innocent individuals will end up in a computer of the Federal Criminal Bureau or a Land police agency.

Typical of the danger of innocents' being caught in the antiterrorist net was the demand by the Federal Criminal Bureau, seeking the whereabouts of terrorists, for electricity plants to release information to it about users who do not charge their electricity bills to their bank accounts but pay directly. It turned out that not only the few terrorists availed themselves of this practice (in their case, to hide the fact of irregular use of electricity in an apartment—gone one day, only to return weeks or months later) but also thousands of innocent persons (fifteen thousand in Hamburg and thirty thousand in Munich alone).[51]

New technologies present an increasing danger of the government's watching over every individual. In March 1987, a security law went into effect that permits the police, with the help of a central motor vehicle register in Flensburg and the use of a high-tech device, to identify instantly the owner of a vehicle, on the basis of its license number, without necessarily stopping it. Thus, authorities will have an increased capacity to gather data about the movements of individuals without their knowledge.[52]

Civil libertarians are also worried about further technological refinements putting people under total computer surveillance. It is conceivable that identity cards will be needed in the future to gain access to banks, work places, and public offices, with computers checking identity and storing data. Thus, the police could gain information not only for its lists of 200,000 people wanted for a host of major and minor crimes but for other people who may be suspect but are innocent.[53] Civil libertarians reject the police argument that more identity checks and data banks increase the security of all; they contend that existing procedures suffice to capture terrorists and other offenders who might use forged passports or identity cards.

In 1987, a television program confirmed the citizens' concern about the police filing more and more information in their computers without telling the public. In this instance, the police added to their file the information that some wanted persons were suffering from AIDS, to ensure that in case of a scuffle with a suspect, their personnel would not run the risk of contracting the disease. The critics contended that there had been no case in which the police ever contracted the virus; for agents to wear rubber gloves in such cases was discriminatory against persons who deserved sympathy and care.[54]

Surfacing time and again in the debates on data banks have been such questions as which persons and what information about them should be stored in files? how long should the data be preserved? who can use it? To protect citizens, Bonn and Länder created the posts of commissioners for data protection. But such a safeguard is no guarantee that the government and Parliament will stop drafting and approving new legislation expanding the sphere of internal security, including the increased use of data banks, at the expense of individual freedoms. When, in 1983, the Bonn commissioner for data protection, Hans-Peter Bull, was too outspoken and too critical of government data policy, Minister of the Interior Zimmermann summarily dismissed him.

As a result of popular criticism of the inherent dangers of data banks, the cabinet approved in December 1988 and sent to Parliament in 1989 a bill that would limit the collection of data in government computers, strengthen the right of citizens to get information on the storage and use of data about them, and provide compensation to them if there is a misuse. The bill also allows the military and federal intelligence agencies to gather data through intelligence methods but restricts such an activity to each service's area of competence. For reasons of national security, the agencies are to be exempt from the requirement to disclose information to citizens.

Zimmermann contended that the bill would offer citizens legal protection "like nowhere else in Europe" and hailed it as "progress in securing basic rights for the individual and in the rule of law." Yet, the four FDP ministers, including Minister of Justice Hans Adolf Engelhard, having reservations about the bill, stated that they would seek amendments in Parliament. Their view, shared by the opposition SPD and Greens, is that the intelligence services should not be exempt from the disclosure requirement. The Bonn commissioner for data protection, Alfred Einwag, said that the proposed measures would be a "step backward" in comparison to current practices if the law's safeguards dealing with data banks are not extended to paper files and data gathering.[55]

The Census Controversy

Closely linked to the debates concerning data banks was the emotion-laden debate over the 1980 census, which for budgetary reasons had to be postponed. In 1982, Parliament passed unanimously, with hardly any discussion, a law authorizing the census for 1983. This action sparked protests by the Greens and citizens initiative groups, which saw the census as another intrusion of the state into the private lives of its citizens. They objected to provisions in the law that would permit police and security agencies to compare the census data with individuals' domicile registration data, already on file with local authorities. Baum, former FDP minister of the interior, assailed CDU/CSU politicans for taking the initiative on the census, given widespread opposition to it, including within the FDP. He reminded them that Hitler had left a legacy of popular sensitivity to the state's prying into individuals' privacy. In defense of the CDU/CSU position, Zimmermann denounced the census critics as "a minority of extremists seeking to undermine the system."[56]

Undaunted by Zimmermann's remark, the critics, who composed a wide segment of the population, petitioned the Constitutional Court to halt the pending census. In April 1983, the court issued such a preliminary injunction; in December it ruled unanimously that the law's language had been too open-ended and did not set sufficient limits on the state's authority to question its citizens. It noted that the government cannot force persons to reveal information such as their telephone numbers in a census. It rejected a single identification number for each citizen, which could then be used to retrieve personal data from different files. The court regarded a provision in the law granting government agencies the right to share data unconstitutional. It also insisted that the federal and Länder commissioners for data protection must at all times be able to check whether precautions such as returning forms in sealed envelopes were being taken during the census. The court's decision, emphasizing the Basic Law's implied power guarantee under Article 2 to the individual of the "right of self-determination regarding personal information," meant that the cabinet and Parliament would need to amend the law to provide further protection against the unlimited collection, storage, use, and transfer of personal data.[57]

In mid-1984, the cabinet approved the draft of a revised law that all parties except the Greens sustained in Parliament in October 1985. SPD-governed Länder officials supported the census, rescheduled for 1987, as a means to update fifteen-year-old information, which in turn would help in the fair distribution of funds to communities. Yet, a public opinion poll published in 1985 showed that opposition to the census continued, as 30 percent of respondents said they would refuse to fill out a census questionnaire. These opponents included nearly two-thirds of Greens voters, one-third of SPD voters, 18 percent of CDU/CSU voters, and 17 percent of FDP voters.[58]

In 1987, the census was taken as scheduled, after a costly propaganda campaign by the government. Although many leaders of the Greens called for a boycott, it fizzled because of popular fear of supporting an illegal action, police harassment of census opponents (e.g., by confiscating their flyers), media rejection of paid advertisements supporting the boycott, and the threat of heavy fines for those refusing to fill out the questionnaire.[59]

The controversy over the census reflects the division within the Federal Republic between adherents of law and order and those desiring maximum freedom for individuals. In this instance, the Constitutional Court tilted toward the latter group by insisting on a census containing maximum safeguards for individual rights. For the Greens, the court's position did not go far enough; they would have preferred a categorical rejection of any census.

Human Rights Defenders

Although popular opposition to the census was strong for a time, the number of groups consistently opposing state infringements on personal freedoms has been more limited—a reflection of the weak civil libertarian tradition in Germany. One such group is the Humanist Union, which does not have a mass membership but has a solid record of fighting for civil liberties causes. It was deeply concerned about the stringent antiterrorist measures and the threats to individual freedoms of the Schmidt and Kohl governments. In 1979, in an open letter to top SPD and FDP authorities and all deputies, it stated, "The more political and legal freedoms the state leaves to its citizens, the more its domestic security increases." It viewed restrictions on freedoms as an opening for the Republic's enemies to put the nation into "twilight," giving grounds for fear about the rise of a police state engaged in torture of terrorists in prison.[60] (The charge of "torture" concerned the terrorists' protracted isolation, lack of daylight, restricted periods of exercise, and so forth, which led to serious psychological and physical consequences.)

Among other human rights groups in the Federal Republic is the German section of Amnesty International, which was upset about the fear of many Germans, given government surveillance, to sign its petitions calling for an end to torture of political prisoners in all countries. In 1979, the International's London headquarters issued a memorandum denouncing the ill-treatment of West German terrorists in prison. The memorandum, sent to the federal and Länder ministers of justice, recognized the need for special security but nevertheless called for a more humane solution to the treatment of terrorists, of whom over one hundred had been put in complete or semi-isolation cells, many for years.[61] Yet, in its 1980 report, Amnesty International, commenting on the antiterrorist legislation, stated that "legislation which [could] be used to restrict political criticism and the freedom of speech of the individual has not led to the adoption [by Amnesty International] of anyone as a prisoner of conscience."[62]

Another human rights group in the Federal Republic is the already-cited Committee for Basic Rights and Democracy, founded in 1979 to promote civil liberties in the Federal Republic. It received the support of about sixty well-known persons in public and intellectual life, who pledged to be active in achieving its goals. The committee not only criticized the 1972 decree but warned about the dangerous consequences of the antiterrorist legislation, the expansion of the intelligence services and the police, and the surveillance capabilities of data banks. The committee has also been concerned about the human rights of women and foreigners. It has issued a journal (since 1983 a yearbook) and documentation, holds conferences, provides help for those affected by government measures, and maintains contacts with other human rights organizations in Europe.[63]

Some citizens initiative groups, whose life span is often shorter than that of established nationwide organizations, also have been concerned about human rights violations. In addition to these one-issue groups, the SPD, FDP, and trade unions have occasionally been in the forefront of the struggle against human-rights restrictions and repression.

To assist some of these groups and publicize possible human rights violations, the Third International Russell Tribunal, which had criticized the 1972 decree in its first sessions (see chapter 5), dealt in its second sessions with censorship, the rights of legal defense in terrorist trials, and the activities of the *Verfassungsschutz*. The tribunal, meeting in Cologne from January 3 to 9, 1979, concluded that Federal Republic authorities were practicing censorship in the media, public libraries, bookstores, universities, and theater; that the antiterrorist legislation constituted a serious threat to human rights; and that the growth and practices of the *Verfassungsschutz* were a threat to the democratic state.[64]

It based these findings on the testimony of a number of specialists, including professors, lawyers, and media people. John Shattuck, then the director of the American Civil Liberties Union (later a vice president of Harvard University), read a statement concerning secret services in a number of countries. He criticized the FBI's intensive investigations of dissident political groups at the expense of economic and organized crime in the United States. He noted that there was evidence of cooperation between the *Verfassungsschutz* and American secret agencies, such as the FBI's request to German intelligence authorities to tap the telephones of some Americans in Berlin and Heidelberg. The tribunal received evidence of the intimidation of dissidents in a letter from an editor of North German Radio who wrote to the tribunal members that she could not appear because, after speaking with a lawyer, she was advised that her job might be endangered.[65]

The tribunal's deliberations and findings received little media coverage, primarily because most editors (and the government) decided that its work constituted an interference in the internal affairs of the Federal Republic. Gerhard Schröder, Juso chief, one of the few political leaders who defended the tribunal, lauded its devotion to the principles of political democracy and its criticisms of state repression. He called on civil libertarians to study the question of which economic and political interests in the Federal Republic stood behind the drive to limit freedoms.[66]

Public Opinion

Public reactions in the Federal Republic to terrorist actions, antiterrorist legislation, and restrictions on individual freedoms varied widely. As shown in the polls on the 1972 decree, the lack of a strong civil rights tradition is mirrored in polls indicating that a considerable segment of the population feels that the constitutional guarantees of free speech and expression should not be extended to political dissidents. In a 1972 poll, only about half of the respondents were sure or fairly sure that communists and Nazis had such constitutional rights.[67]

Terrorist actions generated a government- and media-inspired fear among a majority of the population, which in turn demanded the death penalty for terrorists (according to one poll, 67 percent of respondents).[68] In 1977, nearly two-thirds of the respondents (62 percent) in another poll were willing to accept restrictions on their personal rights through controls and house searches. Only 21 percent were opposed, while the rest were undecided or gave no answer.[69]

In a 1978 poll, 28 percent of respondents stated that the sphere of individual freedoms was being curtailed. Among these respondents, party preference made no significant difference. When asked to identify the cause(s) for this curtailment, 60 percent named terrorist threats; 43 percent, the consequences of economic difficulties, such as unemployment or a shortage of teaching jobs; 40 percent, state measures to combat terrorism; 35 percent, the 1972 decree against radicals; and 33 percent, the increase in suspicions as to who belongs to the circle of terrorist sympathizers.

When asked whether they personally had been affected by the curtailment of individual freedoms, 10 percent answered in the affirmative (projected nationally, this percentage would total 4.5 million of the adult population). Among respondents under thirty, from 15 to 18 percent gave the same answer. In this group, more than one-third of the students and apprentices contended that their freedoms had been narrowed. They were worried about jobs and their future, unlike most of the population, which was optimistic about the future.[70]

In a 1980 poll by the Munich Institute for Youth Research, Market and Public Opinion Research of persons between seventeen and twenty-nine, 54 percent said that freedom of speech existed in the Federal Republic, but 43 percent disagreed, noting that in school and on the job they "do not find it beneficial" to speak freely because they could be at a disadvantage.[71]

If there is cause for concern in these responses, it increases when answers to other questions in a 1978 Infas-Institute poll indicate that only about 20 percent of those interviewed paid attention to politics, while about 30 percent were indifferent.[72] Of course, a similar question in other democracies would produce similar responses, but given Germany's history, the low number of individuals worried about limitations on civil rights and the high number of apathetic and cynical individuals indicates a need to shore up popular commitment to a democratic system. There are indications, however, noted below, that citizens' interest in politics increased in the 1980s.

One indicator of a potential problem was activism among the Right, as seen in the growth of clandestine neo-Nazi groups and anti-Semitic outbreaks in response to terrorist actions. Another indicator was a poll taken in 1977–78, which showed that 26 percent of respondents yearned for a strong leader and 36 percent opted for "a single strong political party" to run the country.[73] With the decline in terrorism in the 1980s, it is doubtful that the percentages choosing such antidemocratic alternatives has remained that high.

Conclusion

This brief survey of the state of civil liberties in the Federal Republic has encompassed a number of the more important restrictions facing the citizens. It has touched on the difficulties encountered by some radicals in the private sector, terrorism producing fear in the population, antiterrorist legislation that has threatened individual rights, limited censorship in the arts and letters, expansion of the police and intelligence apparatus, constraints on the rights of political demonstrators, state surveillance, the controversy over the census, and new data technology that stores more and more information about every resident in the Federal Republic. (The survey has not touched on the human rights or discrimination problems facing the millions of foreigners living in West Germany, including those seeking political asylum, newly arrived ethnic Germans from Eastern Europe and the Soviet Union, women, and minority groups in society, such as homosexuals.)

Civil libertarians have warned that the restrictions on civil liberties are symptomatic of a society that fears challenges to the status quo and suspects potential troublemakers who do not conform to its standards. The restrictions date back to the SPD-FDP government, which precipitously enacted a series of internal security laws. The FDP, with its tradition of upholding individual rights, supported most of the repressive legislation, although it warned CSU minister of the interior Zimmermann (in office from 1982 to 1989) to moderate his extremist proposals to curb the civil liberties of dissidents.[74]

This chapter has focused on numerous instances of repression and increased state surveillance, which the government justified by its need to maintain internal security in the face of extremists threatening the basic order. While the maintenance of security is necessary when there is a real and grave threat to the state, there was no such threat during the terrorist scare. The authorities overreacted to the perceived threat, thereby limiting human rights and marring the Federal Republic's overall good record, equal to that of most other democratic countries, in upholding the civil liberties of its citizens under the rule of law. Such liberties include freedom of speech, press, assembly, and religion and an array of social and economic rights that an independent judiciary is pledged to protect as part of its constitutional task of guaranteeing fundamental rights. Yet, as the next chapter will show, constitutional theory and government practice do not always mesh in the case of political dissenters, especially when the government can pick and choose which and whose rights should be limited.

9

Conclusion

Centuries of experience testify that laws aimed at one political or religious group, however rational these laws may be in their beginnings, generate hatreds and prejudices which spread rapidly beyond control.... Restrictions imposed on proscribed groups are seldom static.

JUSTICE HUGO BLACK, 1950

In the name of promoting internal security, most national governments throughout the world, regardless of political system or ideology, have repressed political dissent that threatens the status quo. Totalitarian and authoritarian systems are the most guilty, but Western liberal democracies must share in the blame. Undoubtedly, repression will be more severe in a dictatorship, where the regime's opponents are likely to be arrested, tortured, and killed, than in a democracy, where the opponents are more likely only to be harassed; but there are disturbing parallels among various political systems in the excesses committed by domestic intelligence services, in state surveillance, and in the state's use of violence.

In the Federal Republic, in normal times, repression of dissidents is more subtle; for instance, in the way the government assails radical groups, which are presumed to threaten governing authorities, whether Christian Democrats or Social Democrats. When the Christian Democrats control the federal government, the Länder, and the cities, frequently they are more authoritarian and ready to restrict civil liberties than are the Social Democrats.[1] For instance, during the reform euphoria period from 1969 to 1972, Brandt's SPD-FDP government enacted a series of laws widening rather than narrowing the sphere of individual liberties.

It was, however, precisely during this period that the coalition agreed, for political and administrative reasons and because of the terrorist scare, to promulgate, together with the CDU/CSU, the 1972 Decree against Radicals. The decree became one of the best-publicized symbolic acts of repression, aimed primarily against communists (labeled extremists or radicals) who wanted jobs in the public sector. Although it was also aimed at neofascists, few were affected. This decree poisoned the domestic climate and led to a decade of protests, street demonstrations, political statements, and court decisions.

Among the causes of protest was the discriminatory nature of the decree; it was designed to exclude one segment of the population from enjoying guaranteed basic rights. This discrimination ran counter to the constitutional provision of the right of citizens to enter professions freely and to hold any political views. While the decree's opponents (the New Left, Jusos, and DKP, among others) cited these provisions to buttress their case that political repression and intolerance existed, the conservatives cited the constitutional provision and civil service legislation affirming the need for public servants to have a special loyalty to the state, stronger than that of the public. In turn, the decree's opponents criticized the concept of a civil service corps, representing the state, which tries to keep aloof from the pressures of society and which, after 1972, began to narrow the parameters of freedom of applicants to enter its ranks.[2]

The Decree's Defenders

Conservative defenders of the decree did not concur with the critics that the decree signified repression, lack of political tolerance, and an erosion of civil liberties. They contended that the legacy of Weimar—when NSDAP and KPD members of the civil service had undermined the republican regime—and the geographic propinquity of a hostile GDR after 1945 that sent its spies into the Federal Republic required a corps of loyal public servants who could be trusted to uphold the free and democratic basic order and the democratic state. As proof of the intent of the drafters of the Basic Law that the new state must not repeat the mistakes of Weimar, the defenders cited the "militant democracy" articles in the Basic Law, granting, among other provisions, power to the Constitutional Court to declare a political party unconstitutional if it is hostile to the FDGO. Public servants are expected to protect the citizenry against extremists who are ready to subvert the pluralist order based on the rule of law in order to establish instead a communist or fascist totalitarian dictatorship, which in turn would extinguish all freedoms.

The proponents argued that the West German and Länder governments must have uniform procedures for loyalty screenings to limit the entry of extremists into the public service. Members of the DKP, which received

GDR assistance, harbor heretical ideas, libel the government as oppressive, and want to overthrow the system. Whether they are nominal members or hold office in the party, they are supporting an organization whose avowed goal is a Marxist-Leninist dictatorship. Hence, CDU/CSU Länder officials bar DKP members from the service because, once admitted in increasing numbers until they formed a critical mass, they could begin to undermine the system and, in an emergency, sabotage installations, cut rail lines, and commit other illegal acts to precipitate the end of democracy.

The defenders furthermore contended that the continuing practice in CDU/CSU-ruled Länder of screening all applicants, as agreed upon in 1972, is the fairest system. The relatively small number of persons who are barred indicates that procedural safeguards to protect the rights of individuals were being observed. The defenders also asked the critics pointedly whether they were willing to keep only neofascists out of the service but allow communists in, on the premise that the latter do not constitute a threat to the democratic system.

The decree's supporters admitted that bureaucratic perfectionism had produced excesses but noted that these were inevitable in the mammoth loyalty screenings that took place. Such excesses, deplorable as they were, had been exaggerated by the critics to give the impression that the government was making potential applicants afraid to stray from the prevailing value system. The decree's implementation, including hiring noncommunist radicals, demonstrates that there is no basis for such fear. Moreover, excesses have in many cases been corrected by court decisions—further proof that the Federal Republic is neither a police state nor on the verge of succumbing to fascism, as charged by some opponents.

The decree's defenders cited the novelist Günter Grass, who, in accord with the view that the Federal Republic is not a police state, once declared: "I wish that other European countries had the courage to look at considerably lesser crimes in their own past and try to come to terms with them. It could be fatal for our neighbors if people keep insisting on the fiction that West Germany is fascist. It could lead to a counterreaction that would be difficult to control."[3]

The defenders also stated, with justification, that the Federal Republic has remained pluralist and democratic, has a functioning system of judicial review, and has seen the rise of citizens initiatives and peaceful protests that are accepted by the government. Moreover, according to the proponents, the government has not engaged in a witch-hunt against radicals who demand systemic reforms. The proponents declared that critics of the decree had overreacted to its minor defects and therefore had given the impression within the country and abroad that the decree, along with antiterrorist legislation, has made West Germany one of the most repressive societies in the West. On the contrary, there is often more discrimination, even if subtler and less overt, against extremists applying for top posts in the civil service in other West European states than in the Federal Republic. As proof that there is no significant repression, the proponents also cite the record of the European Court of Human Rights, which has rejected numerous complaints lodged against the Federal Republic for alleged violations of the European Convention for the Protection of Human Rights.[4]

The Decree's Critics

The critics in the moderate left camp concurred with the defenders that the democratic order is strong and must be preserved but disagreed about limiting the civil liberties of extremists in order to uphold internal security. They believed that allowing a relatively small number of communists and neofascists into the civil service would constitute no clear and present danger to the country. Should their number ever grow to dangerous proportions, then would be the time to bar them. Given the solid support of voters for the democratic parties since 1949, the likelihood of mass backing for the extremist parties is extremely slim. In any case, extremism must be fought on the terrain of politics rather than of civil liberties.

The government should assess why young people join extremist or radical parties and organizations. It would discover that many on the Left are not elitist or authoritarian in the Leninist sense but join the DKP or other communist organizations because of higher moral values (egalitarianism, solidarity, and justice) and because of disillusionment with the political, economic, and social system. Such leftists often provide the impetus for greater freedoms and more democracy. The critics want the state to be more open to reforms, thereby providing greater hope for youth and weakening the possibility of a new generation of terrorists emerging from a subculture of alienated youth.

The Times (London), supporting some of these arguments, contended that the 1972 decree was creating more rather than less dissent. It was difficult "for young people to work through a phase of radical idealism and move on to join the mainstream of society. They feel forced at too early a stage to make a crucial choice between opposition and conformity. If they choose opposition the way back is barred by the unforgiving records which they have accumulated."[5]

This conservative newspaper stated that the screenings and surveillance had taken on a life of their own, creating an atmosphere of distrust and intellectual conformity. "There is a danger that an excess of formalistic zeal in defending the democratic order will undermine its spirit if not its substance. A little more tolerance and pragmatism on the part of the authorities might be conducive to a similar spirit among its opponents."[6]

The Financial Times (London) declared that the Federal Republic was suffering "from a mild bout of authoritarianism." The decree was a "serious blot on the record of what remains one of the more attractive polities of Western Europe."[7]

Gustav Heinemann, former West German president, wrote shortly before his death, "The alarm must be sounded if radical criticism of the constitutional realities is thrown into the same pot as extremism hostile to the constitution."[8] Others denounced the government's mistrust of citizen loyalty to the state and said that citizens are quite capable of withstanding a possible, but most unlikely, subversion by a small group of extremists. The decree's opponents also warned about its aftermath—increasing collaboration between the secret service, police, and judiciary, which will intervene increasingly in the lives of the citizenry rather than protect them against arbitrary acts of the state. The result, Heinrich Böll prophesied, might be that "freedom and democracy will be extinguished in the name of freedom and democracy."[9]

Marxist and leftist critics denounced the decree as an instrument of social discipline, during a time of economic crisis in the capitalist system, against radical noncommunist and communist applicants to the public service. The governing authorities were eager to keep these applicants out of a corps of trusted bureaucrats who could be expected to defend the system against the increasing number of dissatisfied citizens. The bureaucrats remained allied to a declining centrist and conservative population that feared social conflict and change. One American critic noted, "A superstructure of democratic forms and civil liberties has been grafted onto a fundamentally authoritarian and illiberal political culture and society."[10]

The opponents claimed that the Establishment is bent above all on maintaining law, order, stability, and security; weakening Marxist parties and groups; and characterizing their relatively few members as enemies of the Basic Law. In seeking to prevent a socialist alternative to capitalism, the Establishment does not differentiate between the small number of fanatic revolutionaries and the numerous New Left radical democrats. It attempts to cement the societal status quo against a purported enemy—the radicals—whom it lumps together with revolutionaries and terrorists. In its pathological zeal to fight radicals, who to its dismay are not submissive and respectful of authority, it adopted an increasingly authoritarian stance to protect its legitimacy. Thereby it alienated those radical democrats and populists, often the children of bourgeois parents, who lead the struggle for more participatory democracy and responsive government. In 1972, they had no intention of marching through the institutions to destroy them; rather, they wanted to use them as a base to produce democratic changes.[11]

Most of the decree's opponents contended that the radicals are not a security risk; instead, the risk is the authoritarian state that curbs individual liberties. Hence Parliament, the Left, and civil liberties groups must, through publicity, expose the antilibertarian initiatives of the government. According to the opponents, the older, conservative civil servants have an interest in perpetuating such initiatives, because they feel threatened by younger colleagues who do not share their weltanschauung. Thus, the 1972 decree has served in recent years to restrict entry into the civil service to applicants who are conformists, nonactivists, and supporters of the neocapitalist system and who fit into the mold of a loyal corps of public servants. Yet, the critics maintained, these new civil servants may not be ready to defend the democratic order, should the necessity ever arise, but might become instead loyal supporters of an antidemocratic rightist regime. (Polls cited below, however, indicate the contrary.)

Domestic Politics

Defenders and critics of the decree have been engaged in battle since 1972, with some shift in position from defense to criticism among SPD and FDP leaders. But among CDU/CSU leaders and members there has been near unanimity in favor of the decree. The party has received support from numerous conservative newspapers and interest groups, which has strengthened its determination not to yield to pressures for changing its position.

In 1972, few would have predicted how controversial the decree was going to become. At the time, the CDU/CSU sought to conserve the traditional values of a liberal democracy and the power of the dominant capitalist class, which were challenged by the New Left movement. Taking the counteroffensive, the CDU/CSU charged that the SPD, having already absorbed most of the New Left youth into its ranks, would turn further left in its public policies in order to placate its left wing. CDU/CSU officials feared that this shift would adversely affect the interests of the party's business supporters. Therefore, one way, among many others, to prevent the SPD from shifting to the left was to lock it into support for the 1972 decree. The SPD was agreeable to such support, given the initiative that its right-wing officials in Hamburg had taken in 1971 in barring radicals from the public service.

In hindsight, SPD leaders admit that approving the decree in 1972 was one of the greatest blunders they committed in the postwar period. Some years later they claim that they did not foresee the climate of fear, intimidation, apathy, and despair the decree's loyalty screenings would produce, especially in schools and universities. But they backed the decree as long as those primarily affected were DKP or NPD members. Only when a few SPD members were denied jobs in the public service and foreign socialist leaders attacked the decree did the SPD chiefs speak up and join the ranks of those clamoring for more liberalization. Yet, among the SPD leaders, only Lafontaine has abolished the decree in the Saar, a move the Jusos had advocated nationwide almost since its inception and one the Greens supported when they gained Bundestag seats in 1983.

The FDP, with some exceptions, such as Minister Baum's legislative initiative in 1982, followed a hard line against radicals. This policy reflected the wishes of its electoral clientele, made up of the small-business community and other conservative elements. As in the SPD, only its youth branch took a resolute position against the decree.

The trade unions, fearful of being tagged soft on communism ever since the 1950s, originally supported the decree, with the major exception of the teachers union and a few sympathetic industrial unions. The GEW contended that the decree shored up conservative forces intent on blocking the unions' interest in democratizing society, lessening income differentials, and reducing the power of employers. Although some unions passed resolutions calling for its revocation or liberalization and DGB leaders became increasingly critical, the labor movement was not in the forefront of the opposition.

Lacking support from the major political parties and the union federations, the opposition to the decree, led by the DKP and its allied organizations as well as by the noncommunist Jusos and Young Democrats (and in later years also by the Greens), was never strong enough to gain sufficient legislative support for abolishing the decree. Moreover, the DKP's failure to denounce similar restrictions on public service jobs in the GDR and other communist countries weakened its case.[12] Yet, the opposition sparked enough domestic and international protests to win some concessions from SPD-FDP governments to liberalize the decree's administration.

Although the labor courts, especially, frequently ruled against government decisions to bar radical applicants, the upper administrative courts many times backed the administrators. Each court often based its contradictory ruling on different sections of the landmark Constitutional Court decision of 1975, which sustained the decree, but with some reservations. The administrative court rulings were not unexpected, given an affinity of views between conservative judges, who are civil servants, and the conservative civil servants. These judges also reflected, as one writer noted in a different context, the absence in the Federal Republic "of a firmly rooted liberal and individualist tradition, the quest for metaphysical and emotional absolutes and the inability to live with intellectual and political uncertainties."[13] Yet, because of domestic and foreign protests, the appointment of young, liberal judges, and the reluctance of disciplinary courts to support the CDU/CSU position, the administrative courts in recent years have ruled increasingly in favor of radicals, except in the well-publicized postal cases.

An Assessment

In assessing the arguments put forth by the defenders and critics of the decree, I am sympathetic to the defenders' commitment to safeguard the democratic system—the freest in German history—and to prevent the establishment of a totalitarian system. I also concur with their view that the Federal Republic is not one of the most repressive societies in the West and does not stand on the verge of fascism. After all, in the face of significant opposition, policymakers took corrective action to reduce the excesses committed under the decree, indicating the viability of the Bonn democracy. Yet, I am more sympathetic to the case made by those critics, also committed to the democratic system, who believe that the negative features of the decree and the excesses committed under its name call for its revocation.

Their arguments reinforce the thesis of this volume—a democratic government, while protecting its internal security and upholding the rule of law, must provide maximum freedom to political dissenters not sharing the prevalent norms and values. Obviously, persons found guilty, according to due process, of sabotage, conspiracy, espionage, or terrorism should not become or remain public servants. But in West Germany dissenters who could not gain admission to the public service or who were ousted from it were never accused of such acts. Hence, the decree served as a repressive tool, primarily against DKP members who refused to accept the political, economic, and social order. Preventing them from becoming, for instance, teachers, government laboratory technicians, or social workers in a municipal agency limited their civil liberties without increasing internal security.

From this study of the decree, three conclusions may be drawn. First, when conservative-liberal (CDU/CSU-FDP) governments are in power, they may not necessarily restrict civil liberties more than do social-liberal (SPD-FDP) governments because in each instance they have put the highest priority on crisis management and state protection and a lower priority on civil liberties. In 1972, the SPD and FDP matched the CDU/CSU in its eagerness to issue the decree, on the pretext that civil service regulations concerning the political loyalty of those in government employment should be uniformly implemented. Prior to 1972, the SPD and FDP did enact some reform legislation enhancing the civil liberties of all citizens, but these governing parties aborted the reform movement just when the radical students and other youth began to challenge their more status quo policies. As a result, senior SPD and FDP leaders took tough positions against the young dissidents in their own parties, including threats of expulsion. Thus the dissidents faced repression within the SPD and FDP, and some of them again when they sought a position in the public service. Moreover, the SPD-FDP government, until its downfall in 1982, was responsible for passing the tough antiterrorist legislation, evidence once again that it had as few doubts about limiting civil liberties during a period of heightened tension as did the CDU/CSU-led government after 1982.

Yet, by and large the CDU/CSU, well-meaning as it was to protect the democratic system, has been more restrictive of civil liberties. From 1972 until the present, it has unfalteringly supported the decree in the Länder it has governed. It has refused to accept the liberalized guidelines (abandoning the criterion of mere membership in an extremist party as evidence of disloyalty and ending the automatic screening of all applicants) issued in May 1976 and January 1979 by the SPD-FDP governments in Bonn and the Länder. Since 1982, when the CDU/CSU assumed power in Bonn, its ministers have pushed for stricter application of the 1972 decree, only to be stymied by the resistance of the FDP minister of justice. If in the future there is cabinet unanimity to curb further the rights of radicals in the civil service, the mechanism is in place and no new decree need be promulgated.

Second, the state's political culture (the attitudes and values of the masses and of the elite) had an effect on the degree of government repression of its political dissidents. Government leaders of all parties, imbued with strong anticommunist views dating back to earlier decades, could count on the support of a public similarly conditioned. Thus, the specter of communism emphasized by the CDU/CSU (and certainly not exclusively by them) was the prime cause of the decree's promulgation. Most public opinion polls in the 1970s and 1980s showed that a majority of the public, understandably fearful of or repelled by communism, backed the decree or proposals for reforming it but did not want to revoke it.

Third, this study underlines the self-evident thesis that the greater the repression in a democratic political system that prides itself on order and stability, the greater the danger of the system's turning authoritarian. The excesses in implementing the decree, which were bound to occur, given its content and the German penchant for perfectionism, created an increasingly powerful administrative and intelligence bureaucracy responsible for screening millions of persons. With the authoritarian heritage of the bureaucracy, loyalty hearings often turned into inquisitions and contributed to a climate of fear and conformity, especially among a segment of university students. (A climate of conservatism and a shortage of jobs were other contributing factors, but these factors did not preclude massive demonstrations against nuclear energy and defense policies.)

The decree is but one illustration of the danger of an authoritarian government emerging from a democratic base. Chapter 8, dealing with other aspects of civil liberties in West Germany in the 1970s and 1980s, provides ample evidence of repressive legislation, including censorship, and of growing surveillance of citizens. Such an antidemocratic mixture becomes fertile ground for authoritarianism. One way to reduce the chance for its rise is for the Bonn and Länder governments, given the current paucity of loyalty cases, to revoke the decree officially, as the SPD-ruled Saar has already done. But at this stage, despite foreign pressures, including the ILO recommendations, the CDU/CSU will not reverse its policy because of its commitment to the decree. The only positive recent development is that some of the Länder it controls have handled fewer or no dismissal cases.

There is a possibility that the SPD-ruled Länder in which the decree is still in effect (but hardly applied) will revoke it, especially when more young leaders rise to top policy-making positions. The SPD would benefit from the primarily symbolic gesture. Disillusioned and apolitical youth as well as adherents of the new social movements, at present clustered in the Greens, might become more positively inclined toward a party that has already taken steps to bridge the East-West divide by increasing contacts with socialist parties in the Eastern bloc and that pledges to commit itself more fully to the protection of civil liberties at home.

There are other possibilities for civil service loyalty reform, but none that will have enough support in the near future to become law. The Jusos and the Public Service Union (ÖTV), among others, have advocated a major reorganization of the public service. The separate categories of civil servants, salaried employees, and blue-collar workers, with their different requirements of loyalty to the state, would be eliminated. Under this proposal, the civil servants' special pledge of loyalty would be dropped, thereby facilitating the entry of radicals into the public service in the CDU/CSU-governed Länder.

Another reform proposal calls for the restriction of civil servants to administrative posts, as is the practice in most other countries. In such a case, locomotive engineers, postal clerks, teachers, and others would no longer be civil servants and would have less stringent security requirements. Some DGB unions, representing these professions, have remained firm in their opposition to any change that would deprive their members of the special privileges they enjoy as civil servants.

In 1982 the CDU/CSU killed still another reform proposal advanced by the SPD and FDP as the Baum bill. It called for differentiated loyalty requirements depending on the function of the public servant, meaning a more stringent loyalty pledge for top posts and those involving security.

Given the unlikelihood of any changes in the decree's implementation in Bonn and the Länder in the coming years, except possibly its being dropped officially in some SPD-governed Länder, the question should still be posed as to what constitutes an ideal model when internal security and civil liberties requirements clash. My thesis is that without the decree the country's internal security will not be endangered, as shown by the fact that from 1945 on, left and right extremists have held positions in the public service without a problem. Existing laws suffice to convict the few found guilty of subversion or spying for a foreign government. The others do not constitute a "clear and present danger" to the constitutional order as long as they are kept out of sensitive or top-level posts. The continued CDU/CSU practice of loyalty screenings inhibits freedom of expression, critical thinking, and tolerance of nonconformity—characteristics that should be encouraged rather than discouraged in a democratic state.[14]

Hence, to the question of where the line should be drawn between the requirements of internal security and those of civil liberties, my answer is: at the confluence of a minimum level of internal security (e.g., to thwart assassinations by terrorists) and a maximum level of civil liberties (e.g., to abolish the decree). In such a balance, the rights of radicals to work for changes in the system must not be limited by government officials, most of whom have hardly been militant defenders of civil liberties, even though they espouse democratic values. A freer atmosphere would encourage give-and-take discussions between the ostracized leftists and the majority, which sees the enemy primarily on the Left and not on the Right. Such discussions, especially in the Gorbachev era of increasing détente, would change the perception of the average consensus-minded German, socialized by powerful conservative media, that all DKP members are implacable enemies of democracy who are ready to mount the barricades and overthrow the system by force. (Indeed, in 1989, young DKP members, influenced by Gorbachev's reform movements in the USSR, are clamoring for more *glasnost* and democracy within the DKP.) Public discussions in the Federal Republic would also reduce the bitterness and hostility among diverse ideological groups, a hallmark of the country's political culture. More tolerance of diversity would encourage recognition of the contributions that radical democrats, now embittered and alienated, have made in recent decades to improving the system, with its democratic base but relatively weak liberal institutions and lack of strong civil-libertarian tradition. It would provide them with hope that the system can be changed even more in a democratic rather than an authoritarian direction. It would mean that fewer of them, in frustration and protest, become terrorists, *Chaoten*, or *Autonomen*.[15]

The current anti-Left syndrome encourages rightist groups to become active against the Left, a development that is only too reminiscent of the Weimar period. It threatens democracy more than do the small fanatical communist K-groups, most of which have disappeared in recent years. The rightist fanatic groups are numerically weak too, but some have engaged in terrorism. Also of some concern to officials of all parties in 1989 was the unexpected rise in electoral support for the radical-right Republican party. In the West Berlin and European Parliament elections that year the party received over 7 percent of the total vote. (The NPD garnered a surprising 6.6 percent of the vote in the 1989 Frankfurt local election.) The Republicans and the NPD played on the fears of young blue-collar workers that further European integration, a resettlement of ethnic Germans from the Eastern bloc, and a continuing influx of foreigners would have a negative effect on their economic welfare.

A threat to democracy and civil liberties also comes from the state, partly from the lingering negative effects of the 1972 decree, partly from its heavy-handed response to terrorism and the repression of dissidents, especially in periods of crisis. Such repression indicates a low tolerance for domestic conflict and dissent. According to two writers, Germany's emphasis on consensus shows, in psychoanalytic terms, "an inability to face past reality, an inability to mourn."[16] The consequence is an incipient authoritarianism, reinforced by the state's technology-based data-gathering capabilities. In a similar U.S. context, Bertram Gross characterized the trend as "friendly fascism." Such a trend, visible in many other West European states, must be halted in the Federal Republic if the democratic system is to prevail.[17]

West German policymakers have had a chilling effect on the public debates concerning civil liberties, which they deem of less importance than the maintenance of public order at all costs. By their playing off one civil right against another, they are setting the agenda, which in this case study means limiting the rights of dissidents. They might take note of Otto Kirchheimer's assessment of repression. "Should it not," he writes, "be regarded as an elaborately rationalized expression of a deep-seated human need for aggression, violence, exercise of power, and aggressive domination? If so, it would seem all the more noteworthy that whoever advises repression in a democratic society should find himself compelled to grope for a rational validation of each repressive act that is contemplated or taken."[18] The validations are readily given—a crisis situation, endangerment of the state—but their rationality in terms of the decree must be questioned.

Despite this rather gloomy view of the state of some civil liberties in the Federal Republic, it is important to keep in mind that other civil liberties (e.g., freedom of speech, press, assembly, and religion) have normally not been limited in the four decades of West German democracy. Moreover— although it is hardly a consolation—few countries in the world have an unblemished record in their treatment of dissidents and minorities. Because of the need to limit the focus of this study, I have not made a crossnational study of such civil liberties restrictions. My impressionistic view is that in such a comparison West Germany's restrictions are no greater, and some might argue less, than those in other countries. Examples from two states indicate the kinds of problems they have faced: Britain with its Northern Ireland problem and France with its crushing of the 1968 revolt.

In the Federal Republic, there are encouraging signs that the trend toward greater authoritarianism and limits on freedoms has peaked, partly because of domestic protests and partly because of the corrective capacity of the Bonn system. Government officials realized in the 1980s that they had to accept and respond to new dissent and forms of protests, such as massive peaceful demonstrations over environment and peace issues, and make some changes in policy. As a consequence they enlarged the sphere of freedom and strengthened the nonauthoritarian forces.

In terms of this case study, a number of surveys have shown that a new generation of civil servants strongly rejects the attitude of "blind obedience" so characteristic of some of their elders. In one poll of young civil servants, 91 percent supported the democratic system, 79 percent favored greater direct popular participation, and 67 percent criticized politicians for not offering solutions on an appropriate scale to deal with current problems.[19] Even many older, senior-level civil servants, increasingly committed to democratic and pluralist values, reject the hierarchical, traditional model of the *Beamtenstaat* (civil servants' state) and instead try to relate better to the public, accept the idea of teamwork, and become innovative and receptive to new ideas.

Surveys indicate that West German youth has pride in the country's political institutions, although many criticize subtle restrictions on freedom of speech. Other surveys show that West German citizens have become increasingly interested in politics and have shown satisfaction with the democratic system that allows personal freedom (88 percent) and party competition (92 percent).[20] A significant number have participated in citizens initiatives and demonstrations or voted for the Greens, who represent an antiauthoritarian and nonrepressive ideology; few citizens, relatively speaking, have voted for extremist parties in recent elections (although, as noted, radical-right parties made gains in 1989).

The political culture is showing a change, or at least a split, in values. Young citizens, especially the university-educated ones, are less worried about communism, especially in the Gorbachev era, and are espousing postmaterialist, "New Politics" demands: qualitative economic growth, environmental protection, arms control, social equality, and participatory democracy. They are pitted against many unionists and lower-income and older citizens who espouse the materialist "Old Politics" demands: quantitative economic growth, full employment, social security reforms, and law and order. This schism, not as sharply delineated as once thought and not unique to the Federal Republic, has aroused discussions about new governmental policies and contributed to the growth of an active, rather than passive, citizenry, which increasingly challenges the Establishment.[21] Such a new style of citizen politics, healthily less deferential to political elites and skeptical of their performance, it is hoped will nurture the principle that freedoms should be expanded in what has become one of the most stable democracies in the West, which in 1989 celebrated its fortieth anniversary. (This length of time is significant; the Weimar antecedent, for example, lasted only fourteen years.)

Predictions about the future are always uncertain. Whether the Federal

Republic will become more democratic or more authoritarian depends on too many unknown variables, such as the nature and severity of future crises. A good case can be made that both democratic and authoritarian tendencies will coexist in the years ahead but that eventually authoritarianism and repression will decline as a more democratic, more tolerant, and less prejudiced youth moves into positions of responsibility. The probability of this development is reinforced by the inexorable emergence in the 1990s—as a result of the swift collapse in late 1989 of the orthodox communist regime in the GDR—of a united Germany in which the new leaders will have to attach great importance to the preservation and promotion of civil liberties.

Notes

Preface

1. The decree has also been entitled by its defenders as the Decision against Extremists (*Extremistenbeschluss*).
2. The totals, some based on different counting methods, are only estimates, given the lack of reliable data. The 2,250 barred applicants include 1,250 who were denied entry and 1,000 who lost appeals in courts or whose cases were reopened by authorities but, after review, were denied entry. An additional estimated 9,000 individuals were initially barred but, after appeals to the ministries or successful court actions, were admitted into the service (Horst Bethge and Hannes Holländer, "Das bisherige Ausmass der Berufsverbotspolitik und ihre neueren Tendenzen," in *Berufsverbote und Menschenrechte in der Bundesrepublik,* ed. Klaus Dammann and Erwin Siemantel [Cologne: Pahl-Rugenstein, 1987], p. 25; letter by Dammann to author, Jan. 9, 1989). The totals cover the period 1972–86. (See also Bethge, "Möglichkeiten, das Konzept der Neokonservativen zu durchkreuzen: Von der Abwehr der Berufsverbote zur Bürgerrechts- und Demokratiebewegung," *Blätter für deutsche und internationale Politik* 31, no. 9 [Sept. 1986]: 1105; Die Grünen im Bundestag, *Pressemitteilung,* no. 47/87, Jan. 27, 1987; Klaus Dammann, "Das/the/le/il Berufsverbot," *konkret,* no. 3/88, p. 34.)
3. Donald P. Kommers, "The Government of West Germany," in *Introduction to Comparative Government,* ed. Michael Curtis (New York: Harper and Row, 1985), p. 263.
4. John Dornberg in *International Herald Tribune,* Oct. 27, 1985.
5. Henry Steele Commager, *Freedom, Loyalty, Dissent* (New York: Oxford University Press, 1967), p. 77.
6. Isaac D. Balbus, *The Dialectics of Legal Repression: Black Rebels before the American Criminal Courts* (New York: Russell Sage Foundation, 1973).
7. See Alan Barth, *Government by Investigation* (New York: Viking Press, 1955), p. 3; Walter Millis, "Legacies of the Cold War," in *The Price of Liberty,* ed. Alan

Reitman (New York: W. W. Norton, 1968), p. 46; Edwin S. Newman, *Civil Liberty and Civil Rights* (Dobbs Ferry, N.Y.: Oceana Publications, 1967), p. 17.

8. Klaus von Beyme, *The Political System of the Federal Republic of Germany* (New York: St. Martin's Press, 1983), p. 265; see also pp. 266–67.

9. M. Rainer Lepsius, "Institutional Structures and Political Culture," in *Party Government and Political Culture in Western Germany*, ed. Herbert Döring and Gordon Smith (London: Macmillan, 1982), p. 116.

10. Ramsey Clark, "Foreword," in *The Pulse of Freedom: American Liberties, 1920–1970s*, ed. Alan Reitman (New York: W. W. Norton, 1975), p. 18.

Chapter 1: Prelude to 1972

1. Kenneth F. Dyson, *The State Tradition in Western Europe: A Study of an Idea and Institution* (New York: Oxford University Press, 1980), pp. vii–viii.

2. David Southern, "Germany," in *Government and Administration in Western Europe*, ed. F. F. Ridley (New York: St. Martin's Press, 1979), p. 110. See also Hans Rosenberg, *Bureaucracy, Aristocracy, and Autocracy: The Prussian Experience, 1660–1815* (Boston: Beacon Press, 1966); Edmund Brandt, ed., *Die politische Treuepflicht* (Karlsruhe and Heidelberg: C. F. Müller Juristischer Verlag, 1976), pp. 39–40; Bernd Wunder, *Geschichte der Bürokratie in Deutschland* (Frankfurt am Main: Suhrkamp, 1986).

3. James J. Sheehan, "Conflict and Cohesion among German Elites in the Nineteenth Century," in *Imperial Germany*, ed. Sheehan (New York: Franklin Watts, 1976), pp. 67–69.

4. Rudolf Gneist, *Der Rechtsstaat* (Berlin: J. Springer, 1872), p. 12; cited by Leonard Krieger, *The German Idea of Freedom: History of a Political Tradition* (Boston: Beacon Press, 1957), p. 460.

5. Krieger, *German Idea of Freedom*, pp. 6, 7, 36, 468; James J. Sheehan, *German Liberalism in the Nineteenth Century* (Chicago: University of Chicago Press, 1978), p. 43. Gregg O. Kvistad contends that the Decree against Radicals of 1972 cannot be viewed as a civil liberties issue because it does not fit into the Anglo-American liberal concept of "negative" freedom "from" the state, a concept that is foreign to German political tradition ("Radicals and the State: The Political Demands on West German Civil Servants" [Paper presented at the annual meeting of the American Political Science Association, Washington, D.C., Aug. 28–31, 1986], p. 2; see also pp. 11–15; reprinted in *Comparative Political Studies* 21, no. 1 [Apr. 1988]: 95–125). I will deal with this question in subsequent chapters.

6. For a general survey, see Robert J. Goldstein, *Political Repression in Nineteenth Century Europe* (Totowa, N.J.: Barnes and Noble Books, 1983).

7. Richard Bünemann, "Zur Kontinuität der Berufsverbotspraxis von Metternich zu den Ministerpräsidentenbeschlüssen," *Blätter für deutsche und internationale Politik* 20, no. 3 (1975): 319.

8. In 1906, for instance, nearly 47 percent of all ministry civil servants in training came from titled families; a high number, considering the decline in power of the nobility in the previous century (Wolfgang Runge, "Die alte Oberklasse— die neue Beamtenschaft," in *Weimar ist kein Argument; oder, Brachten Radi-*

kale im öffentlichen Dienst Hitler an die Macht? ed. Freimut Duve and Wolfgang Kopitzsch [Reinbek: Rowohlt, 1976], p. 38). See also Hansjoachim Henning, *Die deutsche Beamtenschaft im neunzehnten Jahrhundert* (Stuttgart: Steiner, 1984).

9. Runge, "Die neue Oberklasse," in Duve and Kopitzsch, *Weimar ist kein Argument,* p. 95.

10. Cited by Hans-Helmut Knütter, "Verfassungsfeindliche Beamte in der Weimarer Republik," in *Verfassungsfeinde als Beamte? Die Kontroverse um die streitbare Demokratie,* ed. Wulf Schönbohm (Munich and Vienna: Günter Olzog, 1979), p. 23.

11. Runge, "Die neue Oberklasse," pp. 83–86; Runge, *Politik und Beamtentum im Parteienstaat: Die Demokratisierung der politischen Beamten in Preussen zwischen 1918 und 1933* (Stuttgart: Ernst Klett, 1965), pp. 179–86.

12. See Gotthart Jasper, *Der Schutz der Republik* (Tübingen: J. C. B. Mohr, 1963).

13. Knütter, "Verfassungsfeindliche Beamte," pp. 24–25; Geoffrey Pridham, *Hitler's Rise to Power: The Nazi Movement in Bavaria, 1923–1933* (New York: Harper and Row, 1973), pp. 192–95; E. Brandt, *Politische Treuepflicht,* pp. 90–93.

14. Alfred Grosser, "Brachten Radikale im öffentlichen Dienst Hitler an die Macht?" *Vorwärts,* Feb. 19, 1976; Grosser, foreword to Duve and Kopitzsch, *Weimar ist kein Argument,* pp. 7–13. He fails to note how opposed the conservative civil servants were to genuine democratic reforms. See also *Der Spiegel,* May 3, 1976.

15. Peter Koch and Reimar Oltmanns, *SOS: Freiheit in Deutschland* (Hamburg: Gruner and Jahr, 1979), p. 31. For a general survey, see Hans Mommsen, *Beamtentum im Dritten Reich* (Stuttgart: Deutsche Verlags-Anstalt, 1966); for legal interpretations, see Ernst Fraenkel, *The Dual State: A Contribution to the Theory of Dictatorship* (New York: Octagon Books, 1969).

16. *Reichsgesetzblatt, 1933* 1:518. Arnold Brecht estimated that one-fourth or more of senior civil servants in many agencies quit, were removed, or were demoted ("Personnel Management," in *Governing Postwar Germany,* Edward H. Litchfield et al. [Ithaca: Cornell University Press, 1953], p. 265).

17. Renate Mayntz, "German Federal Bureaucrats: A Functional Elite between Politics and Administration," in *Bureaucrats and Policymaking: A Comparative Overview,* ed. Ezra Suleiman (New York: Holmes and Meier, 1984), p. 177.

18. According to Arnold Brecht, after World War II a total of 53,000 civil servants, including judges, lost their positions in the West German occupation zones, of whom only 1,071 were classified as offenders who could not regain their positions. The others remained eligible for reemployment ("Personnel Management," pp. 267, 271). See also Johannes Feest, "Die Bundesrichter: Herkunft, Karriere, und Auswahl der juristischen Elite," in *Beiträge zur Analyse der deutschen Oberschicht,* ed. Wolfgang Zapf (Munich: Piper, 1965), pp. 104–5; Udo Wengst, *Staatsaufbau und Regierungspraxis, 1948–1953: Zur Geschichte der Verfassungsorgane der Bundesrepublik Deutschland* (Düsseldorf: Droste, 1984), pp. 177–81, 242–44. Karl Loewenstein points to the solidarity among civil servants, who tried to "save as many colleagues as possible from the clutches of denazification" ("Justice," in Litchfield et al., *Governing Postwar Germany,* p. 248).

19. Testimony by Jürgen Seifert (Hanover) at the Bertrand Russell Tribunal; Bertrand Russell Peace Foundation, *Third Russell Tribunal: Berufsverbote Condemned* (Nottingham, England: Russell Press, 1978), p. 11.

20. John H. Herz, "Political Views of the West German Civil Service," in *West German Leadership and Foreign Policy,* ed. Hans Speier and W. Phillips Davison (Evanston, Ill.: Row, Peterson, 1957), pp. 105–6.

21. Wolfgang Zapf, "Die Verwalter der Macht: Materialen zum Sozialprofil der höheren Beamtenschaft," in Zapf, *Beiträge zur Analyse der deutschen Oberschicht,* pp. 82–83. One specialist's proposal at the time—that the civil servants should have the right to resist illegal orders—was not accepted into new civil service legislation after 1949 (see Herbert von Borch, *Obrigkeit und Widerstand: Zur politischen Soziologie des Beamtentums* [Tübingen: Mohr, 1954]).

22. Brecht, "Personnel Management," p. 275. In Germany, civil servants traditionally have been allowed to run for public office while taking leave from their positions.

23. For details, see Donald P. Kommers, "Basic Rights and Constitutional Review," in *Politics and Government in the Federal Republic of Germany: Basic Documents,* ed. Carl-Christoph Schweitzer et al. (Leamington Spa, England: Berg, 1984), pp. 113–19.

24. Karl Loewenstein's writings warning about the dangers of fascism have been influential. See his "Militant Democracy and Fundamental Rights," *American Political Science Review* 31, no. 3 (June 1937): 417–32; no. 4 (Aug. 1937): 638–58, especially p. 652. For commentaries on militant democracy, see Erhard Denninger, ed., *Freiheitliche demokratische Grundordnung: Materialen zum Staatsverständnis und zur Verfassungswirklichkeit in der Bundesrepublik* (Frankfurt am Main: Suhrkamp, 1977); Eckhard Jesse, *Streitbare Demokratie: Theorie, Praxis, und Herausforderungen in der Bundesrepublik Deutschland* (Berlin: Colloquium, 1980); Johannes Lameyer, "Streitbare Demokratie," *Jahrbuch des öffentlichen Rechts der Gegenwart,* ed. Gerhard Leibholz, 30 (1981): 171–76; *Civil Liberties and the Defense of Democracy against Extremists and Terrorists: A Report on the West German Situation,* issued by Atlantic Brücke (Freiburg im Breisgau: Rombach, 1980); Bruno Schmidt-Bleibtreu and Franz Klein, *Kommentar zum Grundgesetz für die Bundesrepublik Deutschland* (Neuwied and Berlin: Luchterhand, 1967); Walter Wiese, *Der Staatsdienst in der Bundesrepublik Deutschland* (Neuwied and Berlin: Luchterhand, 1972), pp. 133–45; Klaus Stern, *Das Staatsrecht der Bundesrepublik Deutschland,* vol. 1, *Grundbegriffe und Grundlagen des Staatsrechts: Strukturprinzipien der Verfassung,* 2d ed. (Munich: C. H. Beck'sche Verlagsbuchhandlung, 1984), pp. 370–71; Wolfgang Michalka, ed., *Extremismus und streitbare Demokratie* (Stuttgart: Franz Steiner, 1987); Martin Kutscha, *Verfassung und "streitbare Demokratie": Historische und rechtliche Aspekte der Berufsverbote im öffentlichen Dienst* (Cologne: Pahl-Rugenstein, 1979), pp. 26–139.

25. Rainer Dobbelstein and Claudius Gellert, "Shades of New McCarthyism in West Germany? A Political and Legal Analysis of the Campaign against Radicals in the West German Civil Service," Part 1, *Revue de Droit Internationale de Science Diplomatique et Politique* 55, no. 1 (Jan.–Mar. 1977): 67.

26. The DGB unions tied the articles to their campaign for greater democratization

in all sectors of West German society, the right to work and a decent life, and a commitment by citizens to participate actively in public and political life (see GEW, "Bundesrepublik Deutschland: Zehn Jahre Radikalenerlass, eine Dokumentation," *Im Brennpunkt*, Apr. 1982).

27. For text of 1953 *Bundesbeamtengesetz*, see *Bundesgesetzblatt* (hereafter referred to as *BGBl*) 1:551–85; for text of 1950 *Bundesbeamtengesetz*, see *BGBl*, 1:279–306. For details, see Udo Wengst, *Beamtentum zwischen Reform und Tradition: Beamtengesetzgebung in der Gründungsphase der Bundesrepublik Deutschland, 1948–1953* (Düsseldorf: Droste, 1988).

28. *Beamtenrechtsrahmengesetz, July 1, 1957*, in *BGBl* 1:667; see also DBB, *Deutscher Beamtenkalendar* (Munich: Jehle, various years); *Beamtenrechtsrahmengesetz, June 17, 1971*, in *BGBl* 1:1025–47.

29. *German Tribune*, Sept. 14, 1975; International Labor Office, Governing Body, GB 235/4/7, 235th session, Geneva, Mar. 2–6, 1987, p. 43.

30. Southern, "Germany," p. 134; *Stuttgarter Zeitung*, Jan. 29, 1975.

31. Brian Chapman, *The Profession of Government: The Public Service in Europe* (London: Unwin University Books, 1959), p. 310. For the relationship of civil servants to politicians, see Günther Schmid and Hubert Treiber, *Bürokratie und Politik* (Munich: Wilhelm Fink, 1975); Joel D. Aberbach, Robert D. Putnam, and Bert A. Rockman, *Bureaucrats and Politicians in Western Democracies* (Cambridge: Harvard University Press, 1981).

32. Southern, "Germany," pp. 134–43.

33. Robert D. Putnam, "The Political Attitudes of Senior Civil Servants in Britain, Germany, and Italy," in *The Mandarins of Western Europe*, ed. Mattei Dugan (New York: John Wiley, 1975), p. 113. See also Mayntz, "German Federal Bureaucrats," pp. 192–94; Kendall L. Baker, Russell J. Dalton, and Kai Hildenbrandt, *Germany Transformed: Political Culture and the New Politics* (Cambridge: Harvard University Press, 1981), pp. 136–59; Kvistad, "Radicals and the State," pp. 14–23.

34. Sebastian Cobler, *Law, Order, and Politics in West Germany* (Middlesex, England: Penguin Books, 1978), pp. 162–63; Dobbelstein and Gellert, "Shades of New McCarthyism," p. 84.

35. Drafts of laws in Deutscher Bundestag, first election period, Drucksache 2846, Jan. 19, 1951; 3335, Apr. 28, 1952 (hereafter referred to as D. BT., el. pd.).

36. Cobler, *Law, Order, and Politics*, pp. 163–64; Alexander von Brünneck, *Politische Justiz gegen Kommunisten in der Bundesrepublik Deutschland, 1949–1968* (Frankfurt am Main: Suhrkamp, 1978), pp. 54–56.

Chapter 2: The 1972 Decree against Radicals

1. Klaus Horn, "Berufsverbote: Ein staatlicher Beitrag zur Unregierbarkeit," *Frankfurter Hefte*, no. 11 (1980): 47–49.

2. D. BT., 8th el. pd., Drucksache 8/2184, Oct. 12, 1978, p. 2; *Innere Sicherheit*, issued by Federal Ministry of Interior (BMI), no. 46, Dec. 8, 1978; Hans Josef Horchem, "Zum Entwicklungsstand des Rechtsextremismus in der Bundesrepublik Deutschland," in *Extremismus im demokratischen Rechtsstaat*, ed. Manfred Funke (Düsseldorf: Droste, 1978), pp. 202–24. In 1972, there were

24,700 members in 129 right-wing organizations (BMI, *Betrifft: Verfassungs-schutz 1972* [Bonn, 1973], p. 13). For a description of right and left extremists, see Horchem, *Extremisten in einer selbstbewussten Demokratie* (Freiburg: Her-derbücherei, 1975).

3. Letter from Minister of Interior Genscher to Bundestag deputy Ostman von der Leyde (SPD), July 21, 1972; cited in Hermann Borgs-Maciejewski, *Radikale im öffentlichen Dienst: Dokumente, Debatten, Urteile* (Bonn–Bad Godesberg: Go-desberger Taschenbuch-Verlag, 1973), pp. 27–28. BMI, *Betrifft: Verfassungs-schutz 1972*, pp. 14–15, gives slightly lower figures. For 1978, see BMI, *Betrifft: Verfassungsschutz 1978* (Bonn, 1979), pp. 21–22; for 1984: BMI, *Verfassungs-schutz 1984* (Bonn, 1985), pp. 132, 135.

4. *Deutsche Zeitung*, Mar. 22, 1974. See also Eckart Spoo, "Erfahrungen mit dem Berufsverbot gegen Radikale im öffentlichen Dienst," *Frankfurter Hefte* 18, no. 3 (1973): 182.

5. *Innere Sicherheit*, Mar. 8, 1978; *Der Spiegel*, May 13, 1973. See also Ossip K. Flechtheim, Wolfgang Rudzio, Fritz Vilmar, and Manfred Wilke, *Der Marsch der DKP durch die Institutionen: Sowjetmarxistische Einflussstrategien und Ideo-logien* (Frankfurt am Main: Fischer Taschenbuch, 1980).

6. BMI, *Betrifft: Verfassungsbericht 1972*, p. 55.

7. D. BT., 7th el. pd., Drucksache 7/3259, Feb. 21, 1975, p. 7. Of the 58 percent of seats captured in 1971, the New Left gained 33 percent, the MSB 8 percent, and the SHB 17 percent. Until June 1972, the SHB had been known as the Social Democratic University League. When the SHB became too radical, the SPD withdrew the party's links to it and forbade it to use the name "Social Demo-cratic." On left extremism, see Kenneth F. Dyson, "Left-wing Political Extrem-ism and the Problem of Tolerance in Western Germany," *Government and Opposition* 10, no. 3 (Summer 1975): 316–29.

8. BMI, *Betrifft: Verfassungsschutz 1972*, pp. 55–56; *Betrifft: Verfassungsschutz 1978*, pp. 67–68. By 1978, the number of left radicals in the public service had risen to 2,309 from 1,307 in 1972.

9. For a chronicle of terrorist acts, see Manfred Funke, ed., *Terrorismus: Unter-suchungen zur Strategie und Struktur revolutionärer Gewaltpolitik* (Bonn: Bun-deszentrale für politische Bildung, 1977), pp. 331–65. For critical commen-taries of the conservative position, see Jürgen Seifert, "Defining the Enemy of the State: Political Policies of West Germany," *New German Critique*, no. 8 (Spring 1976): 50; Milton Mankoff and Monica Jacobs, "The Return of the Suppressed: McCarthyism in West Germany," *Contemporary Crises* 1, no. 4 (1977): 342; Rüdiger Lautmann, "Linksradikal als Stigma," in *Wir Bürger als Sicherheitsrisiko: Berufsverbot und Lauschangriff. Beiträge zur Verfassung un-serer Republik*, ed. Wolf-Dieter Narr (Reinbek: Rowohlt, 1977), p. 289.

10. *Frankfurter Allgemeine Zeitung*, Dec. 10, 1971.

11. Rainer Kessler, "Die Verfassungsloyalität des öffentlichen Dienstes," *Politische Studien* 23, no. 205 (special issue, Oct. 1972): 42; see also 40–41.

12. Spoo, "Erfahrungen," p. 184.

13. D. BT., *Verhandlungen des Deutschen Bundestages*, 6th el. pd., 145th session, pp. 8330–32, 8338–40 (hereafter referred to as D. BT., el. pd., session).

14. *Die Zeit*, July 21, 1978.

15. According to *Corriere della Sera* (Milan) CDU deputy Friedrich Vogel claimed that Brandt, at a meeting with Soviet leader Brezhnev in fall 1971 at Oreanda, Crimea, reached a secret agreement in which Brandt pledged to prevent the Constitutional Court from declaring the DKP illegal (June 5, 1976). For further details on the chancellor's reasons for supporting the decree, see Brandt papers, "Extremisten" file, nos. 13, 16, Friedrich Ebert Stiftung archive, Bonn; cited by Kvistad, "Revolution, Subversion, and German State Employees" (Paper presented at the annual meeting of the American Political Science Association, Augusta, Aug. 31–Sept. 3, 1989), pp. 29–31.

16. Koch and Oltmanns, *SOS*, pp. 30, 166–67.

17. Emnid-Institut, "Die jungen Staatsbürger" (Bielefeld, 1973, hectographed), p. 56; cited by Lautmann, "Linksradikal als Stigma," p. 291. Sontheimer also speculates that without Dutschke's call to march through the institutions, there most likely would not have been any 1972 Decree against Radicals (*Die verunsicherte Republik: Die Bundesrepublik nach dreissig Jahren* [Munich: Piper, 1979], p. 27).

18. Jack Zipes, "From Berufsverbot to Terrorism," *Telos*, no. 34 (Winter 1977–78): 140–41; Kenneth F. Dyson, "Anticommunism in the Federal Republic of Germany: The Case of the 'Berufsverbot,'" *Parliamentary Affairs* 28, no. 1 (Winter 1974–75): 53–54; Wolf-Dieter Narr, "Threats to Constitutional Freedom in the Federal Republic of Germany," *New German Critique*, no. 8 (Spring 1976): 25–26.

19. Grundsatzentscheidung des Senats, Nov. 23, 1971; full text in *Frankfurter Rundschau*, Nov. 24, 1971.

20. Hermann Borgs-Maciejewski, "Radikale im öffentlichen Dienst," in *Aus Politik und Zeitgeschichte*, supplement to *Das Parlament*, B27/73, July 7, 1973, p. 4; Hans Koschnick and Klaus-Henning Rosen, "Der lange Abschied vom Extremistenbeschluss," *Die Neue Gesellschaft/Frankfurter Hefte* 32, no. 10 (Oct. 1985): 941–42.

21. Wehner warned in early 1972, "The fight against communism cannot be misused as a model for the abuse and mistrust of all that is not conservative" (*Die Zeit*, July 21, 1978).

22. Komitee für Grundrechte und Demokratie, *Ohne Zweifel für den Staat: Die Praxis zehn Jahre nach dem Radikalenerlass* (Reinbek: Rowohlt, 1982), p. 44. The authors state that the CDU/CSU threats to ban the DKP were not in earnest because the CDU/CSU never made an attempt in the Bundesrat (upper house of Parliament), in which it had a majority, to have both houses initiate proceedings. Rather, it tried to make political extremism a permanent political issue (ibid.).

23. "Gemeinsame Erklärung des Bundeskanzlers und der Ministerpräsidenten der Bundesländer," Jan. 28, 1972; reprinted under diverse titles, such as "Beschäftigung von rechts- und linksradikalen Personen im öffentlichen Dienst," *Ministerialblatt für das Land Nordrhein-Westfalen, Jahrgang 1972*, p. 342; or "Beschluss der Regierungschefs des Bundes und der Länder," in H. Borgs-Maciewjewski, "Radikale im öffentlichen Dienst," p. 9. Summary in *Bulletin*, no. 15 (Feb. 3, 1972): 142.

24. See, e.g., *Ministerialblatt für das Land Nordrhein-Westfalen*, 1972, p. 342.

25. Werner Holtfort, "Bonner Pilatus: Zur traurigen Geschichte des Radikalenerlasses und des kleinmütigen Versuchs, ihn wieder loszuwerden," *Vorgänge* 19, no. 4 (1980): 19.

26. As I define it, the category of "extremists" includes those communists, fascists, and terrorists who aim for a complete break with the past through revolutionary means without worrying about the costs and the number of victims killed. For a discussion, see contributions by Ossip K. Flechtheim and Manfred Funke in *Extremismus im demokratischen Rechtsstaat*, ed. Funke (Düsseldorf: Droste, 1978), pp. 15–61; and by Martin Kriele and Wolf-Dieter Narr in *Kampf um Wörter? Politische Begriffe im Meinungsstreit*, ed. Martin Greiffenhagen (Munich and Vienna: Carl Hanser, 1980), pp. 351–75. I will employ the terms "radicals" or "extremists," depending on their use in the original source. It must be remembered that the terms lack precision and are used pejoratively by conservatives in the CDU/CSU, SPD, and FDP.

    When I use the term "conservative," I refer primarily to CDU/CSU members, but also those in the SPD and FDP, who seek to preserve existing institutions based on freedom and democracy and who espouse traditional values. For some, such values include authoritarian decision making in institutions. Within the CDU/CSU, there is a liberal or labor wing pushing for economic and social reforms, but hardly on civil liberties issues.

27. On Nov. 15, 1974, Minister of the Interior Werner Maihofer (FDP) told the Bundestag, "We should agree that not just every radical criticism of our existing social order and existing national constitution is to be equated with enmity to the constitution" (D. BT., 7th el. pd., 132nd session, p. 8950).

28. For contrasting views, see Gerhart Maier, *Extremisten im öffentlichen Dienst?* (Bonn: Bundeszentrale für politische Bildung, 1977), pp. 13, 14; Ansgar Skriver, "Innere Sicherheit und Bürgerfreiheit," *Merkur* 32, no. 9 (Sept. 1978): 890; Dobbelstein and Gellert, "Shades of New McCarthyism," p. 69; Thomas Conrad, "Banned in West Germany," *Seven Days*, June 2, 1978, p. 14. I use the term "Decree against Radicals" because it has been widely used in the literature and is less emotionally laden than "Berufsverbot."

29. DKP, DKP-Pressedienst, Düsseldorf, Jan. 19, 1972, reprinted in Institut für Marxistische Studien und Forschungen (IMSF), *Informationsbericht* no. 22, *Berufsverbote in der BRD*, 1976, pp. 94–96; *Unsere Zeit* (DKP organ), Jan. 28, 1972; Hartmut Geil, "Berufsverbot, Wissenschaft, und politischer Prozess," *Marxistische Blätter* 16, no. 2 (Mar.–Apr. 1978): 99–105.

30. Wolfgang Abendroth, Helmut Ridder, Wolfgang Däubler, Gerhard Stuby, and others in "Stellungnahmen von Juristen zu den von der Ministerpräsidentenkonferenz beschlossenen 'Grundsätzen zur Frage der verfassungsfeindlichen Kräfte im öffentlichen Dienst' sowie zur Gemeinsamen Erklärung des Bundeskanzlers und der Ministerpräsidenten der Länder vom 28. Januar 1972," *Blätter für deutsche und internationale Politik*, Parts 1, 2, no. 2 (Feb. 1972): 124–65; no. 3 (Mar. 1972): 246–93; Hans Mausbach, "Sciences and Political Discrimination" (Bund demokratischer Wissenschaftler, n.d., hectographed).

31. dpa [Deutsche Presse Agentur], *Dienst für Kulturpolitik*, Feb. 7, 1972.

32. *Pressemitteilung der Demokratischen Aktion*, Jan. 26, 1973.

33. Resolution zum Ministerpräsidentenerlass, Bundeskongress, Feb. 26–27, 1972, in Jusos, *Bundeskongressbeschlüsse, Jungsozialisten in der SPD, 1969–1976* (Bonn, 1978), pp. 81–82.

34. Bundesvorstand der Deutschen Jungdemokraten, INFO, no. 2, 1972.

35. CDU, *Argumente, Dokumente, Materialen: Radikale im öffentlichen Dienst* (Bonn, 1972), p. 29.

36. *Süddeutsche Zeitung*, Feb. 29, 1972.

37. CDU, DUD [Deutschland-Union-Dienst] *press release*, 26 no. 50 (Mar. 14, 1972).

38. D. BT., 6th el. pd., 188th session, June 7, 1972, pp. 10978, 10991, 11026.

39. *Frankfurter Allgemeine Zeitung*, Feb. 29, 1972.

40. *Vorwärts*, Feb. 13, 1975; *Frankfurter Allgemeine Zeitung*, Apr. 3, 1974; Andrei S. Markovits, *The Politics of the West German Trade Unions: Strategies of Class and Interest Representation in Growth and Crisis* (Cambridge: Cambridge University Press, 1986), pp. 124, 155, 478.

41. Declaration, Oct. 23, 1971, reprinted in GEW, "Bundesrepublik Deutschland; Zehn Jahre Radikalenerlass: Eine Dokumentation," *Im Brennpunkt*, Apr. 1982, p. 9.

42. Cited in SPD, Dokumentation, *Grundsätze zur Feststellung der Verfassungstreue im öffentlichen Dienst, vorgelegt von Hans Koschnick, Stellvertretender Parteivorsitzender, Bonn, 16. Oktober 1978* (Bonn, 1978), p. 17.

43. *Die Zeit*, May 23, 1979.

44. See, e.g., *Ministerialblatt für das Land Nordrhein-Westfalen, Jahrgang 1972*, p. 342, for text of decree. The West Berlin government granted its departments freedom to set their own criteria for employment.

45. CDU, *Argumente, Dokumente, Materialen*, pp. 25–26. See also Hans-Jürgen Schlimke, "Der 'Beurteilungsspielraum' der Einstellungsbehörde bei Einstellung von 'Radikalen' in den öffentlichen Dienst" (Ph.D. diss., University of Münster, 1980).

46. Dyson, "Anticommunism," pp. 63–64; Mankoff and Jacobs, "Return of the Suppressed," p. 347; Hans-Jochen Brauns and David Kramer, "Political Repression in West Germany: 'Berufsverbote' in Modern German History," *New German Critique*, no. 7 (1976): 109.

Chapter 3: The Aftermath, 1973–1976

1. IMSF, *Informationsbericht* no. 42, "Berufsverbote: Neue Entwicklungen—Kritik—Erfahrungen des Widerstandes" (Neuss: Plambeck, 1985), p. 10 (abbreviated English version: "Berufsverbot: Recent Developments—a Critique—the Experiences of the Campaign against 'Berufsverbot'"); *Censorship, Legal Defence, and the Domestic Intelligence Service in West Germany: Conclusions of the Final Session of the Third Russell Tribunal* (Nottingham, England: Russell Press, 1979), pp. 13–14. (Defenders of the decree denounced the statements of the tribunal as "propaganda.") See also Bernd Preis, *Verfassungsschutz und öffentlicher Dienst: Ein Beitrag zum bereichsspezifischen Datenschutz bei den Verfassungsschutzbehörden* (Königstein/Taunus: Athenäum, 1982).

2. Koch and Oltmanns, *SOS*, pp. 38–39, quoting Walter Seuffert. See also pp. 105, 156.
3. Ibid., pp. 133, 201.
4. *Censorship, Legal Defence*, p. 11. See also Joachim Blau, *Zum Ausbau des staatlichen Repressionsapparates seit Ende der sechziger Jahre*, IMSF, *Informationsbericht* no. 29, 1977, pp. 15–16; *Frankfurter Allgemeine Zeitung*, June 27, 1989, p. 5.
5. See, e.g., BMI, *Betrifft: Verfassungsschutz 1978*; for Länder, Baden-Württemberg, Ministry of Interior, *Verfassungsschutzbericht Baden-Württemberg, 1978* (Stuttgart, 1978).
6. *Süddeutsche Zeitung*, Jan. 25, 1977.
7. *Vorwärts*, Oct. 28, 1976.
8. Koch and Oltmanns, *SOS*, p. 161. See also Wolf-Dieter Narr, "Anhörung: Zur Frage, ob ich auf dem Boden der freiheitlichdemokratischen Grundordnung stehe. Ein Psychogramm und verallgemeindere Folgerungen," *Kursbuch*, no. 40 (June 1975): 159–78; Günter Wallraff, "Die 'Anhörer' " and "Der 'falsche Aktenmensch,' " in *Die unheimliche Republik: Politische Verfolgung in der Bundesrepublik*, ed. Heinrich Hannover and Wallraff (Reinbek: Rowohlt, 1984), pp. 191–250; Peter Schneider, *Die Botschaft des Pferdekopfs und andere Essais aus einem friedlichen Jahrzehnt* (Darmstadt and Neuwied: Hermann Luchterhand, 1981), pp. 158–74. In a less serious vein, one author provided the following ten orders to those who did not want to fall under the decree: "Leave politics to politicians; carry the correct party membership card with you; do not live in a commune; do not bother about the political difficulties of your dearest one; do not teach the International song to your children or send them to a progressive kindergarten; do not despair; do not read or collect flyers; forget Article 15 of the Basic Law [dealing with the nationalization of property and firms]; avoid words such as communism, socialism, anarchism; be obedient to your teachers, employers, and other such people" (Ingeborg Drewitz, "Zehn Gebote für alle, die mit dem 'Berufsverbot' gar nicht erst etwas zu tun haben wollen," in *Berufsverbote: Ein bundesdeutsches Lesebuch*, ed. W. Beutin, Thomas Metscher, and B. Meyer [Fischerhude: Verlag Atelier im Bauernhaus, 1976], p. 54).
9. Average based on two hundred cases handled from 1972 to 1976 (*Süddeutsche Zeitung*, Jan. 26, 1977). Another report held the chance of an applicant's success in court at only 20 to 30 percent (*New Statesman*, Apr. 28, 1978).
10. The decree's critics also cited the name of Judge Willi Geiger of the Federal Constitutional Court, who participated in its 1975 decision on the decree. He had been a Land judge and prosecuting state attorney from 1941 to 1943, demanding severe penalties, including death, for some foreign workers. In his 1941 Ph.D. dissertation he had hailed the Nazi ban on Jewish journalists, whose undue influence, he said, had damaged the cultural life of the Germans. In Geiger's case, one supporter of the decree noted that Geiger's distinguished service and politically centrist position on the Constitutional Court, his extensive writings on human rights and basic liberties, and his role as a prominent Catholic intellectual are proof that he is now committed to upholding the democratic system. See Donald P. Kommers, *Judicial Politics in West Germany:*

A Study of the Federal Constitutional Court (Beverly Hills, Calif.: Sage Publications, 1976), pp. 81, 125–27, 182, 271; and letter to author, Mar. 6, 1989. For a critical view, see Horst Bethge et al., eds., *Die Zerstörung der Demokratie durch Berufsverbote* (Cologne: Pahl-Rugenstein, 1976), pp. 19–21; Koch and Oltmanns, *SOS*, pp. 36–37; Heinrich Hannover, "Zeit zum Widerstand," in *Die unheimliche Republik*, by Hannover and Günter Wallraff (Reinbek: Rowohlt, 1984), pp. 12–26, 53–54; 70–73; *Der Spiegel*, Aug. 4, 1975, pp. 32–34. For a list of judges, see Spoo, "Erfahrungen," pp. 181–82.

11. Wolfgang Kaupen and Theo Rasehorn, *Die Justiz zwischen Obrigkeitsstaat und Demokratie: Ein empirischer Beitrag zur Soziologie der deutschen Justizjuristen* (Neuwied: Luchterhand, 1971).

12. See Dorothy Nelkin and Michael Pollak, *The Atom Besieged: Extraparliamentary Dissent in France and Germany* (Cambridge: MIT Press, 1981), pp. 165–66.

13. Günter Frankenberg, "Staatstreue: Die aktuelle Spruchpraxis zu den Berufsverboten," *Kritische Justiz* 13, no. 3 (1980): 276–83; Martin Krutscha, *Verfassung und "Streitbare Demokratie"* (Cologne: Pahl-Rugenstein, 1979), p. 170. In the district and Länder labor courts, panels of three judges preside. Ministers of labor appoint two judges who represent management and unions; the third judge, a professional who is appointed after consultation with management and unions, presides over the court (Markovits, *Politics of Trade Unions*, pp. 36–37).

14. Jesse, *Streitbare Demokratie*, p. 68; *The Economist* (London), Aug. 2, 1975. The weekly based its figures on the decree's critics, who at the time claimed 457 applicants had been rejected. The government totals and the critics' totals usually showed a wide disparity. One explanation is that the total of 457 includes 1972, while the government total of 328, not released until Apr. 1976, excludes 1972.

15. Jesse, *Streitbare Demokratie*, pp. 67–68; *The Nation* (New York), Sept. 11, 1976.

16. Dobbelstein and Gellert, "Shades of New McCarthyism," pp. 70–72, 81; Horst Bethge and Erich Rossmann, eds. *Der Kampf gegen das Berufsverbot: Dokumentation der Fälle und des Widerstands* (Cologne: Pahl-Rugenstein, 1973), pp. 291–92.

17. Narr, "Anatomie eines Berufsverbotes: Dokumente und Anmerkungen zur Nichtberufung von Wolf-Dieter Narr an die Juristische Fakultät Hannover" (n.d. [c. 1975], hectographed); Narr, letter to author, Jan. 8, 1988; *Die Zeit*, June 6, 1975; Dobbelstein and Gellert, "Shades of New McCarthyism," p. 81.

18. *Der Spiegel*, July 23, 1973; *Die Zeit*, July 27, 1973; *New York Times*, Sept. 22, 1973; *Frankfurter Allgemeine Zeitung*, Mar. 15, 1980.

19. *Financial Times*, Dec. 16, 1975.

20. *Der Spiegel*, Nov. 24, 1975; ILO, Governing Body, 1987 Report, pp. 103–5; *Frankfurter Rundschau*, Mar. 14, 1980; *Frankfurter Allgemeine Zeitung*, Dec. 17, 1980. For other cases, see Hanspeter Knirsch, Bernhard Nagel, and Wolfgang Voegeli, eds., *"Radikale" im öffentlichen Dienst: Eine Dokumentation* (Frankfurt am Main: Fischer Taschenbuch, 1973).

21. *Frankfurter Allgemeine Zeitung*, Oct. 19, 1973. Another poll released in February 1976 indicated little change: 55 percent in favor of the decree, 31 percent

opposed, and 14 percent no views. Sixty-five percent opposed the nomination of a DKP member as judge, and 49 percent the appointment of an NPD member as a university professor (*Stuttgarter Nachrichten*, Feb. 23, 1976).

22. *Frankfurter Rundschau*, Dec. 14, 1976.

23. Holtfort, "Bonner Pilatus," p. 18.

24. Among the sponsoring organizations were the League of Democratic Scientists, the Socialist German Working Youth, Marxist Student League-Spartakus, the Socialist University League, Jusos, and Young Democrats (*Die Welt*, Oct. 25, 1978).

25. See Bethge and Rossmann, *Kampf gegen das Berufsverbot; Dokumentation: Vom KPD-Verbot zum Berufsverbot*, issued by Zentraler Arbeitskreis für die Aufhebung des KPD-Verbots; *Sieben Jahre Kampf gegen die Berufsverbote: Bilanz der "Initiative Weg mit den Berufsverboten,"* no. 20 (Hamburg, 1979); IMSF, *Informationsbericht* no. 42, p. 30.

26. Speech given at Ninth DGB Federal Youth Conference, Nov. 19, 1974 (hectographed). See also DGB, *Abwehr von Verfassungsfeinden im öffentlichen Dienst* (Düsseldorf, 1977).

27. GEW, "Bundesrepublik Deutschland," pp. 11–12.

28. Horst Bethge, ed., *Gewerkschaftsstimmen gegen Berufsverbote* (Cologne: Pahl-Rugenstein, 1977), pp. 27–28.

29. Resolution reprinted in GEW Landesverband Hamburg, *Berufsverbote und politische Disziplinierung: Eine Dokumentation der GEW Hamburg* (Hamburg: Verlag Erziehung und Wissenschaft, 1978), pp. 85–86.

30. SPD, *Informationen der Sozialdemokratischen Fraktion im Deutschen Bundestag*, no. 69, Feb. 21, 1973.

31. *Die Zeit*, Aug. 24, 1973.

32. SPD, *Jungsozialisten Informationsdienst*, no. 3, June 1978.

33. *Der Spiegel*, Dec. 8, 1975. For a list of SPD, FDP, and nonparty members affected by the decree, see "Ausgewählte Berufsverbotefälle von SPD- und FDP-Mitgliedern und Parteilosen," issued by Initiative "Weg mit den Berufsverboten" (Hamburg, 1978, hectographed).

34. SPD, *Pressemitteilungen und Informationen*, no. 66/75, Feb. 1, 1975; *Frankfurter Allgemeine Zeitung*, May 10, 1975.

35. SPD, *Parteitag der SPD, 10.–14. April 1973, Hannover*, vol. 1, *Protokoll der Verhandlungen* (Bonn, n.d.), pp. 882–922.

36. SPD, *Pressemitteilungen und Informationen*, no. 319/75; *Dokumentation des SPD-Pressedienstes*, July 1, 1975.

37. *Der Spiegel*, July 7, 1975. See also *Stuttgarter Zeitung*, June 12, 1975.

38. Friedrich-Naumann-Stiftung, *Dokumentation: Extremistenbeschluss* (Bonn, 1979); *Die Zeit*, Aug. 24, 1973; *Der Spiegel*, Aug. 13, 1983.

39. CDU, *Union in Deutschland*, no. 34, Sept. 6, 1973. For a conservative SPD view (and comprehensive documents collection), see Peter Frisch, *Extremistenbeschluss* (Leverkusen: Heggen, 1976).

40. *Deutsche Post-Zeitung*, no. 11, Nov. 1978.

41. See, inter alia, Funke, *Extremismus im demokratischen Rechtsstaat*; Klaus Stern, *Zur Verfassungstreue der Beamten* (Munich: Franz Vahlen, 1974); Hartmut Weyer, *DKP und öffentlicher Dienst* (Bonn–Bad Godesberg: Hohwacht,

1974); Martin Kriele, "Der rechtliche Spielraum einer Liberalisierung der Einstellungspraxis im öffentlichen Dienst," *Neue Juristische Wochenschrift* 32, no. 1–2 (Jan. 10, 1979): 1–8; Jens Brückner, *Das Handbuch der Berufsverbote: Rechtsfibel zur Berufsverbotspraxis* (Berlin: Nicholäische Verlagsbuchhandlung, 1977); Hagen Weiler, *Verfassungstreue im öffentlichen Dienst* (Königstein/Taunus: Athenäum, 1979); BMI, *Innere Sicherheit*, no. 44, July 7, 1978. Prof. Karl-Dietrich Bracher criticized the Left for "overloading the constitutional system with a perfectionist concept of democracy, which amounts finally to a pushing aside of the constitution through its misuse." To protect the Basic Law, said Bracher, the decree must be supported ("Bewahrung und Anfechtung: Zum Streit um Demokratie und Verfassung in der Bundesrepublik," in *Extremismus im demokratischen Rechtsstaat*, ed. Manfred Funke [Düsseldorf: Droste, 1978], p. 425).

42. FRG, Press and Information Office, *Bulletin* (Bonn), Sept. 22, 1973.

43. *Der Spiegel*, Sept. 24, 1973.

44. The CDU/CSU bill was introduced on Feb. 11, 1974, prior to the cabinet's approval of the government bill on Mar. 6. The CDU/CSU jumped the gun because, knowing the contents of the government bill by Feb., it wanted to gain maximum propaganda advantage among the electorate.

45. The forty-one-member Bundesrat does not have coequal powers with the lower house but represents the Länder in legislation directly affecting them, where it has a direct veto, or in other legislation, as in this instance, where it has a suspensive veto. The three to five members, representing each Land, receive voting instructions from their Länder cabinets.

46. For text of the CDU/CSU bill, see D. BT., 7th el. pd., Drucksache 7/2433, Gesetzentwurf des Bundesrates; government bill: Gesetzentwurf der Bundesregierung, July 31, 1974.

47. D. BT., 7th el. pd., 132nd session, pp. 8959–95.

48. Decision of the court's 2d chamber, 2 BvL 13/73, in *Entscheidungen des Bundesverfassungsgerichts* 39 (1975): 334ff., reprinted in *Neue Juristische Wochenschrift*, no. 36 (1975): 1641–52; citation, p. 1642.

49. Ibid.

50. *Frankfurter Rundschau*, July 29, 1975; Jusos, "Erklärung des Bundesausschusses der Jungsozialisten zum Berufsverbots-Urteils des Bundesverfassungsgerichts zum 32.8.1975" (Bonn). For positive commentaries on the decision, see Martin Kriele, "Verfassungsfeinde im öffentlichen Dienst: Ein unlösbares Problem," in *Extremismus im demokratischen Rechtsstaat*, ed. Manfred Funke (Düsseldorf: Droste, 1978), pp. 335–47; Georg Berner, "'Radikalenerlass' und Rechtssprechung," *Politische Studien* 28, no. 233 (May–June 1977): 287–303; Hartmut Maurer, "Die Mitgliedschaft von Beamten in verfassungsfeindlichen Parteien und Organisationen," *Neue Juristische Wochenschrift* 25, no. 14 (Apr. 4, 1972): 601–7; Hans-Hermann Schrader, *Rechtsbegriff und Rechtsentwicklung der Verfassungstreue im öffentlichen Dienst* (Berlin: Duncker and Humblot, 1985). For negative commentaries, see Theo Rasehorn, "Justiz und Verfassung," in *Wir Bürger als Sicherheitsrisiko*, ed. Wolf-Dieter Narr (Reinbek-Rowohlt, 1977), pp. 164–86; Wolfgang Abendroth, "Das Bundesverfassungsgericht und die Berufsverbote im öffentlichen Dienst," IMSF,

Informationsbericht no. 22, pp. 30–36; Hartmut Geil, "Berufsverbote und Staatsschutz?" *Das Argument* 20, no. 109 (May–June 1978): 380–93.

51. D. BT., 7th el. pd., Drucksache 7/4183, "Bericht und Antrag des Innenausschuss," Oct. 21, 1975.

52. D. BT., 7th el. pd., 197th session, Oct. 24, 1975, pp. 13,537–13,600; Drucksache 681/75, Nov. 7, 1975.

53. FRG, *Bulletin* (Bonn), no. 59 (May 21, 1976): 553–54.

Chapter 4: International Reactions

This chapter covers the foreign reactions into the 1980s; subsequent chapters resume domestic developments since 1976.

1. For details, see *New York Times*, June 19, 1976; *Frankfurter Rundschau*, Aug. 11, 1977; Wolfgang Bittner, "Verfassungsfeindlichkeit zur Disposition: Eine Reportage über den Fall Silvia Gingold," in *Extremismus im demokratischen Rechtsstaat*, ed. Manfred Funke (Düsseldorf: Droste, 1978), pp. 376–86.

2. Not all foreign leaders, especially the politically conservative ones, shared these sentiments. In 1981, in an admittedly exceptional case, Gen. Roberto Viola, president of Argentina, announced that he would adopt FRG laws and decrees as a model for keeping out extremists from the state's public service and institutions (*Frankfurter Rundschau*, Jan. 30, 1987). For other foreign reactions, see Andreas Dress et al., eds., *Wir Verfassungsfeinde* (Cologne: Pahl-Rugenstein, 1977).

3. *Vorwärts*, Apr. 17, 1976; Bittner, "Verfassungsfeindlichkeit zur Disposition," pp. 376–86. See also *Sieben Jahre Kampf gegen die Berufsverbote*, pp. 19–21.

4. *Le Monde*, Dec. 5, 1976; *Le Matin*, Nov. 2, 1977.

5. Brauns and Kramer, "Political Repression in West Germany," p. 106.

6. Ibid., p. 107; *The Financial Times*, Dec. 16, 1975.

7. France, National Assembly, Feb. 20, 1984; excerpt reprinted in *Blätter für deutsche und internationale Politik* 29, no. 5 (May 1984): 640.

8. *New York Times*, June 2, 1976.

9. *The Times* (London), July 4, 1975; Alf Enseling, "Das Ausland zur Extremismus- und Terrorismus-Diskussion in der Bundesrepublik Deutschland," in *Aus Politik und Zeitgeschichte*, supplement to *Das Parlament*, B20/78, May 20, 1978, p. 27.

10. *Bielefelder Universitätszeitung*, Apr. 9, 1979, p. 19; Jan Priewe, "Berufsverbote gefährden die Wissenschaftsfreiheit," *Frankfurter Hefte* 35, no. 10 (1980): 43.

11. *The Economist* (London), Jan. 31, 1976. For other press commentaries, see Aktionskomitee gegen Berufsverbote an der Freien Universität Berlin und Komitee zur Verteidigung Demokratischer Rechte, *Bundesrepublik Deutschland: Berufsverbote—Stimmen der Internationalen Presse* (Berlin, 1976).

12. *Süddeutsche Zeitung*, May 29, 1976; *Neue Zürcher Zeitung*, June 8, 1976; *Frankfurter Rundschau*, Oct. 25, 1977.

13. Cited in *Freie Fahrt für den Lokführer Rudi Röder* (Würzburger Bürgerkomitee zur Verteidigung der Grundrechte), p. 26.

14. Ibid. Scheel, in a shortwave message in Dec. 1977, told overseas Germans that

the decree's problems had been highly exaggerated and that few radicals had been rejected.

15. Ingrid Kurz, "Der Anfang vom Ende der Berufsverbote?" *Blätter für deutsche und internationale Politik* 23, no. 11 (Nov. 1978): 1324–25, quoting *Der Stern*, no. 34, 1978. See also D. BT., 8th el. pd., Drucksache 8/2761, Apr. 20, 1979.

16. FRG, German Information Center (New York), *Relay from Bonn*, June 15, 1976; Willy Brandt and Helmut Schmidt, *Deutschland 1976: Zwei Sozialdemokraten im Gespräch* (Hamburg: Rowohlt, 1976), p. 48.

17. *International Herald Tribune*, July 24, 1976; *Relay from Bonn*, June 15, 1976.

18. *The Guardian*, May 29, 1976; *Frankfurter Rundschau*, May 29, 1976. President Scheel denounced Mitterrand's formation of the committee as "cheap polemics" aimed to win votes in France (*International Herald Tribune*, July 24, 1976).

19. SPD, "Dokumentation über die Beschäftigung von Extremisten im öffentlichen Dienst der Bundesrepublik Deutschland" (n.d. [c. 1976], hectographed).

20. European Parliament, Sozialistische Fraktion, Pressereferat, June 11, 1976; SPD, *Pressemitteilungen und Informationen*, 306/76, June 10, 1076.

21. *Süddeutsche Zeitung*, July 23, 1976.

22. *Der Spiegel*, June 28, 1976.

23. Brandt and Schmidt, *Deutschland 1976*, pp. 48–49; *New York Times*, June 10, 1976. According to the *Times*, Horst Ehmke, a close Brandt aide and former cabinet minister, also admitted to having miscalculated politically in supporting Brandt's original 1972 decision.

24. *International Herald Tribune*, July 24, 1976.

25. Ibid., July 30, 1976; *Frankfurter Rundschau*, May 29, 1976; *Süddeutsche Zeitung*, May 31, 1976.

26. *Süddeutsche Zeitung*, June 12, 1976.

27. *Die Welt*, Apr. 1, 1976; *New York Times*, June 10, 1976.

28. Theo Sommer in *Die Zeit*, June 4, 1976.

29. *International Herald Tribune*, July 24, 1976; *Publik-Forum*, July 30, 1976; *Vorwärts*, Apr. 15, 1976.

30. Jusos, *IUSY-Kongress '77, Stuttgart* (Bonn, 1977).

31. *Vorwärts*, Oct. 21, 1976.

32. Members of the council were the writer Ingeborg Drewitz, theologians Hellmut Golwitzer and Martin Niemöller, and professors Wolf-Dieter Narr and Uwe Wesel.

33. D. BT., 8th el. pd., Drucksache 8/1205, Nov. 21, 1977; in reply to a CDU/CSU parliamentary query, Drucksache 8/953, Sept. 25, 1977.

34. Freimut Duve and Wolf-Dieter Narr, eds., *Russell-Tribunal: Pro und contra* (Reinbek: Rowohlt, 1978), pp. 30–40.

35. FRG, *The Bulletin* (English ed.), 5/2, Mar. 15, 1978 (archive supplement).

36. *"For Official Use Only": The Secret Plans of the West German Interior Ministry to Destroy the Russell Tribunal on Human Rights* (Nottingham, England: Russell Press, 1978), p. 8.

37. *Vorwärts*, Oct. 20, 1977; personal interview with Peter Cipa, Bonn Initiative against Berufsverbote, Mar. 12, 1980.

38. Government and agency officials who had been involved in the cases did not

appear, even though they had been invited; professors and journalists favoring the decree also boycotted the proceedings.

39. For details, see *Drittes Internationales Russell-Tribunal: Zur Situation der Menschenrechte in der Bundesrepublik Deutschland,* 3 vols. (Berlin: Rotbuch, 1978); Bertrand Russell Peace Foundation, *Third Russell Tribunal: Berufsverbote Condemned* (Nottingham: Russell Press, 1978).

40. Marion Gräfin Dönhoff in *Die Zeit,* Apr. 7, 1978.

41. *Neue Ruhr-Zeitung,* Apr. 5, 1978; *Bayern-Kurier,* Apr. 8, 1978.

42. *Hannoversche Allgemeine Zeitung,* Apr. 5, 1978.

43. *Le Monde,* Apr. 8, 1978.

44. Council of Europe, Parliamentary Assembly, Twenty-seventh Ordinary Session, May 4, 1976, pp. 57–60.

45. Council of Europe, Parliamentary Assembly, Legal Affairs Committee, AS/Jur (28) 12, July 26, 1976.

46. The government also argued that Article 10 and other articles of the convention do not apply when national security, preservation of order, etc. were at stake (D. BT., 10th el. pd., Drucksache 10/3656, July 18, 1985, pp. 10–11).

47. Council of Europe, European Court of Human Rights, Glasenapp Case (4/1984/76/120), Judgment, Strasbourg, Aug. 28, 1986, p. 28. For commentary, cf. Albert Bleckmann, " 'Berufsverbote' und die Europäische Menschenrechtskonvention," *Die öffentliche Verwaltung* 37, no. 14 (July 1984): 565–77.

48. In a concurring opinion, one judge agreed that there was no technical breach of Article 10 but contended that Kosiek's dismissal was based primarily on the interference with his freedom to express political opinions. In a partially dissenting opinion, another judge argued that even in the case of access to the civil service, Article 10 obviously may apply. See Council of Europe, European Court of Human Rights, Kosiek Case (5/1984/77/121), Judgment, Strasbourg, August 28, 1986; D. BT., 10th el. pd., Drucksache 10/3656, July 18, 1985, p. 11. In 1988, the commission had the case of Rüdiger Quaer pending. Quaer, a teacher on probationary status, had lost his post because of his political activities as a KPD adherent.

49. *Frankfurter Rundschau,* Sept. 14, 1981.

50. EC, Court of Justice of the European Communities, Judgment of the Court, June 28, 1984, *Hans Moser v. Land Baden-Württemberg* (reference for a preliminary ruling from the Arbeitsgericht Reutlingen; Free movement of workers—concept of worker), Case 180/83, pp. 2539–51. See also D. BT., 10th el. pd., Drucksache 10/3656, July 18, 1985, p. 11, in reply to a parliamentary query of the Green Fraktion.

51. EC, European Parliament, Legal Affairs Committee, "Observations on the Rules as to Exclusion from Employment in the Public Service in the FRG," no. 61/80, PE 78.706, July 15, 1982, p. 13.

52. Ibid.

53. European Parliament, Debates, no. 2–330/132, Oct. 9, 1985; question no. 62. See also *Frankfurter Rundschau,* July 9, 1983; D. BT., 10th el. pd., Drucksache 10/3656, July 18, 1985; letter by Alfredo di Stefano, directorate general for research, European Parliament, to author, Apr. 10, 1987.

54. Europäisches Parlament, Ausschuss für Geschäftsordnung und Petitionen,

Sitzung vom 15./16. Oktober 1985, "'Berufsverbote': Der Ausschuss für Geschäftsordnung wünscht sich eine eindeutige Rechtslage."

55. Veröffentlichungen der Vereinigung Demokratischer Juristen in der Bundes-
republik, no. 2/1975, quoted in IMSF, *Informationsbericht* no. 22, pp. 26–29.
See also Bethge et al., *Die Zerstörung der Demokratie,* pp. 251–54; *Sieben Jahre
Kampf gegen die Berufsverbote,* p. 20.

In its session of Mar. 20, 1987, the UN Economic and Social Council renewed
discussion of the decree at a time when the ILO had submitted its report (see
below). The representative of the FRG government was asked whether the
cabinet would accept the report; he referred questioners to the forthcoming
reply to the ILO (UN, Economic and Social Council, Summary Record of the
Nineteenth Meeting [Mar. 20, 1987], p. 9).

56. Weltfriedensrat, *Berufsverbote in der Bundesrepublik Deutschland* (Helsinki,
n.d.); Radio Moscow, German program, Oct. 25, 1977; *Ost-Informationen*
(Bonn), Oct. 26, 1977. The Human Rights Committee of UNESCO, at its
meeting of May 17, 1983, dealt with the 1972 decree anew but deferred action
on two complaints, pending the exhaustion of domestic remedies in the FRG.

57. ILO, GB 210/16/27, 211th session, Geneva. In the Governing Body, 50 percent
of the members are government, 25 percent employer, and 25 percent worker
representatives. The WFTU complaint had been preceded in 1975 by an International Federation of Teachers Unions complaint, which, however, was not
considered.

58. ILO, Governing Body, GB 235/4/7, 235th session, Geneva, March 2–6, 1987,
Report, p. 1.

59. Ibid., p. 75.

60. Ibid., p. 115.

61. Ibid., p. 190. The report is dated Feb. 20, 1987.

62. Ibid., p. 195.

63. Ibid., p. 182.

64. Ibid., p. 205.

65. Internationales Arbeitsamt (ILO), Verwaltungsrat, GB. 236/4/6, 236th session,
Geneva, May 28–30, 1987; appendix, letter from Winfried Haase, FRG representative to the ILO, to ILO director-general Francis Blanchard, May 7, 1987.
The FRG government position was not based on a cabinet decision, but on an
interministerial accord drafted by the Ministry of Labor, with the assistance of
the Ministries of the Interior (BMI), Justice, and Foreign Affairs (personal
interview with BMI official, Bonn, June 5, 1987).

66. Articles 25 and 59 of the FRG Basic Law recognize priority of international over
national law, but Article 59 specifies that an international accord regulating
FRG national matters needs parliamentary approval in the form of a law. In two
decisions (May 20, 1984, and Jan. 20, 1987), the Federal Administrative Court
in West Berlin ruled that a plaintiff could not request delay of a trial until the
ILO report was issued. Even if the report recommends changes in FRG practice,
national laws calling for civil servants' loyalty would not be affected (Bundesverwaltungsgericht, 1. Disziplinarsenat, BVerwG 1 D 114.85; BDiG II VL 4/85;
proceedings of Jan. 20, 1987).

67. Horst Bethge and Klaus Dammann, "Der ILO-Bericht zu den Berufsverboten,"

Blätter für deutsche und internationale Politik 32, no. 5 (May 1987): 586; *Frankfurter Rundschau*, May 30, 1987. See also Klaus Dammann and Erwin Siemantel, eds., *Berufsverbote und Menschenrechte in der Bundesrepublik* (Cologne: Pahl-Rugenstein, 1987), including text of ILO report, pp. 75–370.

68. *Frankfurter Allgemeine Zeitung*, June 2, 1987.
69. *Deutsches Allgemeines Sonntagsblatt*, May 4, 1986; *New York Times*, Sept. 14, 1987.
70. ILO, seventy-fifth session 1988, Report 3 (part 4A), Report of the Committee of Experts on the Application of Conventions and Recommendations, pp. 306–11. See also the Conference Committee report, June 1988 (no pagination), Geneva; Michael Brändle and Klaus Dammann, "Flickenteppich: Zur aktuellen Lage in Sachen Berufsverbote," *Demokratie und Recht* 17, no. 1 (1989): 72–73.

Chapter 5: The Aftermath, 1976–1980

1. "Der Radikalenbeschluss und seine Folgen," *GEW—Neue deutsche Schule*, Oct. 13, 1978; Albert Krölls, "Zehn Jahre Radikalenerlass: Zum (aktuellen) Fortschritt der Berufsverbotspolitik," *Vorgänge* 21, no. 3 (June 1982): 10; Komitee für Grundrechte und Demokratie (KGD), *Ohne Zweifel für den Staat*, p. 127. The totals of rejections are not precise; the KGD cites 1,102 (to 1982); the Initiative against Berufsverbote estimate (to 1987) is 2,250 (Dammann, "Das/the/le/il Berufsverbot," p. 34).

   In 1979, to help the decree's victims, labor leaders, academics, artists, and theologians created the Heinrich-Heine Fund. By 1981, more than 100,000 DM was collected and given to thirty-two ousted individuals for their immediate welfare needs ("Heinrich-Heine-Fonds: Solidarität mit den Betroffenen vom Berufsverbot" [1981, hectographed]).

2. In 1979–80, North Rhine-Westphalia handled 62 cases; the FRG government, 47; Bavaria, 45; Lower Saxony, 40; Berlin, 23; Hamburg, 23; Hesse, 16; Bremen, 9; Schleswig-Holstein, 7; Rhineland-Palatinate, 6; and Saar, 0 (statistics compiled by KGD, *Ohne Zweifel für der Staat*, p. 132; see also pp. 133–37). Cf. the KGD's "Berufsverbotspraxis 1979/80: Die 'Liberalisierung' hat nicht stattgefunden" (Berlin, 1980, hectographed). Also, personal interview with staff member, IMSF, Frankfurt am Main, Feb. 22, 1980.

3. See, for example, Bavarian Ministry of the Interior, *Verfassungsschutzbericht: Bayern 1982* (Munich, n.d.), pp. 153–55.

4. Most numbers for 1972 to 1979 are based on *Verfassungsschutz* yearbooks, calculated by Jesse, *Streitbare Demokratie*, pp. 68–69; for 1980, see *Bonner Rundschau*, Jan. 29, 1982. See also p. 198n.3.

5. *Vorwärts*, Feb. 16, 1978; *The Economist*, Feb. 18, 1978; *Stern*, Oct. 1, 1981.

6. *Vorwärts*, Apr. 20, 1978.

7. "Freie Fahrt für den Lokführer Rudi Röder," issued by Würzburger Bürgerkomitee zur Verteidigung der Grundrechte (Würzburg, n.d., hectographed); *Frankfurter Rundschau*, Apr. 2, 1976; *Vorwärts*, Apr. 15, 1976; *Die Zeit*, Aug. 17, 1979.

8. ILO, Governing Body, 1987 Report, pp. 96–97; summary of 1978 hearing in

Berufsverbote bei der Bundespost: Dokumentation, comp. Ute Post (Hamburg, 1979), pp. 27–28; Bundesdisziplinargericht, Kammer 1, Frankfurt am Main, Az.: I VL 25/83.

9. *Info: West Germany* (issued by New York Committee for Civil Liberties in West Germany), Feb. 1979, p. 11; *Berufsverbot: Ernennungsurkunde* (Berlin: Kant, 1978); *Bürgerversammlung zur Verteidigung unserer Verfassung* (Berlin: Kant, 1978); *Süddeutsche Zeitung,* Oct. 21, 1978; personal interview with Apel, Berlin, Dec. 4, 1979. For other Berlin cases, see *Betroffene melden sich zu Wort* (Berlin: Kant, 1978).

10. Disziplinarkammer bei dem Verwaltungsgericht Hannover, Oct. 9, 1981, Az. DK. A 41/80; Alfred Krovoza, Axel R. Oestmann, and Klaus Ottomeyer, eds., *Zum Beispiel Peter Brückner: Treue zum Staat und kritische Wissenschaft* (Frankfurt am Main: Europäische Verlagsanstalt, 1981); Koch and Oltmanns, *SOS,* pp. 202–3; Wolfgang Nitsch, "Ein 'Staatsfeind' im Gewande des Kritikers? Zum Prozess gegen Peter Brückner," *Psychologie und Gesellschaftskritik* 5, no. 4 (1981): 107–27; *Der Spiegel,* Aug. 15, 1977.

11. *Der Spiegel,* June 16, 1980.

12. *Frankfurter Allgemeine Zeitung,* Jan. 13, 1976; *Süddeutsche Zeitung,* June 10, 1976.

13. See, e.g., Jesse, *Streitbare Demokratie,* pp. 70–71.

14. Deutsche Gesellschaft für Verhaltenstherapie (DGV), *Berufsverbote in der Bundesrepublik Deutschland: Bericht der Kommission "Berufsverbote" über Betroffene, psychische Folgen, und Auswirkungen auf die psychosoziale Versorgung* (Bielefeld, 1979), adapted from pp. 42–44. See also pp. 39–41. The report, issued in German and English, was based on seventy-seven responses; summary in *Neue Praxis* 9, no. 2 (1979): 137–46. See also *Psychologie heute,* no. 1 (1978); *Vorwärts,* Aug. 31, 1978.

15. DGV, *Berufsverbote,* pp. 23–27.

16. Mannheim survey in "Die Schere im Kopf: Untersuchungen zu den Folgen des Radikalenerlasses," *Psychologie heute,* Oct. 1980, cited in Horn, "Berufsverbote," p. 49.

17. Horn, "Berufsverbote," p. 50. See also Klaus Farin and Hans-Jürgen Zwingmann, *Modell Deutschland? Berufsverbote* (Ettingen: Doku-Verlag, 1979).

18. Personal interview with Irmgard and Peter Cipa, Initiative against Berufsverbote, Bonn, Mar. 13, 1980.

19. *Der Spiegel,* Oct. 9, 1978.

20. Eveline Radzom, "Gemerkt, dass ich auch alleine jemand bin," *Deutsche Volkszeitung,* Nov. 17, 1977, p. 16; quoted in Monica Jacobs, "Civil Rights and Women's Rights in the Federal Republic of Germany Today," *New German Critique,* no. 13 (Winter 1978): 170.

21. Jacobs, "Civil Rights and Women's Rights," p. 170.

22. *Bonn General-Anzeiger,* Feb. 29, 1980; author's observations, and personal interview with Prof. Gerald Grünwald, Bonn University, Feb. 28, 1980.

23. List of 178 names printed in pamphlet issued jointly by League of Democratic Academics and Initiative against Berufsverbote, cited in Hans Hermsen, "Politische Repression an den Hochschulen und ihre Folgen: Versuch einer psy-

chologischen Interpretation," in *Politische Psychologie,* ed. Hans-Dieter Klinge-mann and Max Kaase (Opladen: Westdeutscher Verlag, 1981), p. 171; GEW survey (n.d.), cited in Hermsen, "Politische Repression," p. 173.

24. Hermsen, "Politische Repression," p. 185.
25. Wolf-Dieter Narr, "Academic Freedom 1979: The West German Case," *New Political Science* 1, no. 1 (Winter 1979): 50.
26. *Die Welt,* Dec. 13, 1978; Bethge et al., *Die Zerstörung der Demokratie,* pp. 23–24.
27. *Süddeutsche Zeitung,* Apr. 2, 1979.
28. Reprinted in Friedrich-Naumann-Stiftung, *Dokumentation: Extremistenbe-schluss,* p. 32; see also p. 31.
29. Staeck also drew a small label with the inscription "Attention, Attention: Con-tent corresponds to FDGO." For other cartoons, see *links, Sozialistische Zeitung* (Offenbach), no. 73 (n.d.).
30. *Theaterstücke zum Radikalenerlass,* p. 126.
31. Ibid., p. 85.
32. Ibid., pp. 107–14.
33. Schneider, . . . *schon bist du ein Verfassungsfeind: Das unerwartete Anschwellen der Personalakte des Lehrers Kleff* (Berlin: Rotbuch, 1975), p. 22.
34. See Peter Labanyi's review in *Times Literary Supplement* (London), Apr. 22, 1977; Dieter Lattmann, "Freiheit in der Bundesrepublik: Politik und Zeitgeist," in *Extremismus im demokratischen Rechtsstaat,* ed. Manfred Funke (Düssel-dorf: Droste, 1978), p. 458.
35. *Frankfurter Rundschau,* Feb. 7, 1977; June 9, 1980; *Der Spiegel,* Nov. 21, 1977.
36. Komitee Arbeitsgruppe Berufsverbote, KGD, "Berufsverbote 1979/80: Die 'Lib-eralisierung' hat nicht stattgefunden," *Freiheit und Gleichheit,* no. 2 (Oct. 1980): 95–102. The KGD working group members were Bernhard Blanke, Kai Dieckmann, Peter Grottian, Wolf-Dieter Narr, and Albrecht Wellmer.
37. GEW, "Bundesrepublik Deutschland," p. 12; GEW, *Pressedienst,* "Der Radika-lenbeschluss und seine Folgen," Oct. 13, 1978.
38. *DL aktuell,* Oct. 11, 1978.
39. Zentralkomitee der deutschen Katholiken, *Mitteilungen,* Jan. 2, 1979; *Süd-deutsche Zeitung,* Apr. 13, 1976.
40. Some council members did not concur with all recommendations. See Evan-gelische Kirche in Deutschland, "Bericht der Kammer für öffentliche Verant-wortung an den Rat der EKD zur Frage der Beschäftigung von Extremisten im öffentlichen Dienst" (n.p., n.d.). For a less critical position, see Ludwig Raiser, "Der 'Radikalen-Erlass': Prüfstein eines demokratischen Rechtsstaats?" *Zeit-schrift für Evangelische Ethik* 23, no. 2 (1979): 106–17.
41. Personal interview with GEW functionary, Hamburg, Jan. 17, 1980.
42. *International Herald Tribune,* Oct. 24, 1978. See also Narr, "Die SPD, der Radikalenerlass, und kein Ende," *Kritik* 6, no. 19 (1978): 85–92.
43. *Der Spiegel,* Oct. 9, 1978, p. 23. For other press reactions, see Staatliche Presse-stelle Hamburg, *Mehr Toleranz wagen: Ausgewählte Pressestimmen zum Vor-schlag des Hamburger Bürgermeisters Hans-Ulrich Klose zur Lockerung des Extremisten-Beschluss,* 2 vols. (Hamburg, n.d.).
44. *Der Spiegel,* Oct. 9, 1978, p. 23.

45. See "Radikale am Katheder: Was Eltern zu Berufsverboten sagen," issued by Initiative "Weg mit den Berufsverboten" (n.p., n.d.).

46. Text of Koschnick plan in SPD, Dokumentation, *Grundsätze zur Feststellung der Verfassungstreue im öffentlichen Dienst, vorgelegt von Hans Koschnick, Stellvertretender Parteivorsitzender, Bonn, 16. Oktober 1978* (Bonn, 1978). See also Koschnick, *Der Abschied vom Extremistenbeschluss* (Bonn: Neue Gesellschaft, 1979), pp. 9–22; SPD, Bundes-Delegierten-Konferenz und Ausserordentlicher Parteitag der SPD, 9.–10. Dez. 1978, Köln, *Protokoll der Verhandlungen,* pp. 230–55, 411–14. Bremen had a similar plan in force since 1976.

47. Jusos, *Rundschreiben,* A1/79, Jan. 1979, to all *Arbeitsgemeinschaften,* members of the executive committee, Juso secretaries.

48. *Süddeutsche Zeitung,* Oct. 17, 18, 1978.

49. Deutsche Jungdemokraten, *Pressemitteilung,* 6/78, Jan. 27, 1978.

50. FDP, *fdk tagesdienst,* 824/74, Oct. 27, 1978.

51. Friedrich-Naumann-Stiftung, *Dokumentation: Extremistenbeschluss,* pp. 57–59.

52. D. BT., 8th el. pd., 68th session, Jan. 25, 1978, pp. 5365–66.

53. CDU, *Zum Thema: Verfassungsfeinde* (Bonn, n.d.), p. 8.

54. One CSU deputy in the Bundestag declared that the number of leftist teachers kept growing, while the number of rightist teachers was declining. He asked the government to explain this trend and what disciplinary measures were taken against such teachers. The government contended that this was a Länder issue (ibid., pp. 10–11; CSU, *Presse-Mitteilungen,* no. 627/1979, Nov. 8, 1979).

55. D. BT., 8th el. pd., Drucksache 8/2305, Nov. 17, 1978.

56. *Der Spiegel,* Oct. 30, 1978.

57. *Frankfurter Rundschau,* Oct. 31, 1978.

58. For text, see FRG, *Bulletin,* Jan. 19, 1979, pp. 45–47. Title in translation: "Principles for assessing the loyalty to the Constitution of applicants for posts in the public service" (Document: FRG, Translation 105–292/79, n.p., n.d., hectographed). See also D. BT., Drucksache 8/2481 and 8/2482, Jan. 22, 1979.

59. *The Economist,* Jan. 27, 1979; *Christian Science Monitor,* Jan. 29, 1979.

60. *New York Times,* Jan. 19, 1979.

61. *Stuttgarter Zeitung,* Jan. 19, 1979; *Süddeutsche Zeitung,* Jan. 19, 1979.

62. See Zentralkomitee der deutschen Katholiken, *Mitteilungen,* Jan. 2, 1979; Baden-Württemberg, Innenministerium, *Verfassungstreue im öffentlichen Dienst* (Stuttgart, 1979), p. 31; Bayerisches Staatsministerium der Finanzen, *Extremisten beim Staat? Finanzminister Max Streibl antwortet im Landtag* (Munich, c. 1979), pp. 36–37, 40.

63. D. BT., 8th el. pd., 132nd session, Jan. 25, 1979, pp. 10395–432. See also 131st session, Jan. 24th, 1979, p. 10362; Drucksache 8/2481, Jan. 22, 1979. For further CDU arguments, see CDU, *Zum Thema: Verfassungsfeinde,* pp. 9–10. On Feb. 15, in another Bundestag debate, the CDU/CSU introduced a resolution demanding that the government withdraw its guidelines, but to no avail (D. BT., 8th el. pd., 138th session, Feb. 15, 1979).

64. See, e.g., Bayerisches Staatsministerium des Innern, *Schutz für Verfassung, Staat, Gesellschaft: Verfassungsfeinde in den öffentlichen Dienst?* (Munich, 1976). In one tumultuous session of the Bavarian Landtag, one FDP deputy

characterized the CSU as being close to fascism for refusing to liberalize its practice (*Süddeutsche Zeitung*, June 30, 1978).

65. *Frankfurter Rundschau*, Sept. 5, 1980. The Land had introduced a special loyalty-oath requirement in June 1979, which nearly caused a breakup of the SPD and FDP coalition (*Stuttgarter Zeitung*, Oct. 6, 1979).

66. KGD, *Ohne Zweifel für den Staat*, pp. 15–17; KGD, Komitee Arbeitsgruppe Berufsverbote, "Berufsverbote 1979/80," p. 101; *Tageszeitung* (Berlin), Feb. 4, 1981.

67. Hessischer Landtag, 9th el. pd., Drucksache 9/3762, Oct. 30, 1980. According to the federal *Verfassungsschutzbericht* for 1984, the federal government employed 221 left extremists and 111 right extremists, the Länder 1,473 left and 91 right extremists, and the communities 526 left and 54 right extremists (BMI, *Verfassungsschutz 1984*, pp. 22–24, 132, 135).

68. In 1980, Gscheidle's ministry was divided; he remained minister of post and telecommunications, and Volker Hauff (SPD) became minister of transport.

69. *Vorwärts*, July 27, 1978. See also Baum statement in D. BT., 8th el. pd., Drucksache 8/3611, Jan. 24, 1980.

70. CDU/CSU Fraktion im D. BT., Jan. 25, 1980; Apr. 28, 1980; D. BT., 8th el. pd., Drucksache 8/4493, Oct. 1, 1980.

71. *Stuttgarter Nachrichten*, Dec. 4, 1979; *Berufsverbote bei der Bundespost: Dokumentation*, p. 6.

72. *Berufsverbote bei der Bundespost*, p. 15; *Der Spiegel*, Mar. 26, 1979; Sept. 10, 1979.

73. *Der Spiegel*, Nov. 2, 1981.

74. *Frankfurter Rundschau*, June 6, 9, 1980; *Süddeutsche Zeitung*, June 10, 1980.

75. The first category (keeping the radicals out of public service altogether) was supported by 21 out of every 100 SPD supporters, 34 out of 100 FDP, and 46 out of every 100 CDU/CSU supporters (*Der Spiegel*, Oct. 16, 1978, pp. 37–38).

76. The poll also showed that men and women about equally supported the plan, but almost twice as many women as men (37 to 20 percent) had no opinion on the question. Respondents under thirty and those with at least a high school education favored the plan (ibid.).

77. *Die Welt*, Dec. 5, 1979.

78. Elisabeth Noelle-Neumann and Edgar Piel, eds., *Allensbacher Jahrbuch der Demoskopie, 1979–1983* (Munich: K. G. Saur, 1983), p. 260. The responses to the saliency question hardly differed in other years, ranging from 43 percent in 1977 to 40 percent in 1982 (pp. 262, 335, 336). In 1984, in a similar saliency question by the Emnid-Institute, 34 percent of respondents said keeping out radicals was an especially important political problem; 51 percent said that the CDU/CSU can best do the job, while 12 percent chose the SPD (*Die Zeit*, Jan. 11, 1985).

79. In a poll taken in Feb. 1979, the responses to a similar question were 62 percent affirmative, 24 percent opposed, and 14 percent undecided, indicating a slight shift toward the left SPD position (Noelle-Neumann and Piel, *Allensbacher Jahrbuch*, p. 317).

80. The rest were undecided. In 1973, in the first of five periodic polls, 58 percent said no and 18 percent yes (ibid.).

Chapter 6: The Aftermath, the 1980s

1. Peter Grottian, "Werden Berufsverbote wieder sichtbar?" *Vorgänge* 22, no. 2–3 (1983): 106. See also KGD, "Berufsverbote 1979/80," pp. 97–98.
2. Koschnick and Rosen, "Der lange Abschied," p. 942; Bernhard Blanke, "Schutz der Verfassung durch Spaltung der Demokratie?" *Freiheit und Gleichheit*, no. 2 (Oct. 1980): 81; Mankoff and Jacobs, "Return of the Suppressed," p. 350. The Initiative against Berufsverbote issued a tally in 1985 of the total number of bans (6,689) and screenings (2,639,058) from 1971 to April 1985 by Länder and federal government (IMSF, *Informationsbericht* no. 42, p. 11). The tally does not correspond to other totals cited in the preface.
3. D. BT., 10th el. pd., Drucksache 10/3656, July 18, 1985.
4. North Rhine-Westphalia, however, restricted entry to applicants who had been active in such a party (Land Nordrhein-Westfalen, Chef der Staatskanzlei, Mar. 21, 1983; memorandum on cabinet session, Mar. 15, 1983).
5. Bremische Bürgerschaft, Landtag, Drucksache 10/1021, Feb. 7, 1983.
6. Bethge, "Möglichkeiten," pp. 1105, 1107; *The Times* (London), Jan. 28, 1982. After the fall of the CDU-led government in Schleswig-Holstein in May 1988, Björn Engholm (SPD) became minister-president. In July, his cabinet issued an order, comparable to the practice in other SPD-led Länder, stopping the CDU-initiated practice of making routine inquiries from the *Verfassungsschutz* about applicants to the civil service (*Frankfurter Rundschau*, July 13, 1988). The decree was not lifted entirely, even though that seemed to be Engholm's intention before he assumed office.
7. *Süddeutsche Zeitung*, June 26, 1985. For details, see ILO, Governing Body, 1987 Report, pp. 61–62.
8. *Süddeutsche Zeitung*, June 26, 1985; Oct. 25, 1985; *Der Spiegel*, July 1, 1985; CDU/CSU Fraktion in D. BT, *Pressedienst*, June 25, 1985; Bayerische Staatskanzlei, 2/85, July 2, 1985.
9. *Frankfurter Allgemeine Zeitung*, June 26, 1985.
10. *Frankfurter Rundschau*, July 26, 1985.
11. *Süddeutsche Zeitung*, Jan. 12, 1982. The government also appealed the decisions of labor courts in their support of radical salaried employees and workers. Two officials involved in the decree's administration expressed anger at such support (personal interviews with Bavarian Ministry of the Interior officials, Munich, Jan. 17, 1985).
12. GEW, Landesverband Bayern, *Die Demokratische Schule*, no. 1 (Jan. 1982): 29, 35.
13. *Vorwärts*, Apr. 14, 1983. Prior to the issuance of the regulation, the Bavarian branch of the GEW appealed to the union movement to defend the civil liberties of its members and restore constitutional political rights in the FRG. The Land GEW asked its members to pay the equivalent of a monthly union contribution into a solidarity fund for the decree's victims (GEW, Landesverband Bayern, *Die Demokratische Schule*, no. 1 [Jan. 1982]: 5).
14. *Die Zeit*, Sept. 21, 1984. Furthermore, Gerhard Schröder, the SPD candidate for minister-president, announced that if his party won the 1986 election, he intended to reinstate those ousted by the CDU government.

15. *The Times* (London), Jan. 28, 1982; GEW, *Korrespondenz*, Apr. 21, 1983; IMSF, *Informationsbericht* no. 42, p. 36.
16. GEW, "Bundesrepublik Deutschland," p. 7.
17. Bethge, "Möglichkeiten," p. 1106.
18. Of the fifty-six rightist civil servants, fifteen were functionaries in their party organization, and nineteen were candidates for a legislative seat (with many individuals holding a function and running for a seat). Of the seventy-nine leftist civil servants, seven were functionaries in their party, and fourteen were candidates for a legislative seat (D. BT., 9th el. pd., Drucksache 9/1539, Mar. 30, 1982). See BT, *Drucksache* 9/1532, Feb. 12, 1982.
19. Minister of the interior replying to a CDU/CSU question (CDU/CSU Fraktion im D. BT., *Pressedienst*, Apr. 24, 1981; D. BT., 9th el. pd., Drucksache 9/351, Apr. 16, 1981).
20. *Frankfurter Rundschau*, Dec. 4, 1980.
21. In late 1980, the Ministry of Transport, Post, and Telecommunications was split into the Ministry of Transport and the Ministry of Post and Telecommunications.
22. *Der Spiegel*, Apr. 6, 1981.
23. D. BT., 9th el. pd., Drucksache 9/383, Apr. 30, 1981; CDU/CSU Fraktion im D. BT., *Pressedienst*, May 6, 8, 1981.
24. *Stuttgarter Zeitung*, Dec. 6, 1979; *Frankfurter Allgemeine Zeitung*, Mar. 25, 1980; *Frankfurter Rundschau*, Apr. 1, 1980. See also *Wer hat Angst vor dem Postbeamten Hans Peter?* (Stuttgarter Aktionskreis gegen Berufsverbote, Stuttgart, 1981); Erwin Siementhal and H. D. Wohlfarth, eds., *Der Fall Hans Peter: Entlassung eines "Verfassungsfeindes": Dokumentation und Analyse* (Cologne: Ralf Theurer, 1982).
25. Bundesverwaltungsgericht, judgment of Oct. 29, 1981, in *Neue Juristische Wochenschrift*, 1982, p. 779.
26. The GEW supported the center's findings (GEW, *Korrespondenz*, Apr. 21, 1983). See also dpa, *press release*, 2232D/2–3110, n.d.; 202, Oct. 30, 1981, in which SPD chief Brandt contended that Peter's refusal to become a salaried employee was part of the DKP strategy to make him a martyr. See also Peter Czapski, "Zur politischen Treuepflicht der Beamten nach der Entscheidung des Bundesverwaltungsgerichts vom 29. Oktober 1981," *Zeitschrift für Beamtenrecht*, no. 7 (1982): 203–9.
27. *Berufsverbot für den Postbeamten Hans Meister,* issued by Stuttgarter Aktionskreis gegen die Berufsverbote (c. 1979).
28. ILO, Governing Body, 1987 Report, pp. 93–95; Hans-Dietrich Weiss, "Die jüngste 'Extremisten'-Entscheidung des Bundesverwaltungsgerichts," *Zeitschrift für Beamtenrecht*, no. 3 (1985): 70–79; Wolfgang Däubler and H. D. Wohlfarth, eds. *Hans Meister: Postbeamter und Kommunist* (Cologne, 1985). In most other postal cases, the Federal Disciplinary Court also dismissed government charges of disloyalty; individuals were reinstated in their posts if, as in many instances, they had been suspended (IMSF, *Informationsbericht* no. 42, p. 63). See also Martin Kutscha, "Zwischen Vollzug und Verweigerung: Die aktuelle Rechtsprechung in Berufsverbotsverfahren," *Demokratie und Recht* 13, no. 2 (1985): 218–27.

29. *Vorwärts*, July 5, 1984; *Deutsche Post*, Aug. 20, 1984.
30. In reference to Sgt. Norbert Sprör, *New York Times*, Nov. 7, 1978.
31. Glotz, citing Schmidt's 1980 declaration, in SPD, *Sozialdemokraten, Service, Presse, Funk, TV*, no. 169/82, Apr. 2, 1982.
32. For text, see BMI, "Bundeskabinett verabschiedet 'Entwurf eines Dritten Gesetzes zur Änderung beamtenrichtlicher Vorschriften'" (June 16, 1982, hectographed); Bundesrat, Drucksache 290/82, Aug. 27, 1982; FRG, *Bulletin*, June 21, 1982. See also *Der Spiegel*, Feb. 1, 1982.
33. *Frankfurter Rundschau*, June 18, 1982.
34. *Der Spiegel*, Feb. 1, 1982.
35. CSU, *Presse-Mitteilungen*, CSU-Landesgruppe im D. BT., no. 67/1982, Jan. 27, 1982; Alfred Dregger, "Selbstaufgabe der Demokratie? Der Streit um Extremisten im öffentlichen Dienst," *Die politische Meinung*, Jan.–Feb. 1982, pp. 20–25; CDU/CSU Fraktion im D. BT., *Pressedienst*, Feb. 12, Apr. 21, 1982; *Süddeutsche Zeitung*, Apr. 2, 1982; *Münchner Merkur*, Apr. 19, 1982.
36. *Der Spiegel*, June 21, 1982. Peter Conradi, a left-wing SPD deputy, argued the bill was unnecessary if Baum, in his capacity as minister, would instruct Claussen to stop seeking to discharge civil servants unless there was evidence of disloyalty against them. Klaus Thüsing, another left-wing SPD deputy, talked about a possible parliamentary initiative to seek the decree's abolition. The cabinet did not act on either suggestion (dpa, *press release*, Jan. 24, 1982; SPD, *Sozialdemokratischer Pressedienst*, no. 24, Feb. 4, 1982).
37. Bundesrat, press release, Oct. 8, 1982; *Bonner Rundschau*, Sept. 29, 1982; *Frankfurter Allgemeine Zeitung*, Oct. 9, 1982.
38. Personal interview with two officials of the Bavarian Ministry of the Interior, Munich, Jan. 17, 1985.
39. D. BT., Gesetzentwurf der SPD Fraktion, "Entwurf eines Dritten Gesetzes zur Änderung beamtenrechtlicher Vorschriften," Drucksache 9/2058, Oct. 27, 1982 (hectographed); ILO, Governing Body, 1987 Report, p. 153.
40. During the Oct. 1982 negotiations, the participants agreed that Zimmermann should submit a report to the cabinet by Apr. 1983 on the existing practices in all public services, but such a report apparently was not prepared. In spring 1983, the minister informed the Bundestag Committee on Domestic Affairs that the government did not contemplate making any policy changes until the report was finished (FRG, "Ergebnis der Koalitionsgespräche der Regierung Kohl, Okt. 1982" [hectographed]; *Süddeutsche Zeitung*, Mar. 25, 1983; IMSF, *Informationsbericht* no. 42, p. 46; personal interview with BMI officials, Bonn, Aug. 8, 1983; June 5, 1987).
41. Personal interviews with labor-law specialist, University of Freiburg, Jan. 16, 1985; BMI official, Bonn, June 5, 1987.
42. Among the well-publicized cases were Herbert Bastian, Axel Brück, Berthold Goergens, and Wolfgang Repp (Bethge, "Möglichkeiten," p. 1106). See also IMSF, *Informationsbericht* no. 42, pp. 18–19.
43. *Der Spiegel*, Nov. 26, 1979; *Die Tageszeitung*, Aug. 17, 1984.
44. Professors' position detailed in a letter (Mar. 9, 1979) to then Chancellor Schmidt, reprinted in *Berufsverbote bei der Bundespost: Dokumentation*, pp. 22–23.

45. dpa, *press release*, Jan. 31, 1985; *Der Spiegel*, Aug. 27, 1984.
46. FRG, *Monitor-Dienst, Deutscher Teil*, Oct. 3, 1984; DKP, *Pressedienst*, 64/84, Aug. 26, 1984.
47. *Frankfurter Rundschau*, Aug. 30, 1984; SPD, *Informationen der Sozialdemokratischen Bundestagsfraktion*, Oct. 19, 1984; DPG, Bezirksverwaltung Hessen, *Pressemitteilung*, June 18, 1985.
48. dpa, *press release*, Oct. 19, 1984; *Frankfurter Rundschau*, Oct. 12, 1984.
49. D. BT., 10th el. pd., Drucksache 10/2110, Oct. 12, 1984, p. 3; 90th session, Oct. 17, 1984, pp. 6619–21.
50. D. BT., 10th el. pd., Drucksache 10/2207, Oct. 26, 1984.
51. Zimmermann cited figures for 1976, when 4 had been rejected out of 66,997 hired, and for 1977, when 1 had been rejected out of 77,862 hired (D. BT., 10th el. pd., Drucksache 10/3656, July 18, 1985, p. 2).
52. From 1975 to 1980 no permanent civil servant was discharged, but in 1985 ten dismissal proceedings were in progress (ibid., pp. 2, 13).
53. Bethge, "Möglichkeiten," p. 1107.
54. For the Greens' resolution, see D. BT., 10th el. pd., Drucksache 10/4753, Jan. 29, 1986; SPD resolution, Drucksache 10/4758, Jan. 29, 1986; debate, 194th session, Jan. 30, 1986, pp. 14563–71.
55. Die Grünen im Bundestag, *Pressedienst*, no. 47/87, Jan. 27, 1987.
56. SPD, *Informationen der Sozialdemokratischen Bundestagsfraktion*, no. 470, Mar. 19, 1987. See also no. 529, Mar. 29, 1987; D. BT., 11th el. pd., 5th session, Mar. 19, 1987, SPD; *Sozialdemokratischer Pressedienst*, no. 74, Apr. 16, 1987.
57. *Frankfurter Rundschau*, Mar. 3, 1987; DGB, Landesbezirk Baden-Württemberg, Pressestelle, *Information für Presse, Funk, Fernsehen*, no. 93, May 4, 1987; DGB, *Informationsdienst*, no. 17, May 18, 1987.
58. DPG, *Presse-Information*, no. 47/1986, Aug. 14, 1986. See also no. 44/1985, June 24, 1985. In March 1987, DPG chairman van Haaren, in a letter to Minister Schwarz-Schilling, noted that the union fully concurred with the ILO report (*Handelsblatt*, Mar. 26, 1987). The Humanist Union, the Committee for Basic Rights and Democracy, and the Republican Association of Lawyers had asked for a rescinding of the decree as early as 1982 (*Frankfurter Rundschau*, Jan. 27, 1982).
59. *Die Welt*, Aug. 5, 1986; CSU, *Presse-Mitteilungen*, no. 57/1987, Feb. 24, 1987.

Chapter 7: Civil Service Loyalty in Other Countries

1. Information for the West European section of this chapter rests primarily on two major comparative studies: Ernst-Wolfgang Böckenförde, Christian Tomuschat, and Dieter C. Umbach, eds., *Extremisten und öffentlicher Dienst: Rechtslage und Praxis des Zugangs zum und der Entlassung aus dem öffentlichen Dienst in Westeuropa, USA, Jugoslavien, und der EG* (Baden-Baden: Nomos, 1981), written from a liberal perspective; and Karl Doehring et. al., *Verfassungstreue im öffentlichen Dienst europäischer Staaten* (Berlin: Duncker and Humblot, 1980), written from a conservative perspective. See also Eckhard Jesse, "Verfassungsschutz in der Bundesrepublik Deutschland im Vergleich zu anderen westlichen Demokratien," *Politische Bildung* 17, no. 1 (1984): 43–66.

2. Harry Street, *Freedom, the Individual, and the Law* (Middlesex, England: Penguin Books, 1967), p. 234. According to later data, from 1948 to 1961, twenty-four civil servants were dismissed for security reasons, twenty-four resigned, and eighty-three were transferred (Hartmut Schiedermair and Dietrich Murswiek, "Zugang zum öffentlichen Dienst und Verfassungstreue in England," in Doehring et al., *Verfassungstreue*, p. 72; Dieter C. Umbach and Carol Harlow, "Die Einstellung und politische Betätigung öffentlicher Bediensteter im Vereinigten Königreich," in Böckenförde, Tomuschat and Umbach, *Extremisten und öffentlicher Dienst*, p. 255.

3. Street, *Freedom, Individual, Law*, pp. 235–38. See also United Kingdom, *Security Procedures in the Public Service*, Command 1681 (1962); Central Office of Information, *The British Civil Service* (London: Her Majesty's Stationery Office), p. 33.

4. Street, *Freedom, Individual, Law*, p. 238.

5. Ibid., pp. 238–43.

6. Eleanor Bontecou, *The Federal Loyalty-Security Program* (Ithaca: Cornell University Press, 1953), p. 271.

7. Henri Ménudier, "Öffentlicher Dienst und Meinungsfreiheit in Frankreich," in *Verfassungsfeinde als Beamte?* ed. Wulf Schönbohm (Munich and Vienna: Günter Olzog, 1979), pp. 243–44; Charles Fourrier, "Radikale im öffentlichen Dienst Frankreichs," *Beiträge zur Konfliktforschung* 4, no. 1 (1974): 106. For the Barel case, see "Notes de Jurisprudence: Conclusions de M. Letourneur," *Revue du Droit Public et de la Science Politique en France et a l'Étranger*, no. 2 (Apr.–June 1954): 519–38.

8. Ménudier, "Öffentlicher Dienst," pp. 244–45.

9. Fourrier, "Radikale im öffentlichen Dienst," pp. 115, 118; Kay Hailbronner, "Treuepflicht und die Grenzen politischer Betätigung im öffentlichen Dienst Frankreichs," in Doehring et al., *Verfassungstreue*, pp. 103–7.

10. Sabino Cassese and Theo Ritterspach, "Die Kontrolle des Zugangs zum öffentlichen Dienst in der italienischen Rechtsordnung," in *Extremisten und öffentlicher Dienst*, ed. Ernst-Wolfgang Böckenförde, Christian Tomuschat, and Dieter C. Umbach (Baden-Baden: Nomos, 1981), pp. 291–314; Albert Bleckman, "Radikale im öffentlichen Dienst der italienischen Republik," in Doehring et al., *Verfassungstreue* pp. 159–78.

11. Georg Hahn, "Der Zugang zum und die Entlassung aus dem öffentlichen Dienst in Schweden mit besonderer Berücksichtigung der Personalkontrolle," in Böckenförde, Tomuschat, and Umbach, *Extremisten und öffentlicher Dienst*, pp. 455–506; Hannfried Walter, "Die Sicherung eines loyalen öffentlichen Dienstes in Schweden," in Doehring et al., *Verfassungstreue*, pp. 277–348.

12. See note 1 above.

13. Zweites Deutsches Fernsehen program, Aug. 9, 1976, "Radikale im Öffentlichen Dienst," in FRG, Bundespresseamt, *Kommentarübersicht*, Aug. 12, 1976.

14. For a classic neoconservative assessment, see Sidney Hook, *Heresy, Yes—Conspiracy, No* (New York: John Day, 1953). For a perceptive critique of the House Un-American Activities Committee and its crusade against Hollywood

"communists and fellow travelers," see Victor Navasky, *Naming Names* (New York: Viking, 1980).

15. *U.S. Statutes at Large,* vol. 53, part 2, p. 1148; also pp. 1147, 1149.

16. Robert J. Goldstein, *Political Repression in Modern America: From 1870 to the Present* (Cambridge, Mass.: Schenkman, 1978), pp. 300–302; Ralph S. Brown, Jr., *Loyalty and Security: Employment Tests in the United States* (New Haven: Yale University Press, 1958), pp. 21–60.

17. Goldstein, *Political Repression in Modern America,* p. 301.

18. Harold W. Chase, *Security and Liberty: The Problem of Native Communists, 1947–1955* (Garden City, N.Y.: Doubleday, 1955), pp. 41–43. In 1988, the Supreme Court, in a 6–2 decision, ruled that the courts may review the constitutionality of the CIA's dismissal of employees. In 1982, the CIA had contended that one of its employees, a covert electronics technician who was a homosexual, could not be entrusted with national security secrets and ousted him. In separate dissents, Justices Sandra Day O'Connor and Antonin Scalia emphasized the need for the executive branch to have broad authority over national security and foreign affairs (*New York Times,* June 16, 1988).

19. Chase, *Security and Liberty,* p. 303. See also Barth, *Government by Investigation;* Zechariah Chafee, Jr., *The Blessings of Liberty* (Philadelphia: Lippincott, 1956), pp. 25–37.

20. Quoted in *New York Times,* Oct. 2, 1985, upon White's death.

21. See, e.g., Robert Griffith, *The Politics of Fear: Joseph R. McCarthy and the Senate,* 2d ed. (Amherst: University of Massachusetts Press, 1987).

22. Chase, *Security and Liberty,* p. 44.

23. Goldstein, *Political Repression in Modern America,* p. 338. See also Guenter Lewy, *The Federal Loyalty-Security Program: The Need for Reform* (Washington: American Enterprise Institute for Public Policy Research, 1973).

24. *McAuliffe v. Mayor, etc., of City of New Bedford,* 29 Northern Reporter 517 (1892); quoted by Chase, *Security and Liberty,* p. 52.

25. *U.S. v. Lovett,* 328 U.S. 303, 316 (1945); quoted by Chase, *Security and Liberty,* p. 52.

26. John W. Caughey, "McCarthyism Rampant," in *The Pulse of Freedom: American Liberties, 1920–1970s,* ed. Alan Reitman (New York: W. W. Norton, 1975), pp. 167–70.

27. Millis, "Legacies of the Cold War," p. 65. See also Franz Neumann, *The Democratic and the Authoritarian State: Essays in Political and Legal Theory* (Glencoe, Ill.: Free Press, 1957), pp. 187–88.

28. Caughey, "McCarthyism Rampant," pp. 204–5.

29. Brown, *Loyalty and Security,* pp. 180–82.

Chapter 8: Civil Liberties in the Federal Republic

1. Survey by Kiel social scientist Reinhardt Schmidt, cited in Koch and Oltmanns, *SOS,* p. 203. For an overview of how private law affects radicals, see Johann W. Gerlach, *Radikalenfrage und Privatrecht* (Tübingen: J. C. B. Mohr, 1978).

2. *Tagesanzeiger* (Zurich), May 24, 1978; *Info: West Germany,* Oct. 1978, p. 12.

3. Koch and Oltmanns, *SOS,* pp. 203–6.

4. Dyson, "Anticommunism in the Federal Republic of Germany," p. 66; Krölls, "Zehn Jahre Radikalenerlass," p. 11.

5. *Welt der Arbeit*, Nov. 29, 1979. See also *Die KPD informiert: Politische Unterdrückung in der BRD und Westberlin* (Cologne: Rote Fahne, 1978).

6. Koch and Oltmanns, *SOS*, p. 147.

7. Ibid., pp. 39–40.

8. Ibid., p. 21; *Civil Liberties and Defense*, p. 24; John Dornberg, "West Germany's Embattled Democracy: The Antiterrorist Menace from the Right," *Saturday Review: Currents*, June 10, 1978, p. 18.

9. Dornberg, "West Germany's Embattled Democracy," p. 18; Hans-Dieter Schwind, "Zur Entwicklung des Terrorismus in der Bundesrepublik Deutschland," in *Ursachen des Terrorismus,* ed. Schwind (Berlin: de Gruyter, 1978), p. 43.

10. Dornberg, "West Germany's Embattled Democracy," p. 21. See also Irene Dische, "West Germany's War on Terrorism," *Inquiry,* June 26, 1978, pp. 16–19.

11. Cited by Diana Johnstone in *In These Times,* Oct. 5–11, 1977, p. 18; quoted in Zipes, "From Berufsverbot to Terrorism," p. 147.

12. Koch and Oltmanns, *SOS*, p. 21.

13. Zipes, "From Berufsverbot to Terrorism," p. 147.

14. Dornberg, "West Germany's Embattled Democracy," p. 19.

15. *Info: West Germany*, Apr. 1978, p. 6, Schwind, *Ursachen des Terrorismus*, pp. 41–42.

16. Cobler, *Law, Order, Politics*, p. 144. During this period, public attention centered on the incarceration and apparent suicide of Andreas Baader and two others in the Stammheim prison.

17. D. BT., 8th el. pd., 44th session, Sept. 29, 1977, p. 3383. For roll call, see pp. 3384–85.

18. Gerard Braunthal, *The West German Social Democrats, 1969–1982: Profile of a Party in Power* (Boulder: Westview Press, 1983), p. 214.

19. Kommers, "Government of West Germany," p. 261.

20. *Info: West Germany*, Oct. 1978, p. 8; Koch and Oltmanns, *SOS*, p. 52. For a sympathetic view of the police, see Manfred Schreiber, ed., *Polizeilicher Eingriff und Grundrechte* (Stuttgart: Richard Boorberg, 1982); for a critical view, see Heiner Busch et al., *Die Polizei in der Bundesrepublik* (Frankfurt am Main and New York: Campus, 1985); Jürgen Roth, *Ist die Bundesrepublik ein Polizeistaat?* (Darmstadt: Melzer, 1972).

21. Braunthal, *West German Social Democrats*, pp. 214–15.

22. Ibid., p. 215; Dische, "West Germany's War on Terrorism," p. 19.

23. Margit Mayer, "The German October of 1977," *New German Critique*, no. 13 (Winter 1978): 155.

24. Cited (n.d.) in ibid., p. 156.

25. Dornberg, "West Germany's Embattled Democracy," p. 21.

26. Cited (n.d.) in ibid., p. 20.

27. Nelkin and Pollak, *Atom Besieged*, pp. 174–75. *Der Spiegel* broke the story, calling the Traube affair a serious violation of civil liberties (Feb. 28, 1977, pp. 19–34). *Der Spiegel* also has printed numerous other exposés. A major one was run in 1962, when the government raided its offices and arrested two

editors on the charge that the weekly had illegally procured and published secret defense documents. The raid, viewed as a major breach of civil rights, led to the resignation of then Minister of Defense Strauss and another cabinet minister. (For details, see Ronald Bunn, *German Politics and the Spiegel Affair* [Baton Rouge: Louisiana State University Press, 1968]).

28. A conservative correspondent, Egber Kiepert, of the *Reader's Digest,* accused the police of killing his friend, who was innocent (*Globe and Mail*, Sept. 2, 1975).

29. FRG, German Information Center (New York), *The Week in Germany,* Dec. 12, 1986.

30. DGV, *Berufsverbote,* pp. 40–41.

31. For text, see D. BT., 7th el. pd., Drucksache 7/4549, July 1, 1976.

32. Zipes, "From Berufsverbot to Terrorism," pp. 145–46. One confiscated book was that of Michael Baumann, *Wie Alles Anfing* (Munich: Trikont, 1975), published in English by author under name of Bommi Baumann as *Terror or Love? Bommi Baumann's Own Story of His Life as a West German Urban Guerrilla,* trans. Helene Ellenbogen and Wayne Parker (New York: Grove Press, 1979), with perceptive introductory statements by Heinrich Böll and Daniel Cohn-Bendit.

33. The 1886 Haymarket affair in Chicago resulted in the trial of eight anarchists, of whom four were hanged for allegedly throwing a bomb killing a number of police agents and bystanders. For book seizure, see Zipes, "From Berufsverbot to Terrorism," p. 146.

34. Peter Brückner and Alfred Krovoza, *Staatsfeinde: Innerstaatliche Feinder-klärung in der BRD* (Berlin: Wagenbach, 1972), pp. 22–23; *Info: West Germany,* Dec. 1977, p. 7; David Z. Mairowitz, "Scissors in the Head," *Harper's Magazine,* May 1978, p. 30.

35. *Christian Science Monitor,* Dec. 4, 1978.

36. Mairowitz, "Scissors in the Head," p. 30.

37. *Info: West Germany,* Oct. 1978, p. 7.

38. Mayer, "German October of 1977," p. 159.

39. *Info: West Germany,* Feb. 1979, p. 6.

40. Ibid.

41. FRG, *The Week in Germany,* July 5 and 26, 1985; *Nürnberger Nachrichten,* Oct. 1, 1985.

42. *Der Spiegel,* Dec. 29, 1986; *New York Times,* Nov. 4, 1987; *Frankfurter Rundschau,* Nov. 5, 1987.

43. *Süddeutsche Zeitung,* Nov. 6, 1987.

44. FRG, *The Week in Germany,* Dec. 18, 1987; Bundesrat, Drucksache 238/88, May 27, 1988 (Gesetzentwurf der Bundesregierung).

45. FRG, *The Week in Germany,* Mar. 10, 1989.

46. *Censorship, Legal Defense,* pp. 5–6.

47. *Christian Science Monitor,* Jan. 8, 1986.

48. SPD, *Sozialdemokratischer Pressedienst,* vol. 39, no. 1, Jan. 2, 1984.

49. Thomas Conrad, "West Germany Tries McCarthyism," *The Progressive* 42, no. 2 (Feb. 1978): 38.

50. *Bremer Nachrichten,* Feb. 11, 1986.

51. *Unsere Zeitung,* Jan. 30, 1980; cited by "Berufsverbote heute: Eine aktuelle

Bestandsaufnahme der Initiative 'Weg mit den Berufsverboten'" (c. 1980, hectographed); *Die Grünen*, Nov. 21, 1987.

52. *Die Grünen*, Nov. 21, 1987.

53. *Süddeutsche Zeitung*, Feb. 11, 1986. Similar problems have arisen in other countries. For Britain, see Ian Will, *The Big Brother Society* (London: Harrap, 1983).

54. *Die Zeit*, July 17, 1987.

55. FRG, *The Week In Germany*, Dec. 23, 1988. On Apr. 28, 1989, the Bundestag began consideration of the bill (*Frankfurter Allgemeine Zeitung*, Apr. 29–30, 1989).

56. *Die Zeit*, Dec. 30, 1983; cited by Conradt, *German Polity*, p. 67. See also *New York Times*, Apr. 17, 1983.

57. *Handelsblatt*, Dec. 16, 1983; FRG, *The Week in Germany*, Dec. 16, 1983.

58. *Frankfurter Allgemeine Zeitung*, Jan. 21, 1985.

59. *Die Grünen*, Aug. 1, 1987.

60. Humanistische Union, letter, Sept. 10, 1979 (hectographed).

61. Cited in SPD, Jusos, *Gegen den Abbau demokratischer Rechte* (Bonn, 1980), pp. 21–22.

62. *Amnesty International Report, 1980* (London: Amnesty International Publications, 1980), p. 272; cited by Kommers, "Government of West Germany," p. 261.

63. See its journal, *Freiheit und Gleichheit*, no. 1 (Dec. 1979): 107–11.

64. *Censorship, Legal Defense*, pp. 1–24.

65. *Info: West Germany*, Feb. 1979, pp. 5–8.

66. *konkret*, Jan. 1979.

67. *Jahrbuch der öffentlichen Meinung* 5 (1973): 226, cited by Conradt, *German Polity*, p. 68.

68. Emnid poll, n.d., cited by Koch and Oltmanns, *SOS*, p. 54.

69. Unidentified poll, cited by *Civil Liberties and Defense*, p. 47.

70. Infratest survey, cited by *Der Spiegel*, Oct. 16, 1978, pp. 38, 41.

71. Poll cited in SPD, Jusos, *Gegen den Abbau demokratischer Rechte*, p. 14.

72. Poll cited in *Der Spiegel*, Oct. 16, 1978, pp. 41, 44.

73. Unidentified poll, cited by Dornberg, "West Germany's Embattled Democracy," p. 20.

74. In Apr. 1989, Zimmermann, for years a controversial cabinet member, was "demoted" to minister of transport in a cabinet shakeup. Wolfgang Schäuble (CDU) replaced him as minister of the interior (see *New York Times*, Apr. 14, 1989; *Der Tagesspiegel* [Berlin], Aug. 1, 1989).

Chapter 9: Conclusion

1. For similar conclusion, see Manfred G. Schmidt, *CDU und SPD an der Regierung: Ein Vergleich ihrer Politik in den Ländern* (Frankfurt am Main and New York: Campus, 1980), pp. 118–24.

2. Gregg O. Kvistad, "The *Radikalenerlass* and Political Opposition in the Federal Republic of Germany" (Paper presented at Hamilton College Conference on Modern German Politics, Apr. 26–28, 1985), p. 8.

3. Grass interview with *Politiken* (Copenhagen), Dec. 27, 1977; quoted in *Frankfurter Allgemeine Zeitung*, Feb. 25, 1978.
4. *Los Angeles Times*, Apr. 16, 1978.
5. *The Times* (London), Nov. 4, 1978.
6. Ibid., June 12, 1976.
7. *The Financial Times*, Dec. 16, 1975. *Die Zeit* stated that "a free democracy cannot exclude entire groups of citizens from the service of the state simply according to categories determined by the government" (quoted in *New York Times*, Aug. 11, 1975).
8. Quoted in Koch and Oltmanns, *SOS*, p. 177. Jane Kramer, the European correspondent of *The New Yorker*, wrote, "Whatever the lessons of Nazism, a high regard for the rights of citizens in times of social stress is evidently not among them" (Mar. 20, 1978, p. 46).
9. Quoted in Koch and Oltmanns, *SOS*, pp. 26–27.
10. Milton Mankoff, in letter to *New York Times*, Nov. 2, 1977.
11. Mankoff and Jacobs, "Return of the Suppressed," p. 341; Holtfort, "Bonner Pilatus," p. 14; Oskar Negt, "The Misery of Bourgeois Democracy in Germany," *Telos*, no. 34 (Winter 1977–78): 131–35.
12. Peter Conradi, "Wo Gesinnung überwacht und verfolgt wird, ist die Demokratie gefährdet," *Druck und Papier*, Feb. 8, 1982.
13. Josef Joffe, reviewing Walter Laqueur, *Germany Today: A Personal Report*, in *New York Times*, July 28, 1985.
14. See Gordon Smith, *Democracy in Western Germany: Parties and Politics in the Federal Republic* (New York: Holmes and Meier, 1979), p. 209; Barth, *Government by Investigation*, pp. 238–39.
15. For a perceptive analysis, see Dobbelstein and Gellert, "Shades of New McCarthyism," pp. 85–89.
16. Nelkin and Pollak, *Atom Besieged*, p. 168.
17. Bertram Gross, *Friendly Fascism: The New Face of Power in America* (New York: M. Evans, 1980). See also Marcus Raskin, *The Politics of National Security* (New Brunswick, N.J.: Transaction Books, 1979), for a discussion of the national security state with its repressive, authoritarian traits; and Alan Wolfe, *The Seamy Side of Democracy: Repression in America*, 2d ed. (New York: Longman, 1978).
18. Otto Kirchheimer, *Political Justice: The Use of Legal Procedure for Political Ends* (Princeton: Princeton University Press, 1961), p. 172.
19. FRG, *The Week in Germany*, no. 31, Sept. 14, 1984.
20. Polls of 1971 and 1978 cited by Conradt, *German Polity*, pp. 49, 54. See also pp. 46–84.
21. Russell J. Dalton, *Citizen Politics in Western Democracies: Public Opinion and Political Parties in the United States, Great Britain, West Germany, and France* (Chatham, N.J.: Chatham House Publishers, 1988), pp. 118–23; Martin Greiffenhagen, "Vom Obrigkeitsstaat zur Demokratie: Die politische Kultur in der Bundesrepublik Deutschland," in *Politische Kultur in Westeuropa: Bürger und Staaten in der europäischen Gemeinschaft*, ed. Peter Reichel (Frankfurt am Main and New York: Campus, 1984), pp. 67–72; Lewis J. Edinger, *West German Politics* (New York: Columbia University Press, 1986), pp. 319–22. As one

example of the power of an aroused citizenry: in 1989, Kohl's views that the U.S. proposal to modernize a battlefield short-range nuclear weapon in Western Europe be postponed until 1991—after the national election of 1990—was based partly on the strength of West German public opposition to the U.S. proposal (*New York Times,* Feb. 15, 1989).

Bibliography

Public Documents

Supranational

Council of Europe. European Court of Human Rights. Glasenapp Case (4/1984/76/120). Judgment, Strasbourg, August 28, 1986.
————. Kosiek Case (5/1984/77/121). Judgment, August 28, 1986.
European Community. Court of Justice. Judgment of the Court, June 28, 1984. *Hans Moser v. Land Baden-Württemberg* (reference for a preliminary ruling from the Arbeitsgericht Reutlingen; Free movement of workers—concept of worker). Case 180/83.
————. European Parliament. Legal Affairs Committee. "Observations on the Rules as to Exclusion from Employment in the Public Service in the Federal Republic of Germany." No. 61/80, July 15, 1982.
International Labor Office. Governing Body. GB.235/4/7, 235th Session, Geneva, March 2–6, 1987. "Report of the Commission of Inquiry Appointed under Article 26 of the Constitution to Examine the Observance of the Discrimination (Employment and Occupation) Convention, 1958 (No. 111) by the Federal Republic of Germany."

National

Baden-Württemberg. Innenministerium. *Verfassungsschutzbericht Baden-Württemberg, 1978.* Stuttgart, 1978.
————. *Verfassungstreue im öffentlichen Dienst.* Stuttgart, 1979.
Bavaria. Staatsministerium der Finanzen. *Extremisten beim Staat? Finanzminister Max Streibl antwortet im Landtag.* Munich, c. 1979.
————. *Schutz für Verfassung, Staat, Gesellschaft: Verfassungsfeinde in den öffentlichen Dienst?* Munich, 1976.
————.*Verfassungsschutzbericht, Bayern 1982.* Munich, n.d.

Bundesministerium des Innern. *Betrifft: Verfassungschutz* and *Verfassungsschutzbericht.* Bonn, various years.

Deutscher Bundestag. Drucksachen. Bonn, 1972 and ff.

———. "Verhandlungen des Deutschen Bundestages." Bonn, 1972 and ff. Stenographic report.

Great Britain. Central Office of Information. *The British Civil Service.* London: Her Majesty's Stationery Office, 1974.

Hamburg. Staatliche Pressestelle. *Mehr Toleranz wagen: Ausgewählte Pressestimmen zum Vorschlag des Hamburger Bürgermeisters Hans-Ulrich Klose zur Lockerung des Extremisten-Beschluss.* 2 vols. Hamburg, n.d.

Statistisches Bundesamt. *Statistisches Jahrbuch für die Bundesrepublik Deutschland, 1973.* Stuttgart: W. Kohlhammer, 1973.

Political Parties

Christlich-Demokratische Union. *Argumente, Dokumente, Materialen: Radikale im öffentlichen Dienst.* Bonn, 1972.

———. *Zum Thema: Verfassungsfeinde.* Bonn, n.d.

Freie Demokratische Partei. Bundesvorstand der Deutschen Jungdemokraten. *INFO,* no. 2, 1972.

Sozialdemokratische Partei Deutschlands. "Dokumentation über die Beschäftigung von Extremisten im öffentlichen Dienst der Bundesrepublik Deutschland." N.d. Hectographed.

———. *Grundsätze zur Feststellung der Verfassungstreue im öffentlichen Dienst, vorgelegt von Hans Koschnick, Stellvertretender Parteivorsitzender, Bonn, 16. Oktober 1978.* Bonn, 1978.

———. Jusos. *Bundeskongressbeschlüsse. Jungsozialisten in der SPD, 1969–1976.* Bonn, 1978.

———. Jusos. *Gegen den Abbau demokratischer Rechte.* Bonn, 1980.

———. *Parteitag der SPD: Protokoll der Verhandlungen.* Bonn, various years.

Books and Articles

Abendroth, Wolfgang. "Das Bundesverfassungsgericht und die Berufsverbote im öffentlichen Dienst." IMSF, *Informationsbericht* no. 22, *Berufsverbote in der BRD,* 1976.

Aberbach, Joel D., Robert D. Putnam, and Bert A. Rockman. *Bureaucrats and Politicians in Western Democracies.* Cambridge: Harvard University Press, 1981.

Aktionskomitee gegen Berufsverbote an der Freien Universität Berlin und Komitee zur Verteidigung Demokratischer Grundrechte. *Bundesrepublik Deutschland: Berufsverbote—Stimmen der Internationalen Presse.* Berlin, 1976.

Baker, Kendall L., Russell J. Dalton, and Kai Hildenbrandt. *Germany Transformed: Political Culture and the New Politics.* Cambridge: Harvard University Press, 1981.

Balbus, Isaac D. *The Dialectics of Legal Repression: Black Rebels before the American Criminal Courts.* New York: Russell Sage Foundation, 1973.

Barth, Alan. *Government by Investigation*. New York: Viking Press, 1955.

Baumann, Bommi (Michael). *Terror or Love? Bommi Baumann's Own Story of His Life as a West German Urban Guerrilla*. Translated by Helene Ellenbogen and Wayne Parker. New York: Grove Press, 1979. Original edition: Michael Baumann. *Wie Alles Anfing*. Munich: Trikont, 1975.

Berner, Georg. " 'Radikalenerlass' und Rechtsprechung." *Politische Studien* 28, no. 233 (May–June 1977): 287–303.

Bertrand Russell Peace Foundation. *Third Russell Tribunal: Berufsverbote Condemned*. Nottingham, England: Russell Press, 1978.

Berufsverbot: Ernennungsurkunde. Berlin: Kant, 1978.

Berufsverbote bei der Bundespost: Dokumentation. Compiled by Uwe Post. Hamburg, 1979.

Bethge, Horst. "Möglichkeiten, das Konzept der Neokonservativen zu durchkreuzen: Von der Abwehr der Berufsverbote zur Bürgerrechts- und Demokratiebewegung." *Blätter für deutsche und internationale Politik* 31, no. 9 (September 1986): 1102–10.

———, ed. *Gewerkschaftsstimmen gegen Berufsverbote*. Cologne: Pahl-Rugenstein, 1977.

Bethge, Horst, and Klaus Dammann. "Der ILO-Bericht zu den Berufsverboten." *Blätter für deutsche und internationale Politik* 32, no. 5 (May 1987): 582–87.

Bethge, Horst, and Erich Rossmann, eds. *Der Kampf gegen das Berufsverbot: Dokumentation der Fälle und des Widerstands*. Cologne: Pahl-Rugenstein, 1973.

Bethge, Horst, et al., eds. *Die Zerstörung der Demokratie durch Berufsverbote*. Cologne: Pahl-Rugenstein, 1976.

Betroffene melden sich zu Wort. Berlin: Kant, c. 1978.

Beyme, Klaus von. *The Political System of the Federal Republic of Germany*. New York: St. Martin's Press, 1983.

Bittner, Wolfgang. "Verfassungsfeindlichkeit zur Disposition: Eine Reportage über den Fall Silvia Gingold." In *Extremismus im demokratischen Rechsstaat*, ed. Manfred Funke. Düsseldorf: Droste, 1978.

Blanke, Bernhard. "Schutz der Verfassung durch Spaltung der Demokratie?" *Freiheit und Gleichheit*, no. 2 (October 1980): 81–93.

Blau, Joachim. *Zum Ausbau des staatlichen Repressionsapparates seit Ende der sechziger Jahre*. IMSF, *Informationsbericht*, no. 29. 1977.

Bleckmann, Albert. " 'Berufsverbote' und die Europäische Menschenrechtskonvention." *Die öffentliche Verwaltung* 37, no. 14 (July 1984): 565–77.

———. "Radikale im öffentlichen Dienst der italienischen Republik." In *Verfassungstreue im öffentlichen Dienst europäischer Staaten*, Karl Doehring et al. Berlin: Duncker and Humblot, 1980.

Böckenförde, Ernst-Wolfgang, Christian Tomuschat, and Dieter C. Umbach, eds. *Extremisten und öffentlicher Dienst: Rechtslage und Praxis des Zugangs zum und der Entlassung aus dem öffentlichen Dienst in Westeuropa, USA, Jugoslavien, und der EG*. Baden-Baden: Nomos, 1981.

Bontecou, Eleanor. *The Federal Loyalty-Security Program*. Ithaca: Cornell University Press, 1953.

Borch, Herbert von. *Obrigkeit und Widerstand: Zur politischen Soziologie des Beamtentums*. Tübingen: Mohr, 1954.

Borgs-Maciejewski, Hermann. "Radikale im öffentlichen Dienst." In *Aus Politik und Zeitgeschichte,* supplement to *Das Parlament,* B27/73, July 7, 1973.

———. *Radikale im öffentlichen Dienst: Dokumente, Debatten, Urteile.* Bonn–Bad Godesberg: Godesberger Taschenbuch-Verlag, 1973.

Bracher, Karl Dietrich. "Bewährung und Anfechtung: Zum Streit um Demokratie und Verfassung in der Bundesrepublik." In *Extremismus im demokratischen Rechtsstaat,* ed. Manfred Funke. Düsseldorf: Droste, 1978.

Brändle, Michael, and Klaus Dammann. "Flickenteppich: Zur aktuellen Lage in Sachen Berufsverbote." *Demokratie und Recht* 17, no. 1 (1989): 67–73.

Brandt, Edmund. *Die politische Treuepflicht.* Karlsruhe and Heidelberg: C. F. Müller Juristischer Verlag, 1976.

Brandt, Willy, and Helmut Schmidt. *Deutschland 1976: Zwei Sozialdemokraten im Gespräch.* Hamburg: Rowohlt, 1976.

Brauns, Hans-Jochen, and David Kramer. "Political Repression in West Germany: 'Berufsverbote' in Modern German History." *New German Critique,* no. 7 (1976): 105–21.

Braunthal, Gerard. *The West German Social Democrats, 1969–1982: Profile of a Party in Power.* Boulder, Colo.: Westview Press, 1983.

Brecht, Arnold. "Personnel Management." In *Governing Postwar Germany,* ed. Edward H. Litchfield et al. Ithaca: Cornell University Press, 1953.

Brown, Ralph S., Jr. *Loyalty and Security: Employment Tests in the United States.* New Haven: Yale University Press, 1958.

Brückner, Jens. *Das Handbuch der Berufsverbote: Rechtsfibel zur Berufsverbots-praxis.* Berlin: Nicoläische Verlagsbuchhandlung, 1977.

Brückner, Peter, and Alfred Krovoza. *Staatsfeinde: Innerstaatliche Feinderklärung in der BRD.* Berlin: Wagenbach, 1972.

Brünneck, Alexander von. *Politische Justiz gegen Kommunisten in der Bundesrepublik Deutschland, 1949–1968.* Frankfurt am Main: Suhrkamp, 1978.

Bünemann, Richard. "Zur Kontinuität der Berufsverbotspraxis von Metternich zu den Ministerpräsidentenbeschlüssen." *Blätter für deutsche und internationale Politik* 20, no. 3 (1975): 316–23.

Bunn, Ronald. *German Politics and the Spiegel Affair.* Baton Rouge: Louisiana State University Press, 1968.

Bürgerversammlung zur Verteidigung unserer Verfassung. Berlin: Kant, 1978.

Busch, Heiner, et al. *Die Polizei in der Bundesrepublik.* Frankfurt am Main and New York: Campus, 1985.

Cassese, Sabino, and Theo Ritterspach. "Die Kontrolle des Zugangs zum öffentlichen Dienst in der italienischen Rechtsordnung." In *Extremisten und öffentlicher Dienst,* ed. Ernst-Wolfgang Böckenförde, Christian Tomuschat, and Dieter C. Umbach. Baden-Baden: Nomos, 1981.

Caughey, John W. "McCarthyism Rampant." In *The Pulse of Freedom: American Liberties, 1920–1970s,* ed. Alan Reitman. New York: W. W. Norton, 1975.

Censorship, Legal Defence, and the Domestic Intelligence Service in West Germany: Conclusions of the Final Session of the Third Russell Tribunal. Nottingham, England: Russell Press, 1979.

Chafee, Zechariah, Jr. *The Blessings of Liberty.* Philadelphia: Lippincott, 1956.

Chapman, Brian. *The Profession of Government: The Public Service in Europe.* London: Unwin University Books, 1959.

Chase, Harold W. *Security and Liberty: The Problem of Native Communists, 1947–1955.* Garden City, N.Y.: Doubleday, 1955.

Civil Liberties and the Defense of Democracy against Extremists and Terrorists: A Report on the West German Situation. Issued by Atlantic Brücke. Freiburg im Breisgau: Rombach, 1980.

Cobler, Sebastian. *Law, Order, and Politics in West Germany.* Translated by Francis McDonagh and revised from *Die Gefahr geht von den Menschen aus* (Berlin: Rotbuch, 1976). Middlesex, England: Penguin Books, 1978.

Commager, Henry Steele. *Freedom, Loyalty, Dissent.* New York: Oxford University Press, 1967.

Conrad, Thomas. "Banned in West Germany." *Seven Days,* June 2, 1978, pp. 14–15.

————. "West Germany Tries McCarthyism." *The Progressive* 42, no. 2 (February 1978): 37–39.

Conradt, David P. *The German Polity.* 3d ed. New York: Longman, 1986.

Czapski, Peter. "Zur politischen Treuepflicht der Beamten nach der Entscheidung des Bundesverwaltungsgerichts vom 29. Oktober 1981." *Zeitschrift für Beamtenrecht,* no. 7 (1982): 203–9.

Dalton, Russell J. *Citizen Politics in Western Democracies: Public Opinion and Political Parties in the United States, Great Britain, West Germany, and France.* Chatham, N.J.: Chatham House Publishers, 1988.

Dammann, Klaus. "Das/the/le/il Berufsverbot." *konkret,* no. 3 (1988): 34–36.

Dammann, Klaus, and Erwin Siemantel, eds. *Berufsverbote und Menschenrechte in der Bundesrepublik.* Cologne: Pahl-Rugenstein, 1987.

Däubler, Wolfgang, and H. D. Wohlfarth, eds. *Hans Meister: Postbeamter und Kommunist.* Cologne, 1985.

Denninger, Erhard, ed. *Freiheitliche demokratische Grundordnung: Materialen zum Staatsverständnis und zur Verfassungswirklichkeit in der Bundesrepublik.* Frankfurt am Main: Suhrkamp, 1977.

Deutsche Gesellschaft für Verhaltenstherapie. "Auswirkungen des 'Radikalen-Erlasses' im Hochschulbereich: Ein Bericht über eine empirische Untersuchung." *Neue Praxis* 9, no. 2 (1979): 137–46.

————. *Berufsverbote in der Bundesrepublik Deutschland: Bericht der Kommission "Berufsverbote" über Betroffene, psychische Folgen, und Auswirkungen auf die psychosoziale Versorgung.* Bielefeld, 1979.

Deutscher Gewerkschaftsbund. *Abwehr von Verfassungsfeinden im öffentlichen Dienst.* Düsseldorf, 1977.

Dische, Irene. "West Germany's War on Terrorism." *Inquiry,* June 26, 1978, pp. 16–19.

Dobbelstein, Rainer, and Claudius Gellert. "Shades of New McCarthyism in West Germany? A Political and Legal Analysis of the Campaign against Radicals in the West German Civil Service." Parts 1, 2. *Revue de Droit Internationale de Science Diplomatique et Politiques* 55, no. 1 (January–March 1977): 64–80; no. 2 (April–June 1977): 81–113.

Doehring, Karl, et al. *Verfassungstreue im öffentlichen Dienst europäischer Staaten.* Berlin: Duncker and Humblot, 1980.

Dokumentation: Vom KPD-Verbot zum Berufsverbot. Issued by Zentraler Arbeitskreis für die Aufhebung des KPD-Verbots. N.p., n.d.

Döring, Herbert, and Gordon Smith, eds. *Party Government and Political Culture in Western Germany.* London: Macmillan, 1982.

Dornberg, John. "West Germany's Embattled Democracy: The Antiterrorist Menace from the Right." *Saturday Review,* June 10, 1978, pp. 18–21.

Dregger, Alfred. "Selbstaufgabe der Demokratie? Der Streit um Extremisten im öffentlichen Dienst." *Die politische Meinung,* January–February 1982, pp. 20–25.

Dress, Andreas, et al., eds. *Wir Verfassungsfeinde.* Cologne: Pahl-Rugenstein, 1977.

Drewitz, Ingeborg. "Zehn Gebote für alle, die mit dem 'Berufsverbot' gar nich erst etwas zu tun haben wollen." In *Berufsverbot: Ein bundesdeutsches Lesebuch,* ed. W. Beutin, Thomas Metscher, and B. Meyer. Fischerhude: Verlag Atelier im Bauernhaus, 1976.

Drittes Internationales Russell-Tribunal: Zur Situation der Menschenrechte in der Bundesrepublik Deutschland. 3 vols. Berlin: Rotbuch, 1978.

Duve, Freimut, and Wolfgang Kopitzsch, eds. *Weimar ist kein Argument; oder, Brachten Radikale im öffentlichen Dienst Hitler an die Macht?* Reinbek: Rowohlt, 1976.

Duve, Freimut, and Wolf-Dieter Narr, eds. *Russell-Tribunal: Pro und contra.* Reinbek: Rowohlt, 1976.

Dyson, Kenneth F. "Anticommunism in the Federal Republic of Germany: The Case of the 'Berufsverbot.'" *Parliamentary Affairs* 28, no. 1 (Winter 1974–75): 51–67.

———. "Left-wing Political Extremism and the Problem of Tolerance in Western Germany." *Government and Opposition* 10, no. 3 (Summer 1975): 306–31.

———. *The State Tradition in Western Europe: A Study of an Idea and Institution.* New York: Oxford University Press, 1980.

Edinger, Lewis J. *West German Politics.* New York: Columbia University Press, 1986.

Enseling, Alf. "Das Ausland zur Extremismus- und Terrorismus-Diskussion in der Bundesrepublik Deutschland." In *Aus Politik und Zeitgeschichte,* supplement to *Das Parlament,* B20/78, May 20, 1978, pp. 23–37.

Evangelische Kirche in Deutschland. "Bericht der Kammer für öffentliche Verantwortung an den Rat der EKD zur Frage der Beschäftigung von Extremisten im öffentlichen Dienst." N.p., n.d.

Farin, Klaus, and Hans-Jürgen Zwingmann. *Modell Deutschland? Berufsverbote.* Ettlingen: Doku-Verlag, 1979.

Feest, Johannes. "Die Bundesrichter: Herkunft, Karriere, und Auswahl der juristischen Elite." In *Beiträge zur Analyse der deutschen Oberschicht,* ed. Wolfgang Zapf. Munich: Piper, 1965.

Flechtheim, Ossip K. "Extremismus und Radikalismus: Eine Kontraststudie." In *Extremismus im demokratischen Rechtsstaat,* ed. Manfred Funke. Düsseldorf: Droste, 1978.

Flechtheim, Ossip K., Wolfgang Rudzio, Fritz Wilmar, and Manfred Wilke. *Der Marsch der DKP durch die Institutionen: Sowjetmarxistische Einflussstrategien und Ideologien.* Frankfurt am Main: Fischer Taschenbuch, 1980.

"For Official Use Only": The Secret Plans of the West German Interior Ministry to Destroy the Russell Tribunal on Human Rights. Nottingham, England: Russell Press, 1978.

Fourrier, Charles. "Radikale im öffentlichen Dienst Frankreichs." *Beiträge zur Konfliktforschung* 4, no. 1 (1974): 103–23.

Fraenkel, Ernst. *The Dual State: A Contribution to the Theory of Dictatorship.* New York: Octagon Books, 1969.

Frankenberg, Günter. "Staatstreue: Die aktuelle Spruchpraxis zu den Berufsverboten." *Kritische Justiz* 13, no. 3 (1980): 276–94.

Friedrich-Naumann-Stiftung. *Dokumentation: Extremistenbeschluss.* Bonn, 1979.

Frisch, Peter. *Extremistenbeschluss.* Leverkusen: Heggen, 1976.

Funke, Manfred, ed. *Extremismus im demokratischen Rechtsstaat.* Düsseldorf: Droste, 1978.

———. *Terrorismus: Untersuchungen zur Strategie und Struktur revolutionärer Gewaltpolitik.* Bonn: Bundeszentrale für politische Bildung, 1977.

Geil, Hartmut. "Berufsverbot, Wissenschaft, und politischer Prozess." *Marxistische Blätter* 16, no. 2 (March–April 1978): 99–105.

———. "Berufsverbote und Staatsschutz?" *Das Argument* 20, no. 109 (May–June 1978): 380–93.

Gewerkschaft Erziehung und Wissenschaft. "Bundesrepublik Deutschland: Zehn Jahre Radikalenerlass, eine Dokumentation." *Im Brennpunkt,* April 1982.

———. Landesverband Hamburg. *Berufsverbote und politische Disziplinierung: Eine Dokumentation der GEW Hamburg.* Hamburg: Verlag Erziehung und Wissenschaft, 1978.

Goldstein, Robert Justin. *Political Repression in Modern America: From 1870 to the Present.* Cambridge, Mass.: Schenkman, 1978.

———. *Political Repression in Nineteenth Century Europe.* Totowa, N.J.: Barnes and Noble Books, 1983.

Greiffenhagen, Martin. "Vom Obrigkeitsstaat zur Demokratie: Die politische Kultur in der Bundesrepublik Deutschland." In *Politische Kultur in Westeuropa: Bürger und Staaten in der Europäischen Gemeinschaft,* ed. Peter Reichel. Frankfurt am Main and New York: Campus, 1984.

———, ed. *Kampf um Wörter? Politische Begriffe im Meinungsstreit.* Munich and Vienna: Carl Hanser, 1980.

Griffith, Robert. *The Politics of Fear: Joseph R. McCarthy and the Senate.* 2d ed. Amherst: University of Massachusetts Press, 1987.

Gross, Bertram. *Friendly Fascism: The New Face of Power in America.* New York: M. Evans, 1980.

Grottian, Peter. "Werden Berufsverbote wieder sichtbar?" *Vorgänge* 22, no. 2–3 (1983): 100–106.

Hahn, Georg. "Der Zugang zum und die Entlassung aus dem öffentlichen Dienst in Schweden, mit besonderer Berücksichtigung der Personalkontrolle." In *Extremisten und öffentlicher Dienst,* ed. Ernst-Wolfgang Böckenförde, Christian Tomuschat, and Dieter C. Umbach. Baden-Baden: Nomos, 1981.

Hailbronner, Kay. "Treuepflicht und die Grenzen politischer Betätigung im öffentlichen Dienst Frankreichs." In *Verfassungstreue im öffentlichen Dienst europäischer Staaten,* Karl Doehring et al. Berlin: Duncker and Humblot, 1980.

Hannover, Heinrich, and Günter Wallraff. *Die unheimliche Republik: Politische Verfolgung in der Bundesrepublik.* Reinbek: Rowohlt, 1984.

Henning, Hansjoachim. *Die deutsche Beamtenschaft im neunzehnten Jahrhundert.* Stuttgart: Steiner, 1984.

Hermsen, Hans. "Politische Repression an den Hochschulen und ihre Folgen: Versuch einer psychologischen Interpretation." In *Politische Psychologie,* ed. Hans-Dieter Klingemann and Max Kaase. Opladen: Westdeutscher Verlag, 1981.

Herz, John H. "Political Views of the West German Civil Service." In *West German Leadership and Foreign Policy,* ed. Hans Speier and W. Phillips Davison. Evanston, Ill.: Row, Peterson, 1957.

Holtfort, Werner. "Bonner Pilatus: Zur traurigen Geschichte des Radikalenerlasses und des kleinmütigen Versuchs, ihn wieder loszuwerden." *Vorgänge* 19, no. 4 (1980): 13–24.

Hook, Sidney. *Heresy, Yes–Conspiracy, No.* New York: John Day, 1953.

Horchem, Hans Josef. *Extremisten in einer selbstbewussten Demokratie.* Freiburg: Herderbücherei, 1975.

———. "Zum Entwicklungsstand des Rechtsextremismus in der Bundesrepublik Deutschland." In *Extremismus im demokratischen Rechtsstaat,* ed. Manfred Funke. Düsseldorf: Droste, 1978.

Horn, Klaus. "Berufsverbote: Ein staatlicher Beitrag zur Unregierbarkeit." *Frankfurter Hefte,* no. 11 (1980): 46–52.

IMSF, *Informationsbericht* no. 22, *Berufsverbote in der BRD,* 1976; no. 42, *Berufsverbote: Neue Entwicklungen, Kritik, Erfahrungen des Widerstandes,* 1985.

Jacobs, Monica. "Civil Rights and Women's Rights in the Federal Republic of Germany Today." *New German Critique,* no. 13 (Winter 1978): 165–74.

Jasper, Gotthart. *Der Schutz der Republik.* Tübingen: J. C. B. Mohr, 1963.

Jesse, Eckhard. *Streitbare Demokratie: Theorie, Praxis, und Herausforderungen in der Bundesrepublik Deutschland.* Berlin: Colloquium, 1980.

———. "Verfassungsschutz in der Bundesrepublik Deutschland im Vergleich zu anderen westlichen Demokratien." *Politische Bildung* 17, no. 1 (1984): 43–66.

Kaupen, Wolfgang, and Theo Rasehorn. *Die Justiz zwischen Obrigkeitsstaat und Demokratie: Ein empirischer Beitrag zur Soziologie der deutschen Justizjuristen.* Neuwied: Luchterhand, 1971.

Kessler, Rainer. "Die Verfassungsloyalität des öffentlichen Dienstes." *Politische Studien* 23, no. 205 (special issue, October 1972): 40–63.

Kirchheimer, Otto. *Political Justice: The Use of Legal Procedure for Political Ends.* Princeton: Princeton University Press, 1961.

Knirsch, Hanspeter, Bernhard Nagel, and Wolfgang Voegeli, eds. *"Radikale" im öffentlichen Dienst: Eine Dokumentation.* Frankfurt am Main: Fischer Taschenbuch Verlag, 1973.

Knütter, Hans-Helmuth. "Verfassungsfeindliche Beamte in der Weimarer Republik." In *Verfassungsfeinde als Beamte? Die Kontroverse um die streitbare Demokratie,* ed. Wulf Schönbohm. Munich and Vienna: Günter Olzog, 1979.

Koch, Peter, and Reimar Oltmanns. *SOS: Freiheit in Deutschland.* Hamburg: Gruner and Jahr, 1979.

Komitee für Grundrechte und Demokratie. "Berufsverbotspraxis 1979/80: Die 'Liberalisierung' hat nicht stattgefunden." Berlin, 1980. Hectographed. Condensed in *Freiheit und Gleichheit,* no. 2 (October 1980): 95–102.

———. *Ohne Zweifel für den Staat: Die Praxis zehn Jahre nach dem Radikalenerlass.* Reinbek: Rowohlt, 1982.

Kommers, Donald P. "Basic Rights and Constitutional Review." In *Politics and Government in the Federal Republic of Germany: Basic Documents,* ed. Carl-Christoph Schweitzer et al. Leamington Spa, England: Berg, 1984.

———. "The Government of West Germany." In *Introduction to Comparative Government,* ed. Michael Curtis. New York: Harper and Row, 1985.

———. *Judicial Politics in West Germany: A Study of the Federal Constitutional Court.* Beverly Hills, Calif.: Sage Publications, 1976.

Koschnick, Hans. ed. *Der Abschied vom Extremistenbeschluss.* Bonn: Neue Gesellschaft, 1979.

Koschnick, Hans, and Klaus-Henning Rosen. "Der lange Abschied vom Extremistenbeschluss." *Die Neue Gesellschaft/Frankfurter Hefte* 32, no. 10 (October 1985): 939–42.

Die KPD informiert: Politische Unterdrückung in der BRD und Westberlin. Cologne: Rote Fahne, 1978.

Kramer, Jane. "A Reporter in Europe: Hamburg." *The New Yorker,* March 20, 1978, pp. 44–87.

Krieger, Leonard. *The German Idea of Freedom: History of a Political Tradition.* Boston: Beacon Press, 1957.

Kriele, Martin. "Der rechtliche Spielraum einer Liberalisierung der Einstellungspraxis im öffentlichen Dienst." *Neue Juristische Wochenschrift* 32, no. 1–2 (January 10, 1979): 1–8.

———. "Verfassungsfeinde im öffentlichen Dienst: Ein unlösbares Problem." In *Extremismus im demokratischen Rechsstaat,* ed. Manfred Funke. Düsseldorf: Droste, 1978.

———. "Verfassungsfeindlicher Extremismus/Radikalismus." In *Kampf um Wörter? Politische Begriffe im Meinungsstreit,* ed. Martin Greiffenhagen. Munich and Vienna: Carl Hanser, 1980.

Krölls, Albert. "Zehn Jahre Radikalenerlass: Zum (aktuellen) Fortschritt der Berufsverbotspolitik." *Vorgänge* 21, no. 3 (June 1982): 10–19.

Krovoza, Alfred, Axel R. Oestmann, and Klaus Ottomeyer, eds. *Zum Beispiel Peter Brückner: Treue zum Staat und kritische Wissenschaft.* Frankfurt am Main: Europäische Verlagsanstalt, 1981.

Kurz, Ingrid. "Der Anfang vom Ende der Berufsverbote?" *Blätter für deutsche und internationale Politik* 23, no. 11 (November 1978): 1323–31.

Kutscha, Martin. *Verfassung und "streitbare Demokratie": Historische und rechtliche Aspekte der Berufsverbote im öffentlichen Dienst.* Cologne: Pahl-Rugenstein, 1979.

———. "Zwischen Vollzug und Verweigerung: Die aktuelle Rechtsprechung in Berufsverbotsverfahren." *Demokratie und Recht* 13, no. 2 (1985): 218–27.

Kvistad, Gregg O. "Radicals and the State: The Political Demands on West German

Civil Servants." Paper presented at the annual meeting of the American Political Science Association, Washington, D.C., August 28–31, 1986. Reprinted in *Comparative Political Studies* 21, no. 1 (April 1988): 95–125.

———. "The *Radikalenerlass* and Political Opposition in the Federal Republic of Germany." Paper presented at Hamilton College Conference on Modern German Politics, April 26–28, 1985.

———. "Revolution, Subversion, and German State Employees." Paper presented at the annual meeting of the American Political Science Association, Atlanta, August 31–September 3, 1989.

Lameyer, Johannes. "Streitbare Demokratie." *Jahrbuch des öffentlichen Rechts der Gegenwart* 30 (1981): 147–96.

Lattmann, Dieter. "Freiheit in der Bundesrepublik: Politik und Zeitgeist." In *Extremismus im demokratischen Rechtsstaat,* ed. Manfred Funke. Düsseldorf: Droste, 1978.

Lautmann, Rüdiger. "Linksradikal als Stigma." In *Wir Bürger als Sicherheitsrisiko,* ed. Wolf-Dieter Narr. Reinbek: Rowohlt, 1977.

Lepsius, M. Rainer. "Institutional Structures and Political Culture." In *Party Government and Political Culture in Western Germany,* ed. Herbert Döring and Gordon Smith. London: Macmillan, 1982.

Lewy, Guenter. *The Federal Loyalty-Security Program: The Need for Reform.* Washington, D.C.: American Enterprise Institute for Public Policy Research, 1973.

Loewenstein, Karl. "Justice." In *Governing Postwar Germany,* ed. Edward H. Litchfield et al. Ithaca: Cornell University Press, 1953.

———. "Militant Democracy and Fundamental Rights." *American Political Science Review* 31, no. 3 (June 1937): 417–32; no. 4 (August 1937): 638–58.

Maier, Gerhart. *Extremisten im öffentlichen Dienst?* Bonn: Bundeszentrale für politische Bildung, 1977.

Mairowitz, David Z. "Scissors in the Head." *Harper's Magazine,* May 1978, pp. 28–31.

Mankoff, Milton, and Monica Jacobs. "The Return of the Suppressed: McCarthyism in West Germany." *Contemporary Crises* 1, no. 4 (1977): 341–57.

Markovits, Andrei S. *The Politics of the West German Trade Unions: Strategies of Class and Interest Representation in Growth and Crisis.* Cambridge: Cambridge University Press, 1986.

Maurer, Hartmut. "Die Mitgliedschaft von Beamten in verfassungsfeindlichen Parteien und Organisationen." *Neue Juristische Wochenschrift* 25, no. 14 (April 4, 1972): 601–7.

Mausbach, Hans. "Sciences and Political Discrimination." Issued by Bund demokratischer Wissenschaftler, n.d. Hectographed.

Mayer, Margit. "The German October of 1977." *New German Critique,* no. 13 (Winter 1978): 155–64.

Mayntz, Renate. "German Federal Bureaucrats: A Functional Elite between Politics and Administration." In *Bureaucrats and Policy Making: A Comparative Overview,* ed. Ezra Suleiman. New York: Holmes and Meier, 1984.

Ménudier, Henri. "Öffentlicher Dienst und Meinungsfreiheit in Frankreich." In *Verfassungsfeinde als Beamte?* ed. Wulf Schönbohm. Munich and Vienna: Günter Olzog, 1979.

Michalka, Wolfgang, ed. *Extremismus und Streitbare Demokratie.* Stuttgart: Franz Steiner, 1987.

Millis, Walter. "Legacies of the Cold War." In *The Price of Liberty,* ed. Alan Reitman. New York: W. W. Norton, 1968.

Mommsen, Hans. *Beamtentum im Dritten Reich.* Stuttgart: Deutsche Verlags-Anstalt, 1966.

Narr, Wolf-Dieter. "Academic Freedom 1979: The West German Case." *New Political Science 1,* no. 1 (Winter 1979): 47–55.

————. "Anatomie eines Berufsverbotes: Dokumente und Anmerkungen zur Nichtberufung von Wolf-Dieter Narr an die Juristische Fakultät Hannover." N.d. (c. 1975). Hectographed.

————. "Anhörung: Zur Frage, ob ich auf dem Boden der freiheitlichdemokratischen Grundordnung stehe. Ein Psychogramm und verallgemeindere Folgerungen." *Kursbuch,* no. 40 (June 1975): 159–78.

————. "Radikalismus/Extremismus." In *Kampf um Wörter? Politische Begriffe im Meinungsstreit,* ed. Martin Greiffenhagen. Munich and Vienna: Carl Hanser, 1980.

————. "Die SPD, der Radikalenerlass, und kein Ende." *Kritik* 6, no. 19 (1978): 85–92.

————. "Threats to Constitutional Freedom in the Federal Republic of Germany." *New German Critique,* no. 8 (Spring 1976): 20–41.

————, ed. *Wir Bürger als Sicherheitsrisiko: Berufsverbot und Lauschangriff. Beiträge zur Verfassung unserer Republik.* Reinbek: Rowohlt, 1977.

Navasky, Victor S. *Naming Names.* New York: Viking, 1980.

Negt, Oskar. "The Misery of Bourgeois Democracy in Germany." *Telos,* no. 34 (Winter 1977-78): 123–35.

Nelkin, Dorothy, and Michael Pollak. *The Atom Besieged: Extraparliamentary Dissent in France and Germany.* Cambridge: MIT Press, 1981.

Neumann, Franz. *The Democratic and the Authoritarian State: Essays in Political and Legal Theory.* Glencoe, Ill.: Free Press, 1957.

Newman, Edwin S. *Civil Liberty and Civil Rights.* Dobbs Ferry, N.Y.: Oceana Publications, 1967.

Nitsch, Wolfgang. "Ein 'Staatsfeind' im Gewande des Kritikers? Zum Prozess gegen Peter Brückner." *Psychologie und Gesellschaftskritik* 5, no. 4 (1981): 107–27.

Noelle-Neumann, Elizabeth, and Edgar Piel, eds. *Allensbacher Jahrbuch der Demoskopie, 1978–1983.* Munich: K. G. Saur, 1983.

"Notes de Jurisprudence: Conclusions de M. Letourneur." *Revue du Droit Public et de la Science Politique en France et a l'Étranger,* no. 2 (April–June 1954): 519–38.

Preis, Bernd. *Verfassungsschutz und öffentlicher Dienst: Ein Beitrag zum bereichsspezifischen Datenschutz bei den Verfassungsschutzbehörden.* Königstein/Taunus: Athenäum, 1982.

Pridham, Geoffrey. *Hitler's Rise to Power: The Nazi Movement in Bavaria, 1923–1933.* New York: Harper and Row, 1973.

Priewe, Jan. "Berufsverbote gefährden die Wissenschaftsfreiheit." *Frankfurter Hefte* 35, no. 10 (1980): 43–48.

Putnam, Robert. "The Political Attitudes of Senior Civil Servants in Britain, Germany, and Italy." In *The Mandarins of Western Europe,* ed. Mattei Dogan. New York: John Wiley, 1975.

Raiser, Ludwig. "Der 'Radikalen-Erlass': Prüfstein eines demokratischen Rechtsstaats?" *Zeitschrift für Evangelische Ethik* 23, no. 2 (1979): 106–17.

Rasehorn, Theo. "Justiz und Verfassung." In *Wir Bürger als Sicherheitsrisiko,* ed. Wolf-Dieter Narr. Reinbek: Rowohlt, 1977.

Raskin, Mark. *The Politics of National Security.* New Brunswick, N.J.: Transaction Books, 1979.

Reitman, Alan, ed. *The Pulse of Freedom: American Liberties, 1920–1970s.* New York: W. W. Norton, 1975.

Ridley, F. F., ed. *Government and Administration in Western Europe.* New York: St. Martin's Press, 1979.

Rosenberg, Hans. *Bureaucracy, Aristocracy, and Autocracy: The Prussian Experience, 1660–1815.* Boston: Beacon Press, 1966.

Roth, Jürgen. *Ist die Bundesrepublik ein Polizeistaat?* Darmstadt: Melzer, 1972.

Runge, Wolfgang. "Die alte Oberklasse—die neue Beamtenschaft" and "Die neue Oberklasse." In *Weimar ist kein Argument,* ed. Freimut Duve and Wolfgang Kopitzsch. Reinbek: Rowohlt, 1976.

———. *Politik und Beamtentum im Parteienstaat: Die Demokratisierung der politischen Beamten in Preussen zwischen 1918 and 1933.* Stuttgart: Ernst Klett, 1965.

Schiedermair, Hartmut, and Dietrich Murswiek. "Zugang zum öffentlichen Dienst und Verfassungstreue in England." In *Verfassungstreue im öffentlichen Dienst europäischer Staaten,* Karl Doehring et al. Berlin: Duncker and Humblot, 1980.

Schlimke, Hans-Jürgen. "Der 'Beurteilungsspielraum' der Einstellungsbehörde bei Einstellung von 'Radikalen' in den öffentlichen Dienst." Ph.D. diss., Münster University, 1980.

Schmid, Günther, and Hubert Treiber. *Bürokratie und Politik.* Munich: Wilhelm Fink, 1975.

Schmidt, Manfred G. *CDU und SPD an der Regierung: Ein Vergleich ihrer Politik in den Ländern.* Frankfurt am Main and New York: Campus, 1980.

Schmidt-Bleibtreu, Bruno, and Franz Klein. *Kommentar zum Grundgesetz für die Bundesrepublik Deutschland.* Neuwied and Berlin: Luchterhand, 1967.

Schneider, Hans-Peter. "Der Verfassungsschutz: Grundordnungshüter, Sicherheitsdienst, oder Geheimpolizei?" In *Wir Bürger als Sicherheitsrisiko,* ed. Wolf-Dieter Narr. Reinbek: Rowohlt, 1977.

Schneider, Peter. *Die Botschaft des Pferdekopfs und andere Essais aus einem friedlichen Jahrzehnt.* Darmstadt and Neuwied: Hermann Luchterhand, 1981.

———. *. . . . schon bist du ein Verfassungsfeind: Das unerwartete Anschwellen der Personalakte des Lehrers Kleff.* Berlin: Rotbuch, 1975.

Schönbohm, Wulf, ed. *Verfassungsfeinde als Beamte? Die Kontroverse um die streitbare Demokratie.* Munich and Vienna: Günter Olzog, 1979.

Schrader, Hans-Hermann. *Rechtsbegriff und Rechtsentwicklung der Verfassungstreue im öffentlichen Dienst.* Berlin: Duncker and Humblot, 1985.

Schreiber, Manfred, ed. *Polizeilicher Eingriff und Grundrechte.* Stuttgart: Richard Boorberg, 1982.

Schwind, Hans-Dieter, ed. *Ursachen des Terrorismus in der Bundesrepublik Deutschland*. Berlin: de Gruyter, 1978.

Seifert, Jürgen. "Defining the Enemy of the State: Political Policies of West Germany." *New German Critique*, no. 8 (Spring 1976): 42–53.

Sheehan, James J. *German Liberalism in the Nineteenth Century*. Chicago: University of Chicago Press, 1978.

———, ed. *Imperial Germany*. New York: Franklin Watts, 1976.

Sieben Jahre Kampf gegen die Berufsverbote: Bilanz der "Initiative Weg mit den Berufsverboten." No. 20. Hamburg, 1979.

Siementhal, Erwin, and H. D. Wohlfarth, eds. *Der Fall Hans Peter: Entlassung eines "Verfassungsfeindes": Dokumentation und Analyse*. Cologne: Ralf Theurer, 1982.

Skriver, Ansgar. "Innere Sicherheit und Bürgerfreiheit." *Merkur* 32, no. 9 (September 1978): 880–96.

Smith, Gordon. *Democracy in Western Germany: Parties and Politics in the Federal Republic*. New York: Holmes and Meier, 1979.

Sontheimer, Kurt. *Die verunsicherte Republik: Die Bundesrepublik nach dreissig Jahren*. Munich: Piper, 1979.

Southern, David. "Germany." In *Government and Administration in Western Europe*, ed. F. F. Ridley. New York: St. Martin's Press, 1979.

Spoo, Eckart. "Erfahrungen mit dem Berufsverbot gegen Radikale im öffentlichen Dienst." *Frankfurter Hefte* 18, no. 3 (1973): 181–88.

"Stellungnahmen von Juristen zu den von der Ministerpräsidentenkonferenz beschlossenen 'Grundsätzen zur Frage der verfassungsfeindlichen Kräfte im öffentlichen Dienst' sowie zur Gemeinsamen Erklärung des Bundeskanzlers und der Ministerpräsidenten der Länder vom 28. Januar 1972." Parts 1, 2. *Blätter für deutsche und internationale Politik*, no. 2 (February 1972): 124–65; no. 3 (March 1972): 246–93.

Stern, Klaus. *Das Staatsrecht der Bundesrepublik Deutschland*. Vol. 1, *Grundbegriffe und Grundlagen des Staatsrechts: Strukturprinzipien der Verfassung*. 2d ed. Munich: C. H. Beck'sche Verlagsbuchhandlung, 1984.

———. *Zur Verfassungstreue der Beamten*. Munich: Franz Vahlen, 1974.

Street, Harry. *Freedom, the Individual, and the Law*. 2d ed. Middlesex, England: Penguin Books, 1967.

Suleiman, Ezra, ed. *Bureaucrats and Policy Making: A Comparative Overview*. New York: Holmes and Meier, 1984.

Theaterstücke zum Radikalenerlass. Offenbach: Verlag 2000, 1978.

Wallraff, Günter. "Die 'Anhörer'" and "Der 'falsche Aktenmensch.'" In *Die unheimliche Republik: Politische Verfolgung in der Bundesrepublik*, ed. Heinrich Hannover and Wallraff. Reinbek: Rowohlt, 1984.

Walter, Hannfried. "Die Sicherung eines loyalen öffentlichen Dienstes in Schweden." In *Verfassungstreue im öffentlichen Dienst europäischer Staaten*, Karl Doehring et al. Berlin: Duncker and Humblot, 1980.

Weiler, Hagen. *Verfassungstreue im öffentlichen Dienst*. Königstein/Taunus: Athenäum, 1979.

Weiss, Hans-Dietrich. "Die jüngste 'Extremisten'-Entscheidung des Bundesverwaltungsgerichts." *Zeitschrift für Beamtenrecht*, no. 3 (1985): 70–79.

Weltfriedensrat. *Berufsverbote in der Bundesrepublik Deutschland.* Helsinki, n.d.

Wengst, Udo. *Beamtentum zwischen Reform und Tradition: Beamtengesetzgebung in der Gründungsphase der Bundesrepublik Deutschland, 1948–1953.* Düsseldorf: Droste, 1988.

———. *Staatsaufbau und Regierungspraxis, 1948–1953: Zur Geschichte der Verfassungsorgane der Bundesrepublik Deutschland.* Düsseldorf: Droste, 1984.

Wer hat Angst vor dem Postbeamten Hans Peter? Stuttgarter Aktionskreis gegen Berufsverbote, 1981.

Weyer, Hartmut. *DKP und öffentlicher Dienst.* Bonn–Bad Godesberg: Hohwacht, 1974.

Wiese, Walter. *Der Staatsdienst in der Bundesrepublik Deutschland.* Neuwied and Berlin: Luchterhand, 1972.

Will, Ian. *The Big Brother Society.* London: Harrap, 1983.

Wolfe, Alan. *The Seamy Side of Democracy: Repression in America.* 2d ed. New York: Longman, 1978.

Wunder, Bernd. *Geschichte der Bürokratie in Deutschland.* Frankfurt am Main: Suhrkamp, 1986.

Zapf, Wolfgang. "Die Verwalter der Macht: Materialen zum Sozialprofil der höheren Beamtenschaft." In *Beiträge zur Analyse der deutschen Oberschicht,* ed. Zapf. Munich: Piper, 1965.

Zipes, Jack. "From Berufsverbot to Terrorism." *Telos,* no. 34 (Winter 1977–78): 136–47.

Index